The Tao of Immunology

A Revolutionary New Understanding of Our Body's Defenses

The Tao of Immunology

A Revolutionary New Understanding
of Our Body's Defenses

MARC LAPPÉ, Ph. D.

PLENUM TRADE • NEW YORK AND LONDON

Library of Congress Cataloging-in-Publication Data

Lappé, Marc.
    The tao of immunology : a revolutionary new understanding of our
  body's defenses / Marc Lappé.
        p.   cm.
    Includes bibliographical references and index.
    ISBN 0-306-45626-5
    1. Immune system. 2. Immunology--Philosophy.   I. Title.
    [DNLM: 1. Immune System. 2. Immunity. 3. Autoimmunity.   QW 504
  L316t 1997]
  QR181.L35   1997
  616.07'9--dc21
  DNLM/DLC
  for Library of Congress   97-9707
                                                                 CIP

The information in this book is based on research by the author. This material is
for information purposes only and should not be construed as medical advice.
The reader is strongly advised not to self-diagnose and is also advised to check
with a qualified health professional before implementing any intervention. The
author and publisher assume no responsibility for any treatments undertaken by
the reader. Companies, interventions, and products are mentioned without bias
to increase your knowledge only, not as a recommendation, promise of a cure,
mitigation, prescription, or prevention of your medical condition.

ISBN 0-306-45626-5

© 1997 Marc Lappé
Plenum Press is a Division of Plenum Publishing Corporation
233 Spring Street, New York, N.Y. 10013-1578
http://www.plenum.com

10 9 8 7 6 5 4 3 2 1

Printed in the United States of America

For Jacqueline

PREFACE

This book had its origins in hours of deliberation and discussion with friends, colleagues, and mentors over just why we have an immune system. And in talking about it, we spent more time discussing the *philosophy* behind immunity than its biology. As sociologist and critic Ivan Illich once pointed out, the idea of a "system" for immunity did not arise until about 1978. Until then the immune apparatus was considered an isolated, antibody-making unit, rather than an integrated system that was part of the body.

Once as a summer graduate student in 1968, I asked George Snell of the Jackson Laboratory just what was the fundamental purpose of the immune system. (It would be another decade before he was awarded the Nobel prize for his discovery of the biological basis for immune recognition of tissue differences between individuals.) When I asked why so many genes had been assembled to coordinate these immune functions, he paused dramatically. Then he said that he thought that the immune system's primary purpose was to identify the "self." I was floored. Here was a biological scientist giving a metaphysical definition of the system that he had so laboriously dissected. I have teased and struggled with this fundamental question over the ensuing three decades.

It has always seemed to me that our approach has limited the fullest understanding of immunity's intricacies. Too often, our vision has been dictated by a peculiarly Western Zeitgeist. We limited our understanding when we first described the activities of the immune system in the language of modern-day warfare, with "defenses" against outward attacks, "strategies" for containment, and "assaults" against invading organisms.

The language of warfare extended to science fiction constructs of the body as a bastion against a hostile universe, girded by an ever-vigilant immune system. Even as a 12-year-old, I vividly remember reading a science fiction story told from the vantage point of a tissue macrophage, a primitive phagocytic cell. This single cell valiantly (and ultimately suicidally) participated in an all-out battle to wall off an inflamed appendix to save the body as a whole. A later movie entitled *Fantastic Voyage* showed microscopically reduced humans fighting for their lives against the ensnaring tendrils of antibody chains.

Today, we have a little more sophisticated idea of how macrophages work and the complexities of immune recognition in general. But we still lack a fundamental model of the role of the immune system in our interactions with an ever-changing external and internal milieu.

Typically, scientists have embarked on their investigations of biological systems long before they have an overview of how such systems function in the body as a whole. Initial scientific inquiry is often done well using this tabula rasa approach, but once a system is discovered, reflection on its overall meaning appears timely and relevant. With the advent of a near complete inventory of the immune system's actors, this time is now.

My own experience with the immune system as a scientist, a patient, and a sometime student of Eastern philosophy suggested a metaphor for understanding immunity in all of its manifestations. In some ways, the immune system appears to operate with a strange form of inner wisdom, roughly analogous to the forces of nature described in the sixth century BCE by an apocryphal Chinese philosopher named Lao-tzu (literally, the "old philosopher"). In the fabled *Tao-te Ching*,* Lao-tzu emphasized the constant waxing and waning of nature and the subtleties needed to work with it. His sayings have been interpreted to provide a metaphor for the governance of people. But they may apply equally well to understanding the politics of the body. Like good rulers, I have often wondered if the immune system might also sometimes prevail by yielding rather than by opposing.

The *Tao-te Ching* stresses the value of accommodating rather than overreaching; winning through losing; retreating rather than destroying; and prevailing through nonconfrontation. Considering their successful application by powerful generals, the principles enunciated in *Tao-te Ching* have tremendous contemporary resonance. The paradoxical virtue of yielding and nonconfrontational tactics has been adopted by civil rights advocates beginning with Mahatma Gandhi through Martin Luther King. It would be quite remarkable if Lao-tzu's hoary aphorisms proved equally apt, whether applied to an encroaching army or an invading bacterium. After learning about the immune system, see what you think.

Most scholarly texts attribute these later writings to a contemporary of Confucius (551–479 BCE) named Li Erh.

ACKNOWLEDGMENTS

As with all ventures of this scale and scope, the ideas and views expressed herein have deep taproots. In addition to my research exposure to immunology in various laboratories throughout the country, I have been influenced by my immersion in Eastern philosophy, especially the coursework I did while a graduate student at the University of Washington under Professor John Spellman. I cut my eye-teeth in immunology in the laboratory of Dr. Curtis Williams at the Rockefeller University, developer of immunoelectrophoresis. I also was extremely fortunate to have learned basic cellular immunology from Nobel laureate George Snell at the Jackson Laboratory in Bar Harbor, Maine.

My most formative years as a scientist were spent in the laboratory of Dr. Richmond T. Prehm, the father of tumor immunology. I want to give special thanks to Rich for encouraging my inquisitiveness into the counterintuitive elements of immunity and for reviewing the manuscript in its early stages. Similar thanks go to Dr. Arthur Ericsson for his review and suggestions for considering the linkage between the nervous and immune systems.

I gratefully recognize the forbearance and remarkable typing and editing skills of Linda Kalkwarf. I also thank Gordon Smith and Britt Bailey for insights in translating science to the public. In this vein, special thanks to my editor at Plenum, Linda Regan, who digested a densely written earlier version of the manuscript and pushed me toward a (hopefully) more accessible writing style! I also gratefully acknowledge the constant support of my loving family.

I am also deeply grateful to my wife Nichol Lovera, who died in a tragic accident in early 1996, for coaxing me long ago to go back to my roots in Eastern philosophy in my scientific writing.

I give my heartfelt thanks to Ralph Abascal at the Wellness Foundation and Tom Pirtle of O'Quinn and Laminack whose generosity gave me the freedom to write this book. Lastly, the whole process of conceptualizing, writing, and editing this book could not have been done without the continuing love, support, and encouragement of Jacqueline Durbin, my dearest friend and companion.

$\mathcal{C}$ONTENTS

$\mathscr{I}$NTRODUCTION

The classic beliefs about the immune system are dead. Where once it was seen as an omnipotent force that protected the body against microscopic foreign invaders and incipient tumor cells, new discoveries in medicine have forced medical experts to reevaluate its role. Under many circumstances, we now know the immune system to be ineffectual or even self-destructive. In particular, its abject failure to control AIDS, cancer, and a host of newly emergent diseases has shattered its reputation as an invincible protector. It is clearly time to reassess just what the immune system can and cannot do.

Today misconceptions still abound. The immune system is something much more than an apparatus designed to keep the body "clean." Like the central nervous sys-

tem, the immune system, its cells, and its chemical mediators reach virtually every part of the body. The new vision
of the immune system is that of a system that shapes our
relationship to the natural world, changing the microorganisms and cells with which it interacts, even as it
defends the body.

The true nature of the immune system still defies our
best efforts to define it. We have a vast inventory of its
component parts, yet little understanding about how
those components fit together. The simplistic notion that
the immune system exists to keep the body sterile is more
a cultural artifact than a reality. Although it is true that the
blood and the tissues it bathes must be free of bacteria for
optimal existence, the body and its cavities are normally
shot through with hordes of bacteria, parasites, and viruses that have taken up silent residence in one portal or
another. And many chronic diseases, from ulcers to lymphoma, are directly linked to newly discovered bacteria
or viral strains, making them potentially subject to immune control. Other formally intractable diseases like
"shingles" or Crohn's disease, an inflammation of the
intestinal tract, are associated with smoldering viral or
bacterial infections in nerve endings or the body tissues
proper. More and more, we are learning that in many
circumstances, the immune system is often an incomplete
barrier to disease.

Up until now, we may have been asking the wrong
questions about the immune system. The research community has been preoccupied with the molecular structure of all of its components, neglecting the most fundamental questions about the immune system's primordial
functions and origins. We know more about what makes
the immune system "work" than perhaps any other coordinated system in the body—but we still lack a grasp of
why it works as it does. Researchers have discovered that
many of the organs of the immune system receive nerve
endings. Could the immune system be an extension of

the body's network of nerves? Is the immune system designed to be a tumor surveillance system? An antibacterial system? A pregnancy protecting system? A parasite control system? Or is it a general "housekeeping" system that ensures that what is inside is safe and what is outside is kept that way?

Our ignorance of immune functions is further underscored by a growing list of unanswered questions about its capabilities:

- Why doesn't the immune system reject the body's own tissues?
- Why can't the immune system control certain infectious diseases more effectively?
- How does the immune system "bounce back" after being knocked down by physical or psychological stress?
- Why are some pregnancies aborted by immune means whereas most others go to term unscathed?
- Why doesn't the immune system stop cancer more often or does it stop cancer many times in a lifetime?
- Why does the body damage certain organs during the self-directed immune attacks of autoimmune disease and not others?
- Why is there autoimmune disease at all?
- Why does the immune system cause so many skin diseases?
- Why has asthma become so much more prevalent in recent years?[1]
- Why is there asthma in the first place?[2]
- Why is the immune system so vulnerable to sunlight-induced damage?
- Why does the immune system weaken so markedly with age?
- Why doesn't the immune system work better to

stop certain parasitic or bacterial diseases, like malaria or tuberculosis?

- Why does the HIV organism prove to be so potent an adversary to the immune system?
- Why does the immune system of genetically similar people respond so differently?
- Why can we sometimes overcome immune recognition to encourage the body to accept foreign organ grafts?

The number and variety of these unanswered questions suggest we still lack a deep understanding of the fundamental function of the immune system. We do know that early on in embryogenesis, the immune system is uncommitted and "tolerant" of non-self cells. In fact, perfectly normal mice have been produced by joining two embryos at an early stage of their normally independent development. And some fraternal twins, especially freemartin cattle, which share the same placenta, grow up "liking" each other immunologically. When full grown, such animals accept a graft of otherwise foreign fraternal tissue as if it were their own.

Although final answers to this list of questions may prove elusive, enough facts exist to provide direction. For one thing, the image of a single population of immune cells serving as the foot soldiers and defending the body against foreign invasion is almost certainly too simplistic. The "thin white line" of white blood cells that collects in a test tube of clotted blood between the serum and red blood cells contains a vast variety of cell types, each with a highly specific function. And within any one class of white blood cells known as lymphocytes, different variants are the norm. For instance, on their way to becoming mature antibody-producing cells, lymphocytes progress through six different precursor cell types. Similarly, the cells that become cell-killing lymphocytes go through anywhere from six to nine cellular stages. In all, at least 26 types of lymphocytes exist in the body.

Nor is the immune system limited to one type of reaction to foreign cells or antigens. Different reactions to the same challenge can produce wonderfully adaptive reactions, as when antibodies neutralize an invading bacterium, or highly maladaptive ones, as when the system produces an allergic response to peanut or soybean antigens.

Part of the problem in developing a deeper appreciation for the varieties of such immune reactivity lies in how we describe immunology itself.

THE LANGUAGE OF IMMUNITY

One of the obstacles to such new and original thinking about the immune system is our continued reliance on the language of war to describe it. As Susan Sontag pointed out in her seminal book, *Illness As Metaphor*,[3] we readily incorporate features of deadly diseases into our daily language and, more importantly, allow our language to shape our view of the world. This idea, that how we view the world is related to how we organize it linguistically (and vice versa), owes its origins to two visionary anthropologist-linguists, Edward Sapir (d. 1968) and Benjamin Lee Whorf (d. 1956). Sapir and Whorf championed the idea that just as the world influences how we shape our language, our words often change the way we come to view the world.

In the case of the immune system, the metaphor at work is one of war. As Peter Jaret stated in an opening lead for a *National Geographic* article on the immune system: "Every minute of every day wars rage within our bodies."[4]

It is unfortunate that we use this language to describe the immune system because it distorts our worldview of

immunity and strongly influences the way we concep-
tualize it. If the immune system is seen solely as our chief
biological means of defense, we may come to believe that
survival depends on constant vigilance and rigorous
counterattacks. We may adopt the notion that nothing
short of complete victory and utter defeat is acceptable. It
makes good copy, but does it make good sense?

Such a construct perhaps began with the work of the
great nineteenth-century Russian zoologist Elie Metchnikoff (1845–1916). In 1882 Metchnikoff collected some tiny,
transparent larvae of a starfish on the coast of Sicily. Back
at his laboratory, he pierced one larva with a rose thorn.
Then he watched in awe as this primitive starfish mounted
a powerful cellular response to the thorn piercing its flesh
(see Figure One). Metchnikoff watched the influx of highly
aggressive macrophages (literally "big eaters") attack and
partially digest the thorn. He took this behavior as evidence of the general defensive role of the immune system
in warding off parasites and other infectious organisms.
Later, Metchnikoff used the metaphors of attack and defense to describe the primitive cell systems he observed
ingesting and immobilizing potentially harmful foreign
bodies or microbes in higher organisms. I may have made
a similar mistake in 1967 when I interpreted the lymphocytes I saw infiltrating a tumor as if they constituted an
"invasion" hellbent on tumor destruction. In fact, only
some of the tumors so invaded are actually destroyed.
Some T-cell infiltrates, as in inflammatory breast cancer,
may actually signal a worse prognosis.

We now know that the "foreign body response,"
although normal, is often maladaptive, leading to tissue
damage and destruction or producing high concentrations of sometimes noxious chemical mediators known as
"cytokines" (sī'-tō-kīns). Metchnikoff's macrophages
were indeed "walling off" and immobilizing the rose

One.   Primitive macrophages attempt to engulf a rose thorn pressed into the flesh of a transparent starfish larva. Such responses were recognized in 1882 by Russian zoologist Elie Metchnikoff as an example of an innate cellular defense system. Redrawn from "Immunity and the Invertebrates," by Gregory Beck and Gail S. Habicht. © by Scientific American. *All rights reserved.*

thorn—but sometimes, as with the tuberculosis or leprosy bacteria (*Mycobacterium tuberculosis* and *Mycobacterium leprae*), the macrophage actually serves as a *host* for
the bacteria, not a destroying angel. And my tumor-
invading lymphocytes may have stimulated tumor growth
as much as they participated in tumor destruction.

The evidence for these and other seemingly paradoxical actions of the immune system have been there, of
course, for any eyes to see. But the standing paradigm of
the immune system as a defensive apparatus probably
delayed full appreciation of its widely disparate functions.

It is now widely recognized in mainstream science
that sometimes immune reactions can injure as well as
heal. Sometimes the chemicals released by immune cells
are vital to the body's natural healing. Without certain
chemical mediators from lymphocytes, a damaged liver
cannot regenerate.[5] These and other data suggest the constellation of cells and chemicals deployed by the immune
system is much more than a front line of defense against
disease. A new metaphor, drawn from Eastern philosophy, would have these elements playing a much more
intricate and sometimes even passive role in guarding the
body's delicate internal balance against external pertur-
bation. This new vision is what this book explores.

HISTORICAL PRECEDENTS

Since its rediscovery in the nineteenth century, the
immune system has been conceptualized as a bodily defense system. Like the Roman historian Pliny the Elder
describing the shiny shield of Perseus, early immunologists like Louis Pasteur (1822–1895) visualized the body's
immune defenses as an invincible bulwark against invading microorganisms, a barrier that could be raised or

lowered at will to protect against virtually any inimical virus or bacterium. Pasteur's dramatic success in immunizing a child named Joseph Meister against rabies powerfully reinforced his belief in the immune system's ultimate shield against pathogens.

Pasteur's ingenious technique of injecting virulent rabies virus from one rabbit into another and then harvesting the weakened, non-disease-producing form of attenuated virus from the dried spinal cords of the survivors provided a risky but valuable model for many later vaccines. Sabin's famous oral live polio vaccine is a contemporary example. In Pasteur's view, once sufficiently weakened, any virus or bacterium could prime the immune system to neutralize a potential microbial invader. In this model, Pasteur visualized the immune system working to immobilize attacking microorganisms, much as the Greek hero Perseus used his shield as a mirror to turn Medusa's snake-haired visage into stone. By converting the normally noxious proteins on the virus surface into immunity-provoking, beneficial ones, Pasteur neutralized the deadly force of viral attack just as Medusa's gaze transfixed her enemies—and, with Perseus's mirror—ultimately immobilized her own evil force. But this metaphor has a message long neglected by medical practitioners.

Few of us remember that after this famous mythological battle Perseus gave two drops of Medusa's blood to the goddess Athena. One drop had the power to destroy and injure, the other to heal. Myth has it that Athena gave only the "good" drop to Asclepius, the founder of Western medicine. The second drop remained a curse that various gods invoked over the centuries. Like all else in medicine, the immune system too retains the capacity to harm as well as to heal. Recognizing the eternal tension between good and evil, healing and injuring, is a view that must be restored in our conception of the body if we are truly to appreciate and, ultimately, to harness the powers inherent in the body's immune system.

ROOTS OF INVULNERABILITY

Despite some recently recognized shortcomings, many clinicians and immunologists still believe strongly in the ultimate efficacy of the immune system. In its best sense, this belief powers the intensive search for vaccines against malaria, AIDS, and a host of less visible but equally devastating scourges in the Third World. This quest is desirable and urgently needed. But as immunologist Barry Bloom of the Howard Hughes Medical Institute in New York has pointed out, development of vaccines is underfunded and sometimes at odds with chemotherapeutic approaches.[6]

Less enlightened medical professionals ignore the immune system or blindly encourage its "strengthening" without regard to the consequences. Currently, many members of the medical public health community cling to a kind of Maginot line mentality that downgrades the immune system to a simple holding function. This was the belief held by the French in World War II. As long as they remained passively entrenched behind an "impregnable" line of fortified positions (named after its inventor, General Maginot), the country was safe. One of the major risks of such a strategy is that its very passivity ensures that any weakness can be exploited by a mobile foe. And so it is with the immune system. Just as the Nazis outflanked the Maginot line with their blitzkrieg type of warfare and mobile panzer tank divisions, many bacteria and viruses can overwhelm an immune system that is too static, unilaterally focused, or nonspecifically strengthened.

Today's rapidly evolving microorganisms are the equivalent of Germany's panzer corps, a highly mobile and evasive enemy group. Escape from antibiotic control is prevalent among increasing numbers of wild-type bacteria, viruses, and other parasites in nature, from salmonella to HIV to malaria. Almost all extant microorganisms maintain the ability to evolve outside of view of the immune system and some, such as HIV, can evolve even while under active attack. Were the immune system itself simply a passive defense system, it would soon succumb to a more clever foe that quickly evolved to a new, undetectable form.

Fortunately, the immune system itself has tremendous plasticity and can respond to an evolving threat by rapid responses of its own. This revolutionary plasticity ensures that under most circumstances, the immune system can "keep up" with an evolving, novel antigenic strain of a microbe. We now know that the "sharpness" of any given immune response emerges sequentially after the threat of a nascent invasion is sensed. Remarkably, as we will see, this adaptability to home in on an attacker arises *de novo* within the immune system of each individual. Unlike the typical view of evolution as a slow and tedious process of natural selection over generations, the immune system undergoes a remarkably rapid evolutionary response in its antibody production to novel antigenic challenge. This rapid-fire, fine-tuning of the immune system is one of its greatest virtues, a fact to be discussed in Chapter Two.

IMMUNE FUNCTIONS

In terms of immunity generally, we know a few things for sure and others less well. The immune system is not a fail-safe system, and as we will learn, sometimes its actions can do as much harm as good. We also know that without an immune system we would be overwhelmed by opportunistic infections at our first encounter with a highly contaminated world.

Our immune system is indeed an essential and most often highly effective buffer zone between a largely sterile body interior and a noxious, teeming universe of microbial pathogens. But it is not a perfect protective system. Nor could it be expected to be so. Evolution has thrown up an almost limitless variety of cellular types that threaten bodily integrity, from viruses to parasites. A static "perfect" system, as with the Maginot line, would soon be overwhelmed by the sheer variety of attackers. Instead, the immune system has evolved remarkable plasticity to deal with this vast panoply of external threats.

One way to understand what the immune system does is to see what happens when it is absent. Children with a hereditary condition known as severe combined immune deficiency (SCID), in which a functional immune system fails to develop, are beset with fatal bacterial and viral infections soon after birth. David, the famous "boy in the bubble," had SCID. Tragically, when he was finally released into the world at age 12 at his own request, he was overwhelmed with a fatal barrage of infections and died within a few weeks. We also know too well how the loss of "helper" cells in AIDS patients leads to overwhelming opportunistic infections. And we know that organ transplant patients whose immune systems are intentionally weakened experience a wave of otherwise rare tumors of the skin and lymphatic system.

These events provide clues to the essential role some forms of immunity play in vouchsafing our security. When the immune system "works," it appears to do a splendid job of protecting us and eradicating disease. As children, the success of our immune systems is often the tightrope we walk between recovery or death. But this view of "victory" over the microbial world can be pyrrhic, for many viruses and some bacteria have evolved remarkable survival strategies, including some that permit persistence even after the most blistering immune response.

We comfort ourselves by believing that patients once recovered from their childhood disease will live out the rest of their lives free of further damage. But recent developments have shocked the medical community out of complacency. Age-old scourges like polio that were thought to be in submission are not "gone." New symptoms of polio's ravages have mysteriously recurred in patients decades after an apparent full recovery. Former polio victims who seemed perfectly well have experienced devilish recurrences. This "post-polio" syndrome, which includes terrible muscular pain and weakness, may be the result of activated latent poliovirus or the recrudescence of nerve damage.[7] And rheumatic fever, brought on by childhood infection with a streptococcal bacterium, can reappear in adults long after it went into remission. A new strep infection can trigger systemwide illness, a point to be taken up later.

Immune systems can be incapacitated by malnutrition, viral infection, starvation, or stress and can be severely damaged by toxic substances. Under such circumstances, immune strength can wane dangerously, leaving us vulnerable to many previously unknown infectious diseases. Diarrheal diseases like shigella that normally run a relatively benign course can become killers in patients with impaired immunity. And entirely new pathogens, including previously unrecognized amoeba and yeast species, have produced novel diseases in AIDS patients with disturbing regularity. In the past, few if any of these organisms ever triggered disease in healthy, immunologically intact adults.

Clearly, we need much more knowledge to understand what we can do to control disease. We still do not know why healthy children rapidly recover from a disease that can fell an adult. For still inexplicable reasons, childhood diseases like measles, mumps, or chickenpox that produce mild illness in children cause severe, sometimes life-threatening, illnesses in adults. Nor do we know fully how or why most children develop immunity to these diseases that lasts for a lifetime, whereas a few become vulnerable again to one or more childhood illnesses some years or decades later. We do know that a constellation of genes determines the range of responsiveness in any individual, but we don't know the origin of the genes or what they are for.

Similar uncertainties plague viral conditions like hepatitis B or the Epstein–Barr virus (EBV) associated with mononucleosis. Both may produce disease symptoms like lethargy and chronic fatigue in teenagers or young adults, only to wane and disappear some months (or years) later. Others, like the RNA-based group of herpesviruses, can remain in the body for years without provoking an effective immune response. In a few individuals, the infection remains latent and generates more serious disease later.

Even after disease symptoms have abated, residual virus may remain in the body. In the case of hepatitis B virus, infectious particles may linger long after an apparent recovery. Many hepatitis patients who have seemingly recovered from their initial bouts of infection have been found to be silent carriers years later.[8] In one dramatic instance, a patient who had apparently recovered from her infection was found to be harboring live virus inside her body 23 years later.[9] In these instances, the immune system makes antibodies to the virus but somehow permits it to escape.

In several viral illnesses, newly uncovered evidence suggests late-recurring disease may be the norm and not the exception. In such instances, the immune system fails to achieve "sterilizing immunity," a result overlooked in the past. Sometimes residual organisms can lead to untoward consequences. Chronic inflammation with the hepatitis C virus can lead to smoldering inflammation of the liver and, in an unfortunate few, cirrhosis and cancer. In those patients in whom hepatitis B infection remains active, liver cancer can result. Persistent strains of other organisms are dangerous as well. *Helicobacter pylori*, the ulcer-causing bacterium, has been linked to lymphoma, as has EBV.

RHEUMATIC FEVER AS A MODEL

Many of these recurrences of "dead" diseases may be silent reminders that the immune system may not eradicate illness so much as hold it in check. And sometimes, delayed disease results from simmering immune responses, as in the case of hepatitis C disease. Still other delayed diseases that follow an initial bout of infection may result from an immune response gone awry. In these instances, the immune cells charged with pursuing an offending organism attack the body itself or, in the case of hepatitis, the cells that harbor the fleeing intruder. Many autoimmune diseases may be the result of such misdirected assaults.

The classic example is the condition that arises after a bout of streptococcal infection. In this instance, an initial disease that causes a childhood respiratory infection, tonsillitis, or pharyngitis goes on to produce a much more serious disease in adulthood. In about 3 percent of infected children, the strep organism goes on to produce a serious illness characterized by heart disease, skin nodules, swollen joints, and neurological problems of gait and muscular control. These symptoms comprise a disease known as rheumatic fever. In this illness, an immune-damaged nervous system may progress to Sydenham's chorea, a debilitating nervous condition in which coordination fails entirely.

One theory for rheumatic fever is that the offending bacterium shares an antigen with heart muscle, particularly that lining the aortic valve. The resulting immune reaction destroys the aortic tissue as well as the bacteria. Keep in mind that the essence of immunity is to recognize and respond to foreign proteins, typically with antibodies. Sometimes this response to bacteria can inadvertently cross-react with look-alike proteins in the body proper.

Although this model is still just a theory of how rheumatic heart disease occurs after a strep infection, it is supported by the facts. Group A *Streptococcus* bacteria carry surface antigens that do in fact mirror those of several body constituents. Many patients with rheumatic heart disease have antibodies in their blood that "cross-react" or bind with heart tissue *and* the bacterium, resulting in tissue damage even as the infection is being cleared. In keeping with this idea, bacterial growth on the heart valves can damage heart tissue, revealing the vulnerable cross-reacting antigens within the valve tissue to the immune system.

A paradox is why so many strep patients get later heart disease whereas others (up to 15 percent) become "silent" carriers of strep organisms and remain well. According to the *Cecil Textbook of Medicine*,[10] once the immune system has been challenged with organisms that cross-react with heart antigens, it may put the patient at increased risk for heart disease well into adulthood and perhaps indefinitely. For young adults who have had a childhood bout with a strep throat, especially if there was some evidence of early heart involvement, this threat is so real that every time they undergo a dental or surgical procedure, they receive a course of prophylactic antibiotics. This medical decision hinges on the mistaken belief that strep patients can avoid developing auto-immune reactions altogether by suppressing new bacterial infection. In addition to selecting for resistant bacteria, the antibiotic regime may miss the few bacteria that trigger the immunological memory from the first strep infection. It is this triggering that reactivates an immune reaction that damages the heart.

These simple medical observations raise at least two evolutionary quandaries: Why does the surface of a bacterium come to look like a human cell? And how does nature permit people to get so sick years *after* they seem to recover?

IMMUNITY AND HEART DISEASE

First, rheumatic fever is a dramatic, albeit indirect, killer. From 25 to 40 percent of *all* cardiovascular disease and resulting disability in developing countries is the indirect consequence of earlier bouts with strep.[11] This fact strongly suggests that natural selection should be working to increase the proportion of people who are resistant to strep infections. If a strep infection reduces the viability and reproduction of genetically sensitive people, over time it would leave behind a population more resistant to strep's damaging effect. But apparently, this selection is not effective, for a large number of people, as many as 78 per 100,000 in U.S. Hispanic communities, still get sick with rheumatic fever.

One explanation for the prevalence of rheumatic heart disease is that unlike childhood rheumatic fever, the coronary manifestations occur late in life. Patients who have had an episode of acute rheumatic fever are particularly prone to developing the heart manifestations of this illness only if they get a *second* bout of the disease.

About one in five patients who get this secondary strep infection will develop a recurrence of rheumatic fever. In addition to the heart symptoms experienced by about half of those patients, some 75 percent will experience episodes of arthritis, 10 percent skin manifestations, and 15 percent neurological or gait disorders.

Researchers have also identified other conditions where a self-directed immune reaction has been linked to heart disease or other abnormalities. Hughes disease is a case in point. In this disease, antibodies to the body's own low-density lipoproteins increase the risk of plaques forming in arteries—and, strangely, there is also an increased likelihood of miscarriage, perhaps from blood clots in the placenta. Chronic viral infections, particularly in cases of cytomegalovirus, have also been linked to an increased risk of narrowing the heart's major blood vessels.[12] Additional data suggest that strokes may be associated with abnormal immune reactions.[13] Finally, new evidence suggests that immune-mediated inflammation may cause some forms of artery-narrowing atherosclerosis.[14]

All of this disease is evidence for the ferocity of an unleashed autoimmune attack. Much of this illness and potential disability suggests either that the immune system is not doing its job or that evolution has failed to protect the body from severe, sometimes devastating, illness. As is usual in such quandaries, the truth exists somewhere in between these possibilities. In a childhood strep infection, the immune system appears to do an admirable job in protecting young lives. The fact that late-arising disease occurs sometime after adulthood is merely evidence of an evolutionary maxim: Natural selection, the process by which environmental factors permit the survival of some but not all individuals, cannot protect or save offspring of genetically vulnerable individuals from illnesses that arise *after* those persons have already passed the age of reproduction. Under such circumstances, any genetic predilection they may have had to getting strep will have been passed on to their children.

A more radical and as yet speculative idea that would also explain a renewed population of strep-susceptible hosts each generation is that somehow a strep infection in childhood is *protective* against certain other late-arising diseases. For instance, a strep infection may increase the body's surveillance against the early stages of heart disease by putting more lymphocyte "police" at the site of incipient damage. Were such surveillance to prove effective, it might increase the survival advantage of strep-infected persons over those whose hearts were not so patrolled. The rationale behind this unorthodox idea is the observation made by the late Earl Benditt of the University of Washington that many if not most of the thickened heart blood vessel walls start from small nests of cells that look like early tumors. A modest, strep-encouraged, heightened immune surveillance directed toward such cells in heart vessel walls could suppress incipient plaque clones, giving the rheumatic fever patient a paradoxical survival *advantage*. This as yet untested idea could be challenged by following the outcomes of heart disease (other than valvular) in strep patients: If I am right, acute rheumatic fever patients should have *less* heart disease (other than valve problems) than do their normal counterparts.

This model underscores a fundamental truism. If all self-directed, autoimmune conditions arose only after menopause, there would be few selective disadvantages to having them. But some of the most destructive autoimmune diseases (to be discussed more fully in Chapter Six) arise in childhood and early middle age. This includes juvenile arthritis, juvenile diabetes, lupus erythematosus, and multiple sclerosis. It is also noteworthy that for the most part autoimmune disorders affect women preferentially over men. The ages for which this female predominance occurs are paradoxically centered around the reproductive years, raising serious questions about how some adverse immunological phenomena evolved.

A partial explanation is afforded by the fact that pregnancy ameliorates many forms of autoimmunity. It is now clear that the symptoms associated with many autoimmune diseases, like lupus erythematosus, let up appreciably during pregnancy, only to flare anew after the period of birth and lactation. For this reason, autoimmunity may not compromise reproductive success as much as might be expected, and the genes permitting its recurrence in the next generation may be perpetuated.

IMMUNOLOGICAL SELF-INJURY

New data suggest immune strength may in fact be a trade-off between hyperreactive, autoimmune reactivity and complete anergy wherein real threats are ignored. The most recent discovery supporting this view is *C3F*, a variant of a gene that controls the production of complement (a system of proteins that function as an immunological aid). As implied by its common definition, complement aids and abets immune reactions. *C3F*'s real evolutionary "value" was discovered serendipitously. During a search to uncover the basis for a strong propensity to migraine headaches in certain fair-skinned groups, researchers initially believed *C3F* was a relatively trivial gene. Early data seemed to confirm this view: It flags a predisposition to allergic reactions to strawberries or lobster. But *C3F* has since been found to be a master gene that links hyperactivity of the immune system to heart disease, arthritis, and hypertension.

The *C3F* gene is intimately associated with powerful immune responses. People who carry this gene are vulnerable to all sorts of immune-mediated organ damage resulting from self-directed immune attacks. The injuries appear to result from cumulative, immunologically mediated inflammation in organs like the heart and blood vessels that produce extra wear and tear over a lifetime.[15]

The possible importance of this gene as the master controller of immune strength cannot be overemphasized. In the United States, approximately 35 percent of the Caucasian population and lesser numbers of African Americans (about 7 percent) carry this critical variant. Something has to explain the extraordinary prevalence of a disease-associated gene. One clue is that those who carry the *C3F* gene appear to have a heightened degree of immunological efficiency. Carriers appear to have an increased resistance to many forms of infection as a result of a hypervigilant immune system. Indeed, a Faustian bargain seems to have been struck by natural selection: Individuals with the *C3F* gene escape some of the risks from infectious disease but are more prone to develop more extreme forms of immune overactivity, including autoimmune disease, arthritis, and long-term tissue injury from inflammation. This state of affairs is akin to the circumstances leading to the extra casualties experienced by Gulf War troops: In both instances, an overwhelming superiority of "firepower" succeeds in suppressing an enemy but inadvertently produces collateral damage. Just as more Allied troops died from "friendly fire" than from enemy assaults in the Gulf War, more tissues in the body of a *C3F* carrier may be damaged by the overkill from an excessively aggressive immune system than by natural attrition.

The reason for this hyperreactivity remains obscure, but researchers believe it is linked to an overresponse to antigenic stimulation. When the body's immune system reacts in an individual carrying the *C3F* gene, the overreaching intensity of infiltrating immune cells damages joints, bones, and other cellular targets. The resulting injuries suggest that many disabling diseases may result from damage to innocent bystanders from an otherwise "healthy" immunological attack.

A DOUBLE-EDGED SWORD

The second line of evidence for the double-edged sword of immunity comes from what is known about the development of some key infectious diseases. Microbiologists have long known that some organisms cause damage only *after* the immune system is brought into play. In diseases like lymphochoreomeningitis where inflammation of the membrane around the brain can cause swelling and brain damage, the damage ensues after the immune system mounts an abortive reaction to the initial viral incursion. Most of the damage to the brain results from the inflammatory changes brought about by the immune system and *not* the virus itself. As proof of this assertion, animals whose immune systems are so weakened that they *cannot* mount an immune response to the virus retain healthy brain tissue even in the presence of live virus. Most dramatically, such immunologically "crippled" animals with the meningitis virus stay well while their immune-intact, virus-infected littermates die.

Based in part on examples like these, I am asserting that much of the damage, sickness, and ill health we experience when under assault from microbial organisms is the result of our incomplete, overreactive, or mistimed immune reactions. As partial support for this radical notion, consider the new evidence that chronic fatigue syndrome, a persistent debilitating illness, is caused by the body's own faulty or incomplete response to an acute infection. New data from two studies[16] show that a prior viral or bacterial infection can lead to a long, drawn-out illness accompanied by unrelenting fatigue and, in time,

to a syndrome of chronic disability. The suspected cul-
prits are the cytokines, chemical alarm substances released by immune cells during chronic inflammation. In
fact, it is now recognized that inflammation per se is the
most primitive reaction from the immune system and can
lead to a general feeling of illness. Chronic inflammation
is commonly accompanied by a flood of blood-borne
chemicals that cause malaise, fatigue, fever, a host of
nonspecific aches and pains, and, in at least one disease
(relapsing fever), death. Like many of the body's reactions to infection, some of these symptoms may reflect
useful adaptations. For instance, fatigue may be a protective mechanism that encourages the body to rest and heal.

The idea of the immune system as a double-edged
sword is not new. With the advent of Austrian organic
chemist Karl Landsteiner's discovery of blood groups in
1923, it was clear that antibodies could also produce cellular damage. The ability of blood serum from different
people to break down or burst red blood cells (a process
termed "lysis") was used as a basis for classification of
blood types, with type O having the fewest antibodies
and AB the most. For this reason, someone with type O
blood can be a "universal donor" whereas someone with
AB can only donate blood to another type AB person. Red
blood cell destruction was soon found to be a real biological problem and not merely a test-tube artifact. Rh-
incompatible pregnancies (in which the mother was Rh
negative and her fetus Rh positive) are a case in point:
Fetal Rh-positive-provoked antibodies from the Rh-negative mother can cross the placenta and enter the fetal
circulation, producing a sometimes fatal breakdown or
hemolysis of fetal blood. In the 1960s, this catastrophic
consequence prompted the first heroic efforts of intrauterine therapy with transfusions of "compatible" blood.
Today, Rh disease in Rh-negative mothers is preventable
through an injection of Rh antibodies (known as Rho-

gam™) before or just after delivery of a firstborn Rh-positive fetus.

But why would the immune system have evolved to engage in such aggressive behavior? Answers are few and far between. In the early 1900s most researchers agreed with French immunologist Louis Pasteur that aberrant immune reactions were artifacts, completely atypical of what went on in the human body. Others, like German physician and scientist Paul Ehrlich, were genuinely concerned that the immune system could turn on the body itself and do serious damage. In a few rare instances of uncontrolled autoimmune disease, Ehrlich's concerns have proved all too real.

The reason why the immune system engages in self-destructive behavior is elusive. Among the explanations offered by some clinicians is that an autoimmune reaction is always secondary to a more vital function, that of clearing the body of naturally occurring and life-threatening microorganisms. In this model, autoimmunity is an unfortunate overreaction of a hypervigilant immune system. The *C3F* system just discussed would be such an example. The immune system's occasional overresponsiveness has been likened to the reactions of an army under siege, "lashing out blindly against an unseen and unmeasured enemy . . . using deadly force in the wrong time or place."[17]

Another explanation for the apparent maladaptive nature of autoimmunity is that it results from incomplete efforts of the immune system to dislodge pathogens. Just as a child will often throw a tantrum if he cannot resolve a seemingly simple problem, an immune system that can't throw off an unwanted invader may "lose it" and overrespond to the imagined threat. As partial proof of this possibility, a small number of children who cannot dislodge a gastrointestinal bacterium like salmonella go on to develop juvenile arthritis.

These observations offer the first titillating glimpses of a system that normally operates like a kind of gyroscope, deviating if perturbed but always returning to a certain ground state. When the deviations are extreme, the system can lose its balance altogether. In this sense the immune system is a kind of modern-day cybernetic machine that fluctuates between stimulating and suppressing, eradicating and enriching, annihilating and restoring. In the extreme of its ability to do good or harm, it is akin to the Hindu goddess Shiva whose two faces of creation and destruction undergird the Indian belief in the duality of the universe. Much of the evidence for these paradoxical immune reactions can be gleaned from a close look at the most common human diseases in which immunity plays a role.

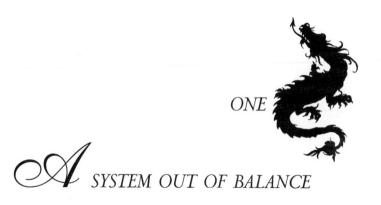

ONE

𝒜 *SYSTEM OUT OF BALANCE*

New patterns of disease have forced us to rethink our assumptions about the immune system's simple function as a defensive system. AIDS is a contemporary example. Although this disease is often presented as the archetype of the consequence of a failed immune system, it offers some strange contradictions, which will be explored at length in Chapter Thirteen. Here it suffices to observe that infection with HIV leads not only to a progressive deterioration of the immune system itself but also to paradoxical flareups of autoimmune disease. At one level, AIDS gives all of the appearances of a progressive state of immunological exhaustion. In AIDS patients the destruction and regeneration of the archetypal immune cell (the thymic lymphocyte T cell) occurs at an accelerating rate.

Initially 10 billion cells may need to be replaced each day. Later, as the disease progresses, the number may reach 200 billion! Over time, the immune system loses its ability to regenerate altogether. But even as the system runs down (and the rate of decline differs radically from patient to patient), other elements of the immune system are heating up with autoimmune reactions against body tissues like the salivary glands a common side reaction. In AIDS, because one type of immune cell escapes unscathed, it can continue to function. Ironically, this surviving cell type may even attack the dwindling main population of immune cells itself![1]

AIDS AS A MODEL

The AIDS epidemic has thrown this otherwise philosophical debate about the nature of immunity into sharp relief. As we will see in the chapter on AIDS, it is starkly evident that a failing immune system opens the body to a horror of opportunistic infections. By this account, anything that reinforces this flagging vital system would be presumed to be beneficial. But paradoxical evidence suggests that vulnerability to HIV may be *heightened* when the immune system is stimulated. It has long been recognized that people who also carry malarial parasites, tubercle bacilli, or other infections that stimulate their immune systems and thereby make more cells available for HIV infection are more—not less—vulnerable to AIDS.

Further evidence for this paradox comes from recent studies of AIDS patients who were given tetanus boosters in a misguided effort to strengthen their waning immunity. The results provide evidence that for survival in AIDS, less immunity may be better than more. In these tetanus-treated AIDS patients, the heightened level of immunity achieved after vaccination, rather than reducing viral load, led to a doubling or even greater increase in HIV.[2] More critically, following a booster shot, the white blood cells of HIV-negative volunteers showed a dramatic *increase* in susceptibility to infection with HIV in tissue culture.

In AIDS patients, it may be that these "booster" shots stress an already beleaguered immune system to the breaking point or simply increase the number of cells in harm's way for HIV. Whatever the explanation, this scary study suggests that the conventional wisdom that blindly creating a more powerful immune system *automatically* means longer-term survival, be it for AIDS patients or patients with other diseases, sometimes may be dead wrong. In AIDS as elsewhere, we may need to reexamine the cues from the immune system: Stronger may not always mean better, and weaker may not mean worse.

Some of these new and provocative data begin to make sense of other paradoxical findings in the AIDS research community. The young AIDS patient who underwent profound immunosuppression so as to receive a baboon bone marrow transplant has proven to be a surprisingly resilient survivor. Despite the fact that his bone marrow was never colonized with baboon cells, a year after his own immune system was virtually destroyed, this immunosuppressed patient is doing amazingly well, according to his treating physicians at the University of California San Francisco and Stanford. Although this case represents only a single patient, taking some of the non-specific responsiveness *out* of the immune system so that it can fight the variegated types of HIV more selectively may prove to be a viable option for AIDS treatment. But to do any of the required manipulations clearly demands a much more sophisticated understanding of how the immune system works than we now have.

AGING AND IMMUNITY

One often overlooked reality is the intrinsic ability of the immune system to "learn." The immune system has the remarkable capacity to improve with time. It does so by sharpening its responsiveness and retaining immunological "memory" of its prior contacts with the microbial world. For as yet unknown reasons, this memory can deteriorate, much as a tightly woven cloth becomes moth-eaten with time and use. In most species, this system develops serious flaws and gaps within a few years after the peak of its maturation. For some, immunity's protective shield against microbial invasion begins to wane once we pass the age of childrearing.

Once the immune system has mounted a successful response, some clinicians also mistakenly believe that it "remembers" how to respond indefinitely should a repeat challenge occur. In actuality, although the so-called "memory" cells of the immune system are extraordinarily long-lived (15–20 years or more), immunological memory fades just as does its neurological counterpart.

Until very recently, clinicians have relied on the assertion of infallibility of immunological memory to assure us that vaccinations provide indefinite protections against repeated bouts with illness. Unfortunately, the immune system commonly loses or distorts "remembered" information, leaving us vulnerable to reinfection in our later years when assailed by organisms like the tetanus-producing bacterium that we once could champion with ease.

ORIGINS

At birth, we are quite defenseless against many common pathogens and rely instead on the passive transfer of antibodies ingested with the colostrum in mother's milk from our digestive tract into our bloodstream. With each encounter with a pathogen, the system adjusts, gains strength, and sharpens its attentiveness to the external world. As we will see, if these natural bouts with infection are bypassed or replaced with artificial immunizations, the system appears to become unbalanced, allowing asthma and other reactions to ensue. As we age, the immunological memory of these past encounters also wanes, and autoimmune reactions become more common. Aristotle Onassis (1906–1975), for all his wealth, could not stem the onslaught of myasthenia gravis, an autoimmune disease in which antibodies are directed against the junctions between nerves and muscles. He died of this disease at the age of 69.

Over time, the immune system sometimes becomes so flawed that it "loses track" of friend and enemy, and misdirected attacks, like allergies, become more common. More ominously, as we pass into maturity, what began as an unmatched defense system may actually serve to stimulate or create certain disease processes, including cancer and autoimmune diseases directed against vital organs like the thyroid gland.

To understand how parts of the immune system decline while others flourish, we must understand the intricacies of its design.

The earliest precursors of the immune system can be found in the early embryo in the tissues surrounding the aorta and then spread to the nourishing yolk sac.[3] Although it varies enormously in its rate of maturation from species to species, for most higher animals, a functioning immune system first appears in late fetal life, around 7 months for humans. As the immune system matures, it "recapitulates" the phylogeny of its origins, retracing the gradual emergence of a sophisticated immune system with each stage in evolution.

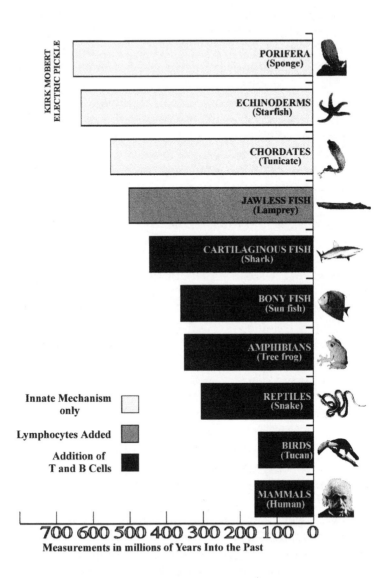

KIRK MOBERT
ELECTRIC PICKLE

PORIFERA
(Sponge)

ECHINODERMS
(Starfish)

CHORDATES
(Tunicate)

JAWLESS FISH
(Lamprey)

CARTILAGINOUS FISH
(Shark)

BONY FISH
(Sun fish)

AMPHIBIANS
(Tree frog)

REPTILES
(Snake)

BIRDS
(Tucan)

MAMMALS
(Human)

Innate Mechanism
only

Lymphocytes Added

Addition of
T and B Cells

700 600 500 400 300 200 100 0

Measurements in millions of Years Into the Past

In embryonic development, the first components of the system to appear are those found in primitive life forms. First, simple cell-engulfing macrophages like those found in the hydra and sponges arise, followed by antibody-producing cells that can be found in early vertebrates like the hagfish. In time these are followed by more complex cell-to-cell recognition and antibody-making systems common to higher vertebrates like reptiles and bony fishes. (See Figure Two.)

What emerges within a few months of birth is a highly plastic, flexible, and changing universe of integrated subsystems. We now know that all components of this system must act in harmony to achieve even the most modestly effective ends against often highly adaptive targets. The entire system must respond in a matter of days to keep pace with the incredibly rapid rate of replication of many invading pathogens. A typical bacterial strain may divide once every 20 minutes, producing over 1 billion descendants in just 10 hours! Given the fact that mutations arise only about once every 100,000 to 1,000,000 human cells and that the mutation rate of microorganisms such as HIV and its variants approaches 1 million times that of human cells, evolutionary change in some pathogens can be extraordinarily rapid, making them moving targets for an attacking immune system.

←——

Two.   Time of origin of immunological capabilities. Horizontal axis shows, in millions of years before the present, when different versions of immune systems emerged. Bars extending from the right show the form of immunity that different groups of animals (phyla) achieved. The jawless fishes, notably the lampreys, probably had the first lymphocyte-based immune systems. As shown by the black bars, all of the phyla from the cartilaginous fish upwards have all three immune apparatuses. Adapted from "Immunity and the Invertebrates," by Gregory Beck and Gail S. Habicht. Copyright © by Scientific American. *All rights reserved.*

As we will see in the next chapter, the immune system ultimately relies on its own ability to use enhanced mutation rates to generate varieties of antibody-making cells that can anticipate the ever-changing cell surfaces of these and other invading organisms. But a first response to a novel microorganism or foreign tissue may take up to a week or 10 days to become fully effective. In the meantime, nonspecific defenses must suffice. Only with the heightened secondary response of a previously primed immune system can defenses be marshaled in as few as 2 to 4 days. No wonder failure is as much a possibility as success in the early stages of many disease processes.

Yet failure is not a word that evolution respects. For any higher vertebrate to survive to reach reproductive years, it must effectively dance away from a myriad of pathogenic assaults from its embryonic phases, into adolescence and sexual maturity. The immune system is a remarkably effective system for accomplishing this objective. In doing so, it may nonetheless sow the seeds for misfortune arising in later years, as we have seen for diseases such as rheumatic fever.

NATURAL FORCES

The immune system, like all else in living systems, is shaped and limited by the forces of natural selection. Natural forces selected organisms whose bodies and blood serum could stave off the short-term threats to physical integrity posed by incursions of voracious parasites or disease-causing microorganisms. A second tier embodied in the acquired immune response ensured a lasting reaction to prevent any recurrence of a given invasion. At the same time, the immune system has had to be sufficiently fine-tuned to guarantee that any reaction against one organism did not so co-opt the system that it could not defend against another. Nor, as we have seen, could it be so hyperreactive that it became allergic to every new antigen it encountered or so aggressive that its attacks could turn back and damage the host.

In practice, these and other checks and balances on our natural defenses have ensured that the immune system is neither infallible in distinguishing self- from non-self nor necessarily 100 percent effective in battling disease-causing organisms when it encounters them. Natural selection has ensured that the immune system is good, but not so good that it wipes out *every* infectious organism, whether benign or harmful. If it did, over time only the most hyperaggressive virulent disease-causing organisms would find susceptible hosts, putting us all in harm's way.

In a kind of twisted evolutionary logic, it is "good" for us that so many of the germs on the planet are allowed to flourish in and on our bodies. Often they tend to serve as kind of a passive buffer zone against more noxious organisms. Some germs even produce their own natural antibiotics, keeping more dangerous organisms at bay. This idea, that the immune system must permit the survival of some disease-causing organisms and tolerate their modest disease-causing abilities (think of the common cold) so that it does not inadvertently select for the very worst pathogens, is a relatively new one. If all humans were immune to every common pathogen, it would open the door to those rare microorganisms for which we had no innate resistance. Organisms like Ebola virus or the other hemorrhagic viral types like dengue might gain a still greater toehold in the human population than they already have. This state of affairs could arise simply because an omnipresent immunity would be taxed to the maximum, leaving too few uncommitted variant lymphocytes to cover new infectious risks.

INVULNERABILITY

In theory the immune system's vast repertoire of possible responses provides that no "Andromeda strain" (a hypervirulent germ invented by author Michael Crichton) can catch us unawares. But as the Ebola epidemic shows, this is only true as long as host and pathogen have had sufficient time to evolve together. Totally "new" organisms, such as *Ebola zaire*, can and do still catch us unprepared. But their very lethality—limiting the number of survivors who can pass along the epidemic—has ensured that miniepidemics of Ebola and related viral strains only break out in isolated pockets. Despite its fearsome reputation, only 23 Ebola outbreaks with about 5000 deaths have occurred worldwide through 1996.

The immune system's sword against cancer has also proven to be blunter than expected. As with its bacterial and viral (especially HIV) counterparts, nonspecifically stimulating immunity to control cancer has proven disappointing. Bacterial extracts such as bacillus Calmette-Guérin (BCG) have worked only when instilled directly into a tumor, or in the case of early bladder cancer, into the urinary cavity itself. As I will show in the chapter on cancer, the immune system may paradoxically *stimulate* cancer cells even as it is being conscripted to fight them.

Such cautionary notes have failed to deter some New Age nutritionists and researchers who tout often unproven immune stimulants to turn the tide in our "battle" against cancer or simply to improve health. As many perceptive clinicians know, by the time a tumor is palpable, any real battle has long since been lost. And success in boosting immunity with nutritional supplements has rarely been well documented. More to the point, if some immune stimulation may produce untoward effects, any blanket recommendation to "tone up" the immune system may prove to be bad advice. The alternative, to have tightly honed, genetically specific immune responses tailored to individual tumor antigens, is just now being explored.

In this light, it may be crucial to our well-being to acknowledge the immune system's limitations as well as its much touted strengths. The immune system is not omnipotent. Sometimes the body's failure to recognize some antigens altogether is simply the result of genetic variation within the immune system itself. At others it may misfire and not mount an immune response because it lacks critical receptors in the human antigen recognition system (HLA).

The knee-jerk reaction that such lapses are dangerous and need repair may be dead wrong. Sometimes the wisdom of the species of the body itself dictates reserve and prudence rather than all-out assault. As we saw with the disastrous results of tetanus "boosters" to wake up latent immunity in AIDS patients, sometimes a dampened reaction is better than a provoked one.

The old idea of an immune system standing as a constantly vigilant bastion against every disease has given way to a much more fluid and dynamic model. As recently as 20 years ago, clinicians and researchers assumed that they understood the basic "philosophy" of immunity: once recovered, ever cured. Indeed, the very word "immunity" conjures up images of a permanent state of protection. Unfortunately or fortunately, the immune system often falls short of this ideal.

It is equally shortsighted to think of the immune system as infallible. In this view, the immune apparatus provides a way to anticipate every possible assault by affording the body a response to every imaginable antigen. Researchers like Jonas Salk, who invented the first polio vaccine, viewed the immune system as such a failsafe program. In theory, all that was needed to beat polio was to provide enough of the killed, virulent poliovirus to dupe the immune system into thinking it was under assault. We now know that the Salk approach, although effective if given early and repeatedly, affords only a limited, transient immunity. Were it not for the development of alternative long-lasting vaccines containing live virus, some adults would still be getting polio. The flawed philosophy of using killed viral particles as the vaccine itself gave rise to the Cutter Laboratory disaster in the mid-1950s when over 500 vaccinated children contracted polio from incompletely inactivated, virulent polio vaccine.

Many immunologists now believe that a weakened, mutating strain of live polio—the Sabin vaccine—provides a much more realistic body exposure to a changing assault. The lasting immunity produced affords most immunized children a long-lasting protection against reinfection. The success of the Sabin vaccine confirmed earlier studies in Egypt that demonstrated how early childhood infection, with wild-type virus while the infant was still protected by maternal antibodies in the milk, could produce lasting immunity.

But even this more daring and subtle challenge to the immune system is not without its detractors. Many immunologists point to the few cases each year of vaccine-produced polio as evidence of the failure of this approach. Typically, most of these cases occur in immunologically compromised children or adults who cannot mount an effective immune response and are overwhelmed by even the weakened viral strain. But the handful of such cases nationwide every year (no more than four to six typically) was originally overshadowed by the almost universal protection afforded to the whole at-risk populations. For instance, *no* cases of polio—vaccine induced or natural— were reported in California in 1996! Now, however, the only cases of polio reported tend to be Sabin vaccine related. With these statistics in mind, the newest protocols are a compromise that combine the strengths and weaknesses of both forms of vaccination. In 1996–1997, the

CDC recommended a preliminary series of two killed, Salk vaccine shots followed by one with attenuated live virus (the Sabin approach).

OVERVIEW

We now know that the immune system does not serve as a Maginot line against invasion of foreign organisms. Nor does it usually work well enough to destroy all of the aberrant, genetically disparate cells that comprise a typical malignancy. Sometimes when the body gives the appearance of having won a battle against an invading cancer, what has actually happened is a kind of Mexican standoff. On one side, you have the triumphant immune cells, bristling with antibody "weapons," while on the other, you have the nearly vanquished but now hidden cancer cells, lying in wait just as do so many latent microorganisms, ready to spring forth once immunity has waned.

We are increasingly learning of situations where an infection is ostensibly "cured" by the body's immune response, only to leave pockets of resistant organisms capable of producing silent infections years later. Such a circumstance is typical following the implantation of a prosthetic device like a hip or breast implant or artificial heart valve. The surfaces of such implants often become covered with a "biofilm" of contaminating microorganisms suspended in a proteinaceous coating impervious to most antibodies. Usually, the microorganisms are held at bay as long as the immune system remains strong and intact. But should immune strength wane or become dysfunctional, pathogens can escape from their privileged sites and undergo a resurgence, sometimes leading to a local response or to overwhelming systemic infection. An analogous series of events may happen with AIDS. Here, latent virus that has been held in check by an initial immune reaction may become sequestered in lymph nodes. From there, forays of virus and resulting destruction of immune cells may permit reemergence of latent viral particles, further immune depression, and the onslaught of opportunistic infections.

As we will see, the struggle to keep our immune systems on alert and functionally intact is a silent one, waged daily against minor incursions of bacteria or viruses. When the system breaks down and infectious organisms gain a toehold, the battle is often described as a war, with the outcome survival itself. Though such military imagery is commonly used, the standard military analogy is often insufficient to describe the complexity of immune reactions.

IMMUNE ASSAULTS

The quest to understand this process is all the more urgent because of recent evidence that our immune systems are themselves under unprecedented attack. Not only are viruses like those responsible for AIDS and its related diseases suddenly rampant, but chemicals and radiation that assault the integrity of the immune system are now permeating our environment. Where this list was once limited to carcinogens like benzopyrene found in coal tar and diesel particles, immunosuppressants now include diethylstilbestrol (DES), the hormone given to millions of pregnant women in the 1950s and 1960s, and workplace chemicals and sensitizers like the isocyanates used in manufacturing plastics and related chemicals (methyl isocyanate) dispersed among tens of thousands of residents in the horrendous industrial accident at Bhopal, India, in 1984. As I will show, new data suggest that a long list of massively used pesticides must now be added to this list of classic immunosuppressants.

In combating many of these unprecedented epidemics we have begrudgingly learned a new lesson of humility. The tragedy of AIDS has helped us understand the intricacies of immunity in unparalleled ways. This knowledge has grown exponentially in the last two decades. We now have an almost complete inventory of the immune system's cellular and chemical actors. Yet by itself, this knowledge has proven ineffectual. Much of what makes for an effective, coordinated immune response to AIDS still remains a mystery. A current review lists 12 unanswered immune questions that require answers before AIDS will be controlled, including the fundamental one of whether immune changes represent the causes or effects of an HIV infection.[4]

Nor do we understand the process of autoimmunity by which the immune system attacks itself. Why do autoimmune diseases like lupus erythematosus seemingly strike at random, crippling young adults—especially women—in the prime of their lives? Immune deficiency diseases affect the very young, often the result of genetic failures to "patch in" or repair one critical component of their immune system.[5] At the other end of life, each of us must cope with flagging immune systems that decay and lose their "edge" with each passing year once we pass into old age. (Subtle evidence of immune depression can be seen as early as age 45–50 in many persons as revealed by reduced antibody responses to standard test antigens.)

For all our knowledge, we lack a fundamental understanding of how the immune system develops prenatally or how it deteriorates with age. We continue mistakenly to permit chemicals into our biosphere that damage immunity or create environmental conditions that weaken it. Even the subtle depletion of the ozone layer by chlorofluorocarbons (CFCs) and other chemicals may be having secondary effects on our bodies. The resulting depletion permits hazardous ultraviolet light to impinge on our skin, killing outright many of the system's key cellular participants, like the so-called Langerhans cells (discussed below), and weakening others.

And when the body's immune system overreacts we are almost helpless in the face of autoimmune onslaughts in which the body's tissues are attacked from within. When we do respond, for instance to bouts of asthma, skin rashes, or allergies, we more often than not use a corticosteroid or antihistamine sledgehammer to cure the problem. Such "cures," particularly when they involve potent steroids such as methylprednisone, can lead to dependency, immune depression, and destruction of bone and other tissues through activation of bone-destroying cells (osteoclasts). Whereas topical cortisone-containing creams generally have too little (0.5 to 1.0 percent) cortisone to affect the body as a whole, parents using the newest 2.0 percent formulation must be made aware of the danger of exposing too much skin to cream treatments because of the real possibility of immune depression in their children from dermal absorption.

Even as we describe the key mediators of the immune response in ever finer detail, we still lack a rudimentary knowledge of how to restore damaged or aging immune systems. Although the very first forays into treating rare forms of severe immune deficiencies with genetic engineering proved promising, as when National Institutes of Health researchers rescued two young girls who had SCID, researchers have failed to develop a broader approach for treating other, more common, hereditary immune disorders. We do know how to knock out the immune system to permit foreign organ grafts like liver, heart, and kidney to survive, but we do not fully understand the mystery of why those grafts are successful, nor why that success is sometimes followed by a rash of new skin tumors. And even though we have known about the existence of antigens in various cancers for more than four decades, we are still years away from a spectrum of effective cancer vaccines that will work consistently against all types of tumors.

Clearly we need sharper thinking about the nature of the immune system and its vulnerabilities if we are to stem the early tide of new immunosuppressant chemicals that now threaten some species. As I will show, many now face an unprecedented wave of exposure to immunotoxic chemicals and radiation. What would a 10 percent depression of immune competence mean for these endangered species, especially the amphibians currently at risk of die-off from excessive UV exposure and perhaps chemical toxicants? And what about the people in the developing world who face reemergent diseases like dengue, cholera, and malaria in such increasing numbers? How will the almost certain immunologically crippling effects of heightened doses of radiation, both ultraviolet and classic, affect people in those regions of the world like Australia and Chernobyl, respectively, that are most vulnerable to assault?

To make any progress at all in our battle to save the immune system, we first have to acknowledge our ignorance. We have always assumed that the immune system was "the way" the body dealt with infection. Indeed, a core problem of Western medicine generally may be its assumption that health is a matter of strength and that each "system" acts independently to shore up the body.

Slowly, we may grudgingly acknowledge that the full panoply of immunological activities touches virtually every aspect of our biology, from self-identity to pregnancy, and that survival requires recognition of interdependency.

INTERCONNECTEDNESS

It is now almost doctrinaire to point out something the Chinese have known for millennia: All organ systems in the body are interconnected and interdependent. At a core biological level, the immune system is inextricably linked to the neural and endocrine systems that integrate our behavior and interactions with the world as a whole. Indeed, we are just now beginning to glimpse the linkage of the immune system and its myriad cellular stations and chemical identifiers with the deepest roots of each person's biological individuality.

What we do know is almost bewildering in its complexity. The immune system is an incredibly busy place. It somehow takes stock of all of the normal tissues in the body on a regular basis, retains a memory of past encounters with foreign substances and organisms, and then adjusts itself—especially during pregnancy—to tolerate what would otherwise be an alien presence. Each of us is subjected to a constant rain of foreign material, much as detritus falls incessantly to the bottom of the ocean. Dead cells, encroaching microorganisms, foreign foodstuffs and pollen, incipient tumors, and parasites enter the body's portals on a daily basis. Somehow the immune system parses through this incredible morass of novel and foreign material and sorts out that to which it must respond and that to which it must adapt, much like a quality control engineer on the assembly line. And as we will see, tolerance is as important to an ever-vigilant immune system as is aggression. To understand just how the immune system manages to be both a boon and a bane to our existence requires a deeper understanding of its fundamental nature.

TWO

*B*ASIC IMMUNOLOGY

Anyone who watches what the immune system does would conclude the function of immunity is in some way linked to recognizing "foreignness." As we have seen, the immune system copes with an ever-changing panoply of potential pathogens, many with remarkably adept and rapid evolutionary adaptability. To do this well, the system must have tremendous variability and high specificity in its response. Much of this flexibility is ensconced in the 209 genes embedded in three major tissue-recognition regions of the human genome.[1] Many of the genes code for proteins that enable their holder to bind a particular group of viral or parasite antigens.

Why such variability? For one thing, this enormous diversity of genes minimizes the likelihood that a given virus could escape immune surveillance and threaten the population as a whole. Novel laureate Rolf Zinkernagel, in his 1996 Lasker Award lecture, stressed this point as the primary reason for the existence of so many different tissue- or surface-recognition molecules in the human population.[2] An immune response can recognize and inactivate *simultaneously* two or more invading organisms, be they virus, bacterium, or parasite, demonstrating that this recognition system has remarkable adaptive properties.

Typically, the immune response involves antibodies that home in on a surface component of a pathogen. When it works well, the ensuing destruction or inactivation of the invading organism can be lifesaving. When it fails, or worse, when the immune system turns against the body's own constituents, it can be harmful or fatal. This last element, the root of autoimmune disease (the topic of a separate chapter), increasingly appears to result from failure to distinguish certain bacterial or viral antigens from those antigens of the body itself. Perhaps most quixotic of all, the immune system appears to vary between the sexes.

SEX DIFFERENCES

As a general rule, females of every mammalian species studied express stronger immunity to a given antigenic challenge than do males. On closer scrutiny, females generally outperform males in terms of immune strength throughout their lifetime, but especially after puberty. Given the limited genetic differences between males and females, such a realization is simultaneously one of the most dramatic and perplexing phenomena in nature. Although researchers have identified the probable hormonal contributions to this difference, it remains an evolutionary paradox.

From an evolutionary viewpoint, it is unclear why either sex should hold an immunological advantage over the other. In a heterosexual species, the general rule is males and females must survive in equal numbers to ensure a balanced sex ratio during the reproductive years. Natural selection and the exigencies of mammalian reproduction have generally operated to keep the sex ratio at 1:1. How can this balance be achieved if males are in fact immunologically inferior—and hence subject to more infectious deaths, for instance—than females? To ensure a balanced sex ratio, nature initially produces more males than females at conception. In part this is because males begin to die at a higher rate than do females soon after they are conceived. In addition to a greater loss of XY embryos, the newborn death rate is higher for males than for females. To compensate for these early losses, in most human groups about 106 males are born for every 100 females, a sex ratio of 51.46 percent.

Estrogens in women or females generally are linked to stronger immune responsiveness. Conversely, as males mature, it is clearly a disadvantage to have a surfeit of testosterone—or some other factors associated with maturation of the testes. Compared with females, adult male mice, for instance, are hampered in their ability to recognize and reject dissimilar skin grafts, a surrogate test of the general strength of their immune systems. In a series of early studies with Nobel laureate George Snell and immunologist Ralph Graff on the effect of the gonads on this sensitive measure of immune strength, I found that only half as many males as genetically identical females could recognize and reject certain foreign skin grafts.[3] If such males were orchiectomized (a polite, technical term for castration), their immune strength became more like that of their female counterparts. Interestingly, removing the ovaries of the female mice did nothing to improve or diminish their immune strength, suggesting that substances in the testes were adversely affecting male immunity. This likelihood was underscored by transplant studies in which ovariectomized (ovaryless) females were given male gonads. Under such circumstances, the "female" mice reverted to the male pattern of delayed and incomplete rejection of their skin grafts.

Perhaps most interestingly of all, simultaneous removal of *both* the adrenal glands (found above the kidneys) and the sex glands (either ovaries or testes) produced an immunologically *superior* animal, whether male *or* female! At the onset, between a third to a half of all intact animals of either sex were incapable of rejecting their skin grafts. Removal of the adrenal glands *with* the testes or ovaries enabled 83–89 percent of the animals (male and female, respectively) to reject their test skin grafts, suggesting that minimizing the amount of corticosteroid hormones (which are found in the adrenal gland) also improves immune competence. (This point is taken up again in Chapter Seven on stress.)

The simplest interpretation of these historic studies was that hormones secreted by the testes and the adrenal glands normally suppress a full-blown immune response, which makes the body less vulnerable to autoimmunity but also more open to external disease. Certainly, from what we know about the immune-suppressing effects of stress, this finding accords with the literature. More recent studies have confirmed that both sex and adrenal hormones are potent modifiers of the immune response. Estrogens generally support or stimulate immune reactions whereas testosterone and hormones from the adrenal gland suppress it.

THE "MALE THING" AND AUTOIMMUNITY

These data suggest that nature has permitted male immune competence to lag behind that of females. Indeed, male morbidity and mortality from infectious diseases, especially in the very young and very old, exceeds that of females in virtually every culture studied. Life expectancy for males consistently falls below that of females by some 10 percent. In developed countries, this difference may be even greater, with life expectancy in men averaging 76–78 years and in women 83–85 years. Some of this deficit is presumed, but not proven, to be linked to diminished immunological strength and competence.

One explanation for such a paradoxical loss of life and vitality is that somehow male immune depression is an evolutionary trade-off. Perhaps males give up some of their immunological competence in order to deal with and respond to the typically higher stresses associated with male cultural roles. If being a "tough guy" entails manufacturing lots of adrenocorticosteroids as well as testosterone, immune depression may be a secondary consequence of needing to be able to show androgenic steroid-supported aggression in do-or-die situations.

This model presupposes that the necessity of withstanding the repetitive stresses of male existence has led to a heightened production of adrenal and testicular hormones. From an evolutionary viewpoint, we also have to believe that such male-dominant exigencies outweigh the adaptive edge of a strong immune system. But this idea is not completely heuristically satisfying. The paradoxical loss of immune strength in half of the population has to have a positive value. One place to look for such value is in the risks of a hypervigilant immune system. What if being immunologically "on the edge" all the time were a *dis*advantage in some way? A hint in this direction can be gleaned by looking at autoimmune disease. With the limited exception of rare conditions like ankylosing spondylitis, which results in a crippling arthritis of the spine, women outnumber men in almost every category of autoimmune disease. As mentioned earlier, females are more likely to have lupus erythematosus, Sjögren's disease, multiple sclerosis, and scleroderma than are males. But for women, this extra "cost" of hyperimmune vigilance appears to be an acceptable trade-off in terms of health: Women experience fewer episodes of blood poisoning and pneumonia and other infectious disease complications than do men.

The true explanation for sex differences in immunity is obviously more complex than this. The answer goes beyond a simple "male dominance is good," "immunity can suffer" argument. Given the centrality of immunity it is less than evident why it is a good thing for certain sex hormones to incapacitate immune reactions, no matter how harmful rare autoimmune diseases are. Perhaps being able to have sex or stress hormones transiently depress immunity is an important evolutionary fixture of human development. If powerful immune reactions are not all that they are cracked up to be (part of the major thesis of this book), then permitting transient or even semipermanent immune depression during the years of peak male, and to a lesser extent female, sexuality may be a blessing in disguise.

For one thing, the transient depression of immune strength seen in pregnancy may be essential for protecting the fetus (more about this below). And recall that semen carries large numbers of lymphocytes. It may be crucial that these lymphocytes be immunologically weakened, perhaps by their exposure to male hormones. For men, *not* sending a cascade of primed, immune-ready lymphocytes into the female reproductive tract at the time of intercourse may be essential for protecting women against some male sexually transmitted diseases, or even so-called graft-versus-host reactions where the male lymphocytes might attack the female's own cells. If immunologically activated male cells did traverse the vaginal canal, it might also impair the local mucosal immunity needed by women for protection against bacterial infections. Perhaps males let up a little in immune strength so as not to threaten female immune integrity. Much of this lost reactivity is in diminished antibody production. To understand how this might be so, it is first critical to understand the fundamentals of antibodies.

ANTIBODIES

The immune system demonstrates remarkable affinity to its targets. Each time an exposure to a novel substance or bacterial/viral product occurs, the immune response appears to mold itself to the invader. In the main, this remarkable property depends on special molecules known as antibodies that lock onto their antigenic targets. The original interpretation of the antigen–antibody reaction was that the amino acid chains of antigens "fit" corresponding protein chains in antibodies. In support of this idea, antibodies were found to bind chemically to their targets. The nature of the bonding involved weak reactions analogous to some of the chemical bonding observed in other chemical reactions.

For this reason and because so many of the early antigen–antibody experiments (circa 1910–1930) were performed in test tubes, antibodies and their reactions were not unexpectedly described in the language of chemistry. In one sense, this early chemicalization of immunology was unfortunate because it deflected experiments away from understanding the biological and naturalistic, adaptive functions of the immune system toward more mechanistic models. Antigen–antibody reactions were described by some German immunologists like Heidelberger with the same steady-state equations applied to chemical reactions. When an antibody–antigen reaction occurred in test tubes or petri plates, the resulting complex would take one of three forms: It could stay in solution, precipitate, or form a kind of matrix or gel. The resulting complexes were all antigen–antibody mixtures of one kind or another. In language reminiscent of high school chemistry, the ability of antibodies to tie up certain antigens was described as a process of "neutralization" where they bound with antigens until an equilibrium was reached, much as bases dripped slowly into colored acid solutions cancel each other. Group reactions could occur because most antibodies contain *two* antigen-binding sites, like the docking stations on a space station, permitting clusters of antigen–antibody complexes to form. A few antibodies, such as those involved in allergic reactions known as IgE, have four such sites.

One of the predictable consequences of this chemicalized worldview was that the great diversity of antibodies produced by the body was described in strictly chemical terms. In the early 1940s, these antibody–antigen complexes greatly impressed early Nobel prize-winning protein chemists like Linus Pauling. In keeping with his work on enzymes and the structure of the hemoglobin molecule, Pauling believed molecular mechanisms gave antibodies their ability to mold themselves to antigens. In Pauling's model, antibodies took on the conformation of an antigen, much as a copy of a coin is made using a mold.[4]

In this case, the logic of Pauling's molecular biology was uncharacteristically flawed. There would simply not be enough antigen around to account for every molecule of antibody, even if antigens were used repetitively. Moreover, it was a cumbersome system, requiring the positioning and immobilization of templates each time an antibody was needed. No, something far richer and ingenious was needed to ensure that antibodies were "made" with just the right target specificity following exposure to a novel antigen.

CLONAL SELECTION

The theory that postulated just how the immune system accomplishes this delicate task of sorting its targets was originally developed by researchers in the early 1950s and published in book form in 1957. The progenitor of this "clonal selection theory" was Niels Jerne of Denmark. His views were later championed by Sir Macfarlane Burnet in Australia and Malcolm Talmadge in the United States. The Pauling protein folding model postulated that each competent cell would be able to make many different antibodies as long as templates were available. In contrast, the Jerne model predicted only one antibody type per cell. Jerne postulated each lymphocyte would be selected for antibody production by virtue of having a genetically unique property of antigenic recognition, much the way one soldier could be culled from the ranks to "volunteer" for duty by matching his name to a duty roster. In its earliest stages of development, the antibody-producing white blood cell would be able to respond to one or at best two or three related antigenic determinants. The cell did this by making antibodies that it was genetically *pre*programmed to produce. Jerne envisioned literally hundreds of thousands of genetically unique immune cells, embedded in their lymph node or splenic "homes," lying spiderlike to be tripped into action by contact with a novel antigen.

At first blush, this model seems preposterous. How could such genetic diversity exist among cells that, at least initially, began life with genetically identical instructions? And given the limitations on space within lymphoid tissue, how could the body afford to have a small handful, perhaps even just one lymphocyte precursor for any given antigenic specificity? Certainly that was an inefficient way to muster support for a concerted attack on bacteria! Then there was the problem of antibody volume. Only when stimulated by a powerful matching antigen could the progenitor lymphocyte or clone expand into an antibody-producing microfactory. How would there be enough time for the formidable population of cells needed to make even a few microliters of antibody?

We now know that a series of rapid cellular divisions permits rapid genetic changes and rearrangements in the antibody "repertoire" of primordial lymphocytes, much as all of the parts of a new symphonic score get subdivided into individual musical instructions for individual instruments. The conductor elicits a response from the appropriate musician just as an antigen provokes a single lymphocyte with the proper genetic score to play out its antibody. Following such an antigenic "cut," the special lymphocyte expands to produce millions of descendants in a short period, each a genetic replica of the other. In this way, highly specific antibodies can be produced in number and kind proportionate to the continuing presence of the inciting stimulus.

DISTINGUISHING "SELF" FROM "NON-SELF"

Sir Macfarlane Burnet along with Talmadge added another element to Jerne's "clonal selection theory." Burnet recognized the intrinsic danger of preexisting reactivity: If lymphocytes encountered the body's own antigens, they could be stimulated at the wrong time for the wrong reasons, and the body could open up and attack itself. To counter this possibility, he posited that the body became "self-tolerant" during neonatal life by a process of elimination of potentially self-reactive clones. In this model, key cellular components of the immune system would police themselves to eliminate any cells with the capacity to react against the body's own tissues.

The exact mechanism through which the immune system accomplished this was unknown in Burnet's time, but we now have remarkable affirmation of the accuracy of his vision. In the last few years researchers have discovered that during the early stages of their maturation, primordial lymphocytes are channeled through the thymus, the central gland of the immune system located just below the thyroid gland at the front of the neck. There, virtually all of the precursors of the immune cells of the body that are destined to become autoreactive cells are eliminated. Like kids coming to football practice for the first time, newly arrived precursor cells are partitioned into two groups: one that is destined to sit on the sidelines, the other to play. During passage through the thymus, those precursor cells that carry surface markers that bind to *self antigens* die or become inert, while those with cell surface markers that will enable them later to identify enemies of the body are allowed to live.

A corollary of this elegant model is that presentation of *any* antigen early enough in development (when this process largely takes place) will lead to destruction of the respective self-reactive cell. The critical test of Burnet's theory was put to experiment by Rupert E. Billingham, L. Brent, and Peter Brian Medawar in 1953. The Billingham team posited that if a newborn mouse were presented with cells other than its own during the "check-in" phase of immune development, potentially reactive cells would encounter this "foreign" tissue and die: As a result, the mouse would become tolerant toward non-self tissue.

In dramatic fashion, the Billingham team showed that this would indeed happen: Cells from a black mouse injected into a newborn white mouse made the white one "think" it was black as well as white. Months later the white mouse would readily accept skin grafts from the same otherwise alien black donor. Later, Medawar showed that removal of the neonatal thymus would also leave the mouse vulnerable to accepting foreign tissue from virtually any mouse of the same species. But because the thymus was the only way station at which potentially self-reactive lymphocytes could "check in," over time extirpation of this critical gland also permitted the development of self-reactive lymphocytes that attacked the mouse's own tissues.

Although refinements of this concept have shown that an animal need not be exposed solely during the neonatal period to induce tolerance, the basic features of this model of elimination of these precursor cells* or "thymocytes" have held up.[5] Once cleansed of potentially self-reactive lymphocytes, the immune system can carry out a plethora of surveillance and elimination activities with a minimum of risk.

*The key element in the process of cleaning out self-reactive cells from the lymphocyte pool appears to be linked to the way in which antigens are presented to developing thymocytes. We now know that this antigen presentation process is carried out in a manner analogous to a fraternity or sorority selection process. By word of mouth, certain recognized candidates pass muster while "different" pledges are chummed out. Similarly, antigens are made "familiar" by being referred by antigen-processing cells (APCs). If they are "right," they are accepted and antibodies are made. If they are "wrong," APCs give signals to thymocytes that either trip their internal "self-destruct" mechanism or cause functional paralysis wherein the cells are rendered nonreactive.

NATURAL SELECTION IN THE IMMUNE SYSTEM

This process of mutation and subsequent selection is very much akin to Darwin's idea of natural selection. In the instance of the immune system, an environmental agent (here an antigen) works to favor the proliferation or growth of only one of many genetically preadapted cell types. By having an extraordinarily high mutation rate, responsive immune cells are programmed to "imagine" an entire universe of potential antigens. An antigen selects a responsive cell, much like darkness favors rare albino life form, by finding the one mutated cell that will respond to its presence.

The body's way of preventing T cells from responding to its own constituents is also a form of Darwinian evolution. Through adult life as new variants of T cells emerge via mutations in special "variable genes," a wide range of potential reactivity appears in the constellation of lymphocytes. Whenever an inadvertent "match" arises with a native histocompatibility antigen, that cell lineage is destroyed, ensuring that the respective antigen cannot be a target of an autoimmune response.[6]

The mechanism whereby contact with an antigen results in cell death rather than cell growth is known as "clonal deletion." This process is analogous to the destruction of heat-sensitive bees in a hive on a hot summer day—all but those genetically preadapted to resist heat and respond positively to the new environment die.

As discussed above, clonal deletion occurs primarily in the thymus gland and is responsible for expunging the body of potentially self-reactive cells. For this reason, the thymus gland is properly considered the central organ of the immune system. This fact, known since about 1960, did not prevent some well-intentioned pediatricians from prophylactically irradiating perfectly healthy thymus glands from newborn children, often girls, in the mistaken belief that this initially large, heart-shaped gland located just below the sternal notch somehow interfered with normal breathing. If the mouse experiments are right, in time many of these now middle-aged women will develop autoimmune disease. Many have already developed thyroid cancer.

To recap, the thymus gland's primary function is in generating and selecting a rich population of T cells ("T" stands for thymus-derived) that will be able to patrol the body effectively. To do so, the thymus must both activate a sufficiently broad range of reactive T cells and simultaneously restrict others for responding to the major histocompatibility complex (MHC) antigens that define "self." To do this latter task, the thymus both orders the above-described destruction of potentially autoreactive T cells and induces others to a kind of cellular paralysis to ensure self-tolerance. (The details of this process may be of interest to science-oriented readers, whereas others may wish to move ahead to the next subheading.)

ONTOGENESIS: DEVELOPMENT OF THE IMMUNE SYSTEM

The first stages of the maturation process begin during embryonic development. The differentiation of the rudiment of thymic tissue into a functional outer layer (the cortex) and inner one (the medullary compartment) involves a series of sequential steps. First, migratory precursor cells move from the bone marrow to the thymus where they become thymocytes. These cells in turn move from the outer region of the thymus (the cortical region) and then, as they mature, to the medullary compartment where the cells run through the previously described selection process to either be activated—or destroyed. Different varieties of immune cells thus pass through the microenvironment of the thymus where they acquire the "marching orders" that tell them what functions to perform in the body. At a microscopic level, these orders are inscribed by special molecules on their cell surfaces that define their range of reactivity.[7]

The most common sites to find T cells are the lymph nodes. A highly specialized subgroup of cells assist T cells in mediating immune reactions. These critical cells are known as helper T cells (also identified as CD4$^+$ cells). (These helper T cells are the ones targeted by the HIV organism.) Other T-cell subpopulations assist the body in dampening immune reactions so that the latter do not persist indefinitely. These cells are known as T suppressor cells.

Another group of cells is destined to make antibody-producing cells. These are called B cells (named after the bursa of Fabricius in the chicken discovered by the seventeenth-century anatomist Fabricius). B cells go through their own process of maturation, usually within the bone marrow, during which various forms of antibody are expressed on their surfaces. Eventually, a mature antibody-producing B cell emerges known as the plasma cell. The degree and number of such plasma cells is controlled by certain chemical mediators and, ultimately, by the form of antigen itself. As will be discussed below, one important stimulant of the immune system is the class of substances known as "superantigens."

THREATS TO BODILY INTEGRITY

Increasingly, researchers have become aware of direct and subtle threats to the body posed by certain aberrant cells that may grow outside of immunological control. These cells include not only tumor cell populations, but also variants of cells that grow outside of the organ they normally occupy. A typical example are the cells of the uterine lining that produce a florid form of cell overgrowth known as endometriosis where uterine cells lodge in the wall of the body cavity. Others include cells from the embryo that are inadvertently implanted and may produce a cancerous growth known as choriocarcinoma. The immune system appears to have the capacity to recognize and destroy such aberrant cells. We now know that the immune system also targets other cells for destruction, such as damaged or dying ones that have lost growth-controlling signals or receptors. Such accidental variants can pose a grave risk to the normal internal balance of cell numbers and division. In some circumstances, genetic changes (such as the loss of the *P53* gene, the one associated with a high risk of many forms of cancer) can generate cells with the capacity for unlimited growth. On those occasions when new genes are activated and "foreign"-appearing cells arise—as in the developing embryo—it is important for the body's immune system *not* to respond and thereby threaten the survival of an emerging vital organ or tissue. In part, the immune system achieves this by being among the last organ systems to mature during embryogenesis.

To serve an internal surveillance function, the immune system must thus walk a delicate tightrope. On the one hand, the system must draw a sharp enough distinction to "miss" an otherwise normal variant of a vital body constituent but still "hit" an offending cell that poses a genuine risk to bodily integrity. When confronted with an internal threat from a virus, it must mount a response that is so powerful and focused that it leads to the destruction of the offender but one that is not *so* powerful that it destroys adjacent nontarget cells or is misfocused on one of the body's own constituents.

RECOGNITION

Research immunologists recognize that to respond both appropriately and effectively, the immune system must be able to distinguish genuine from bogus threats from within and outside the body and then remember how to repeat the process. It must also be able to temper its response so that the nature of the reaction is appropriate to the threat.

Ultimately, immune recognition depends on the ability of the system to thread a molecular needle, distinguishing foreign "antigens" that are usually proteins or combinations of sugars and proteins (glycoproteins) from otherwise identical ones that may arise on the body's own tissues. In practice, making such distinctions can be more difficult than it sounds. With the exception of some bacterial and plant cells, the building blocks of the cell walls of all higher organisms are essentially identical. For this reason, the feat of distinguishing self components (which must not be attacked) from foreign ones (which must be) can be a treacherous undertaking.

The immune system usually accomplishes this feat with remarkable precision. As we saw, the process of culling any self-reactive cells from the pool of potential immune respondents leaves most of the lymphocytes of the body primed and ready to direct their attention toward bona fide threats—and not the body proper. Occasionally, the system mismatches a target and attacks the body's own cellular components, as when the body attacks the lining of heart valves after a strep infection.

TWO LEVELS OF RESPONSE: THE FIRST TIER

Normally, such aberrant reactions are stymied by an elaborate system of checks and balances embedded in a two-tiered system. The first tier, sometimes known as the "innate" or intrinsic immune system, is a vestige of an evolutionarily old apparatus, one that ensured that body fluids included chemicals or cells that would prove inimical to invasion by infectious or parasitic organisms. The strengths of this innate system reside in its broad spectrum of virus-killing activity and its ready-made toxicity to infectious organisms.

As a front line response, the innate system presents a kind of broadside defense that rapidly and nonspecifically clears out newly arriving bacteria or other pathogens. It does so with a host of ready-made molecules, including so-called "defensins." These molecules are found in many insect orders and are toxic to a broad array of potential microbial threats. Hemolin, present in certain insects such as moths and grasshoppers, is a substance that functions like a primitive antibody. It binds to the surface of certain microbes and thereby assists the body in removing them. The silk moth (*Hyalophora cecropia*), for example, expresses cecrophin, a small peptide that can kill bacteria.

Other nonspecific defenses exist at the various boundaries between the self and the outer world: In frogs, magainin (from the Hebrew word for shield) is a skin protein that provides amazing protection against otherwise disease-causing, waterborne bacteria. In humans, the skin's "acid mantle" affords excellent protection against many forms of potentially pathogenic bacteria. And mucosal membranes secrete varying levels of a general antibody (IgA) into mucus, entrapping an indeterminant number of bacteria and viruses that might otherwise invade normal tissues.[8]

Overall, having this "on call" immune system gives the body a head start, just as having an emergency room provides a speedy, although sometimes nonspecific, front line for a hospital. Thereafter, refinements in immune responses help hand-tailor the reaction to bacteria and viruses. The innate system is augmented by preformed antibodies (opsonins) along with a substance (complement) that assists the breakdown of bacterial cell walls. Serum also contains white blood cells with many-lobed nuclei (polymorphonuclear cells) and macrophages (named from the Greek root, "big eaters"), which can envelop offending bacteria into their cellular interiors and digest most of the ingested cells.

Included in the list of cellular actors are bacteria- and tumor-neutralizing cells, the natural killer (NK) cells. NK cells, like the protagonists of the movie *Natural Born Killers*, are ostensibly preordained to kill. They are "natural-born" enemies of tumor cells. During the early stages that normally precede development of full-blown cancer, NK cells may actually seek out and kill incipient tumor cells incubating in the recesses of the body. We know this in part because a light brown strain of "beige" mice that are genetically deficient in NK cells develop many more spontaneous tumors than do their normal counterparts.

This innate system can be called the Minutemen of the Body because it requires no preparation time to get up to speed in marshaling its defensive activities. Some variant of this system is present in virtually all multicellular organisms studied. As might be expected from a system designed for rapid response, the innate system includes many substances that are preformed and released by hair-trigger responses, often within minutes or hours of a bacterial invasion, much as a Minuteman missile is designed to respond to any unidentified attacking missile.

But like the early versions of this defense system, the immune system components can misfire, releasing physiologically overwhelming amounts of pharmacologically active substances. In some instances, such as an allergic or anaphylactic response to an antigen, the response can be so exaggerated as to threaten the body itself. In some forms of allergic reactions, so much histamine can be released that the body's blood vessels may dilate catastrophically, leading to loss of blood pressure, fainting, tissue swelling, and possibly death from asphyxiation.

INTERFERONS

A related quick response system exists for controlling viruses. Within hours after an initial viral infection, the body produces a surge of chemicals known as interferons. Now known to be several related molecules, the first-line interferons are termed type I. Interferons work like the Luddite's proverbial wrench, effectively blocking the cell's DNA-synthesizing machinery. This blockage keeps the body's cells from making the genetic material of the virus. Interferons also stimulate the immune system's cellular repertoire by encouraging the proliferation of key T cells. This rapid response system "buys time" for the host by limiting viral spread and replication while the more time-consuming process of custom designing an antibody or a cell-mediated killing response unfolds. The end point, commonly a new cadre of lymphocytes geared up to kill virally infected cells, may take a week or more to be ready to interact with invading viruses.

Type I interferons also serve as chemical messengers or cytokines, encouraging the proliferation and activation of NK cells. The newest finding is that these interferons also assist immune defenses in the long run by reinforcing the production of an effective T-cell response and improving immunological memory.[9] This discovery helps to explain the adaptive function of the massive T-cell proliferation often seen following viral infection and may help explain, in part, the initial waxing and waning of the immune response in AIDS. To coordinate all of these reactions, the immune system works with a finely tuned set of checks and balances.

THREE

$\mathcal{C}$HECKS AND BALANCES

THE SECOND TIER

An evolutionarily "newer" component of the immune system is known as the adaptive immune system. As discussed in Chapter Two, this double-armed system is found in all vertebrates from the primitive lamprey upwards (see Figure Two). It provides a more specific but slower response to invasion by potentially harmful bacteria or parasitic microorganisms than does the preformed defense system circulating in the blood or body cavity. After initial contact, the adaptive immune system responds specifically to each potential threat by making a highly selective antibody. In so doing, it "acquires" the knowledge of how to respond even more vigorously should there be a second exposure.

This evolutionary more recent system offers a highly specific, tailor-made response to any persistent pathogen in the environment. As such, it usually produces either circulating antibodies known as IgG or IgA (pronounced by reading the letters) or specifically programmed cells (lymphocytes) that home in on the offender. As we have seen, the resulting antibodies have a highly specific structure that permits them to bind to antigens on the surface of bacteria or other offending agents.

Remarkably, a reasonably full description of this two-armed antibody/cell killing system has only been achieved in the last three decades. Most recently, researchers have uncovered a close collaboration between these types of immunity, making the "two-armed" distinction somewhat arbitrary. In general, the immune system relies on the bone marrow-derived B cells to make antibodies and the thymus-derived T cells to carry out cell-to-cell killing of viruses, parasites, and certain tumor cells. Each B or T cell has a specific receptor on its surface that defines and limits its reactivity to one particular type of antigenic configuration. A typical antigen is a small amino acid chain or molecule from a larger protein usually derived from a fragment of the surface of a bacterium or virus or, more rarely, from a pollen grain, foodstuff, or synthetic chemical.

ANTIBODY PRODUCTION

Normally, the antibodies produced by the immune system are designed to destroy invading pathogens by binding and breaking apart the integrity of the threatening organism. In the presence of complement, a kind of chemical booster, binding with an antibody leads to a molecular-level explosion, literally ripping apart the cell wall of a potential invader. Immune-activated lymphocytes and their helper cells perform a similar function using a form of antibody to mark cells for subsequent killing in a cellular "kiss of death." After binding to the marked surface of offending cells such as those of a parasite or tumor, the cell-killing lymphocyte destroys them either by activating their own internal self-destruct system or by directly killing the targeted cells with packets of cellular enzymes.

THE BIG PICTURE

All of this is clear enough at a molecular or cellular level. But how does the immune system "know" when and what to respond to? If the immune system's primary function is to isolate and inactivate invading organisms, it must be able to make antibodies that anticipate a whole universe of rapidly evolving microorganisms, each with an extraordinarily wide variety of antigenic types. The immune system's dilemma is to make these antibodies rapidly. As described earlier, it does so by encouraging the dramatic high-speed microevolution of potential antibody-forming cells so that within a matter of days, a custom-designed antibody is available to defend the body.

THE B-CELL SYSTEM

The details of how the immune system does this remarkable bit of chemical legerdemain are fascinating. We already know that antibodies are assembled and secreted by B cells and, by chance alone, some B cells are preformed with an initial predilection for making antibody that binds to a given antigen. The antibody-producing B cells with the best "fit" for the challenge antigen are first stimulated to divide by contact with antigen. They then migrate from the center of their resident lymph nodes to the nodes' surface, and then interact again with target antibody. Those with the best fit are stimulated the strongest, until more and more highly refined and highly "tuned" target cells are selected. In this way, eventually a dominant clone of high-affinity antibody-producing cells is generated.

This highly selective process is triggered by a burst of single-cell mutations after the initial detection of an antigenic challenge. Once provoked by initial contact with a broadly "matching" antigen, B cells respond with a dramatic increase in their mutation rate for those genes that control one of the two binding regions on the antibody. Rapid mutational change at this genetic locus that controls the "variable region" of the antigen-binding sites on antibody molecules eventually creates a cell with a "best fit" of high-affinity antibodies, much as a dress designer winnows through his line of spring clothes based in part on how much response each outfit generates on the runway. In time, a single colony of millions of genetically identical B cells is produced that elaborates a single, potent antibody directed at a specific antigenic marker.

CELLULAR IMMUNITY

The production of a specific cellular response in the T-cell system also involves activation of a cadre of cells. Rather than produce a ready made protein, designed to directly attack parasites, viruses, or aberrant cells (e.g., tumor cells) that infect or arise within the body, T cells will not respond to antigenic challenge if the protein fragments are presented to them "raw." T cells recognize a novel antigen if and only if it is presented to them by a specialized antigen-presenting cell bearing a distinct cell surface receptor. This receptor is coded by genes of the major histocompatibility complex. Often, these two systems work in tandem, marking the offending agent with antibodies and then targeting the pathogen for destruction by activated cells much the way a "smart" bomb homes in on a laser-marked target. In the body, the immune system does its targeting through the services of the antigen-processing cell (APC).

APCs are usually macrophages that engulf and digest large fragments of proteins like those described earlier from bacterial cell surfaces. Recently discovered APCs include the endothelial cells that line blood vessels and the supporting cells of the central nervous system known as glial (glē'-al) cells. The APCs display these smaller, predigested peptide fragments in a receptor embedded in a unique molecular cleft on their surface. This cleft or presenting region is a folded protein whose configuration is determined by the histocompatibility genes.

In part each body preselects and favors the presentation of certain peptides by having its own set of cell-specific codes determined by the histocompatibility or MHC system. This code consists of cell surface constituents made up of major histocompatibility complex (MHC) molecules. Much as all supermarket products carry bar codes for identification, it is the histocompatibility (literally, tissue compatibility) marker that flags "self" cells and distinguishes them from non-self invaders. By marking the cell surfaces of all of the body's nucleated cells, histocompatibility antigens of one type, the so-called MHC Class II proteins, provide molecular "badges" for all body constituents. We now know that the previously described process of self-tolerance involves these badges. Emergent lymphocytes that carry matching badges that would otherwise lock onto the body's own constituents are eliminated early in development and selectively culled during adult life by traversing the thymus gland's selection system described earlier.

DETAILS OF CONSTRUCTION

The surface configuration of the T cell carries an MHC-coded protein that serves as a kind of molecular glove designed to hold a prospective antigen in its groove or palm. A given protein fragment antigen is usually about nine amino acids long. With 20 amino acids, the total number of antigens is 9^{20} or 12 billion billion molecules. Because of this mind-numbing array of potential antigens that can fit different grooves in the T-cell system, each person has a wide repertoire of MHC proteins capable of binding with the most varied cell-surface configurations likely to be thrown up by potential viral pathogens or other threats.

A primary function of Class I MHC glovelike proteins is to provide a binding site for viral peptides early on in a viral infection. The presence of such surface holders on our body's cells works like a sticky resin from tree sap to trap a virus particle at a sensitive cell surface. Once so held, the cell swings into action, releasing chemicals that assist in neutralizing viruses. Were it not for this tailor-made defense system, it is likely that we would quickly be overwhelmed by the explosive growth of viral populations.

As Duncan Adams from the University of Otago Medical School in Dunedin, New Zealand, has argued, we are usually protected from such explosive viral replication by having large numbers of ready-made, cytotoxic T lymphocytes (CTLs) that recognize virally infected cells and kill them on the spot.[1] Some scientists liken these CTLs to the antiterrorist squads in the army. Both are prearmed and dangerous, charged with the responsibility of springing into action within minutes. As in real warfare, a second wave of responders supplants this "quick knockdown" system. In all, some 24 types of killer T cells have been identified, each with a subtly different mission or activity.

IMMUNOLOGICAL MEMORY

Once an initial immune response has occurred, a small number of the most highly "tuned" antibody-making cells persist while the remainder die off in a matter of days to weeks. These are the memory cells of the immune system. Some may last a lifetime, but most live 15–20 years. Should there be a subsequent attack, these cells remain primed to respond in a matter of hours or days, retaining the ability to proliferate and release antibodies in what is called an "anamnestic" response.

This ability of the immune system to bounce back stronger the second time around is its hallmark. Immune cells "remember" their initial immunological specificity, retargeting a potential invader with a highly specific attack that is characteristically speedier and stronger than the first, tentative response months or years earlier. It is this memory system that provides lasting immunity and resistance to reinfection with organisms like mumps or measles that we had as children.

This memory attribute of the adaptive or "acquired" system gives it a distinct advantage over the older, innate one: Up to an age of about 45–50, the acquired system gets better from experience. The cells in the acquired immune system can remember what antigen they have responded to, and as a result they are primed to initiate a powerful, "second-set" response should a repeat exposure occur. In the case of an organ transplant, for instance, if a person has already rejected a kidney with a particular antigenic marker, he will do so even faster (a so-called second-set reaction) if a second kidney carrying the same marker is implanted. Often, this marker is common to many potential donors. This is, in part, why it is so difficult to find a second or third useful donated organ after an initial transplant has failed.

As with second-set reactions, this long memory can be painful. If an immunological memory has set in, even a transient exposure to the same or a cross-reacting antigen some years later can trip the immune system's secondary response, leading to a renewed flood of antibody and/or cellular assailants. These facts help account for the finding that many individuals develop arthritis or other autoimmune reactions following reinfection with bacteria such as salmonella. Such persons commonly experience a reactivation of their arthritis should they get another infection, a point discussed at length in Chapter Six.

This belated but powerful second-set response nonetheless has tremendous evolutionary value. It means that if one is exposed as an infant or child to say a measles or chickenpox virus, a later, adult encounter with the same agent is likely to be quickly aborted. Unlike the primary immune response that often takes weeks to set up, the secondary response is ready within days.

In the case of grafts of foreign tissue, for instance, my own research in the 1960s showed that the immune system's ability to recognize a skin graft that deviated only slightly from the body may take weeks to set in. But once in place, the immune reaction to even that slightly deviant tissue could be mustered within 8–10 days, destroying the target tissue even as it is healing into place in the body.

Because of the grave bodily risks of preexisting immunity for transplant patients, researchers have expended a tremendous amount of effort attempting to subvert permanently the immune response to foreign tissues. In an effort to quash the primary immune response, potential recipients of a grafted organ, say a kidney, may undergo weeks of immune suppression prior to their transplant. But in a small number of patients, an immune reaction nonetheless sets in, and surgeons are faced with a particularly vexing problem. Because of the existence of already committed, long-lived memory cells, an entirely different approach must be taken to abolish the immune reaction. This is typically accomplished by using the immune system itself. By immunizing animals with human thymocytes or lymphocytes, highly potent, immune-suppressing antibodies can be produced. If injected into the bloodstream of an organ transplant recipient, such antilymphocyte antibodies can knock out a large portion of the otherwise resistant lymphocytes that threaten graft survival.

Like most things in life, having immunological memory is thus both a blessing and a curse. It allows the body to fend off life-threatening toxins like that of the tetanus-causing bacterium as long as there has been a prior exposure or immunization. But immunological memory also ensures that last spring's allergy to pine pollen will recur with disturbing regularity this year and for all foreseeable ones, unless the immune system is somehow deactivated.

DETAILS OF THE T-CELL SYSTEM

As discussed earlier, the majority of the lymphocytes that circulate in the blood are first initiated by passage through the thymus. Those lymphocytes that survive this cellular gauntlet become mature T cells. Although there are literally two dozen subtypes, most of the T cells of the body can be divided into just two kinds: those that are adjunct or "helper" T cells, assisting the so-called cytotoxic (cell-killing) T cells. The cells responsible for these tasks are known as $CD4^+$ and $CD8^+$ cells, respectively. Their survival is of critical importance in AIDS, because it is the number of residual $CD4^+$ cells that determines whether or not the patient will have sufficient immunological strength left to fend off invading pathogens including HIV and other opportunistic microorganisms. (More about this in Chapter Thirteen.)

One subgroup of T helper cells known as Th1 (for T helper type 1) cells assist the cell-killing T cells; another known as Th2 (T helper type 2) cells assist the antibody-forming B cells. Helper cells provoke their targeted tissues (T or B cells) to undergo a burst of mitotic activity. The resulting cellular divisions increase the number of potentially reactive cells geometrically.

The helper type 1/helper type 2 distinction is of more than academic importance: If the immune system is driven toward making antibodies (the Th2 direction) during a tuberculosis (TB) infection, the resulting powerful antibody response may produce serious collateral damage from large masses of dead tissue as it works to rid the body of TB-infected cells. A more successful outcome in TB is likely when the immune system favors Th1 or *cellular* reactions against the TB bacterium.[2]

Cellular reactions that favor the cell-killing lymphocytes are also sought after in tumor-destroying strategies. A recent discovery from research in mice suggests that a shift toward the Th1 type of reaction may be cleverly manipulated. Certain chemicals can directly provoke the production of a strong cellular immune response in which Th1-type reactions predominate and thereby increase the odds of conscripting a favorable reaction against some cancers.[3]

CYTOTOXIC T CELLS

Sometimes after being activated by Th1 cells, otherwise benign T lymphocytes can turn particularly nasty. The Jekyll and Hyde transformation of T cells can produce a particularly aggressive population of cytotoxic T cells. Cytotoxic (i.e., toxic to cells) T cells go after tissues or cells that have a specific foreign, non-self antigen displayed on their surfaces. As we have seen, the most commonly targeted cells are those infected with viruses or foreign cells such as those in an organ transplant or neoplastic (tumor) cells.

And here a military analogy may prove useful. By colluding with helper cells, T cells are guided toward preselected targets, much as a modern-day gunner uses a laser beam to "paint" the target for a missile. In this way, there is little if any chance of indigenous cells—even ones closely related to the target—falling prey to "friendly fire." So effective are these targeting systems that a T cell can attack an infected cell displaying a viral surface protein that differs by only one amino acid from a normal body cell a few micrometers away. A further limitation usually ensures fail-safe operation of this system. T cells can only be provoked to kill their targets if the targets carry certain releaser surface molecules,[4] just as a second key system prevents the mistaken activation of a missile.

KEEPING THE SYSTEM UNDER CONTROL

A further system of checks and balances ensures that antibodies and activated cells work in proportion to the perceived threat. An intricate variety of feedback loops regulate immune responses, stepping them up when the threat is large (say a massive bacterial infection) and toning them down when the threat abates. This complex, highly integrated system is designed to thwart foreign invaders, while sparing the body's own tissues from the collateral damage of excessive inflammation. It also spares the body from self-directed attacks by eliminating autoreactive cells and by activating so-called "suppressor cells" that hold potentially self-damaging lymphocytes in check. Such actions are very much akin to the tenets of Taoism, which encourage moderation and tempered responses to achieve victory.[5]

Given the potent cell-killing ability of certain activated lymphocytes and NK cells, it stands to reason that the immune system would require means of suppressing as well as enhancing and activating these agents of destruction. And indeed it does. Were it not for certain chemical messengers (cytokines) that dampen the immune response, potentially out-of-control "runaway" immune reactions would ensue and perpetuate an immune response days or weeks after its effects had been achieved. This immune homeostasis is essential for survival.

KEY ACTORS

Many of the subcellular, chemical messengers that control the type, intensity, and duration of an immune attack have been characterized in the last decade. The key chemical messengers of the immune system are the interleukins (literally, "between white blood cells") that carry information from cell to cell. The most important interleukins (IL), designated according to the sequence of their discovery, are IL-1, IL-4, and IL-12. When confronted by invasive organisms such as bacteria or viruses, macrophages release substantial amounts of both IL-1 and IL-12. IL-1 encourages the proliferation of T cells and invites more macrophages to the site of infection (see Figure Three), whereas IL-12 provokes the transformation of T cells into active mediators of *cell*-mediated immunity. Conversely, when the invading microorganism is a parasite, the first line of defending cells releases IL-4, a hormone that pushes immunity in the direction of *antibody*-mediated immunity.

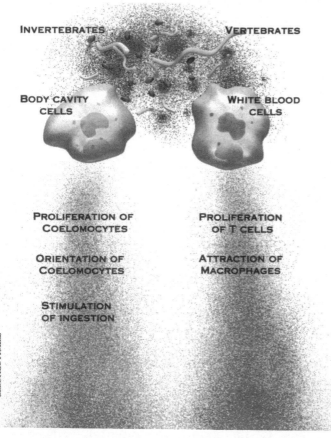

STIMULATION OF INTERLEUKINS
BY MICROORGANISMS

INVERTEBRATES   VERTEBRATES

BODY CAVITY   WHITE BLOOD
CELLS   CELLS

PROLIFERATION OF   PROLIFERATION
COELOMOCYTES   OF T CELLS

ORIENTATION OF   ATTRACTION OF
COELOMOCYTES   MACROPHAGES

STIMULATION
OF INGESTION

KIRK MOBERT
ELECTRIC PICKLE

Three. Common reliance on cytokines in primitive and more "advanced" macrophages. Interleukin 1 from invertebrates like the sponges resembles the same chemical found in humans. IL-1 has served similar defensive purposes across millions of years of evolution, pointing to its wide adaptive value. Adapted from "Immunity and the Invertebrates," by Gregory Beck and Gail S. Habicht. Copyright © by Scientific American. *All rights reserved.*

The immune system uses these and other inter-leukins to raise or lower the level of cellular or humoral immunity. This bifurcation of responses mirrors the existence in nature of two general types of threats to human well-being. One threat is that posed by potentially "hot," quick-acting viruses and bacteria that must be met head-on by a front line, *cellular response*. The other is generally a more insidious threat, brought on by the slowly increasing load of parasites that the body bears. In this case, a protracted *antibody response* makes sense as a means of offsetting the generally chronic burden posed by parasitic disease.

STRATEGIC CONSIDERATIONS

Different ends are championed by each of these two defensive strategies. Having an immune system that is fundamentally oriented toward cellular immunity may be tremendously valuable to people who are vulnerable to assault by viruses or certain disease-causing bacteria. Such a system has the advantage of being able to ferret out cells that have been invaded by viruses or pathogens like the TB bacillus. If only antibodies were present, such a cellular refuge would be an impregnable obstacle to an immune response. Once sequestered, the TB bacillus, and many viruses, can only be destroyed by actually attacking the cell that harbors them. For those viral and bacterial pathogens that have learned this intracellular trick, it makes sense for the body to rely on a cell-mediated or Th1-type response to get them, since only in this way can infected cells be expunged.

By contrast, where *parasitic disease* is rampant, having an antibody-dominated response makes more sense. Here, antibodies produced by B cells may hold a parasite in check, even as the body slowly accommodates to its presence. Such a response may have been essential in the early days of human evolution as a means of staving off parasites and latent bacterial infections.

Other evidence points to an equal role in some parasitic infections for cellular immune reactions. Parasites like the one responsible for sleeping sickness seem to be best held in check by an effective cellular response. Parasite-infected experimental animals that rely exclusively on the antibody arm of their immune system hang on but stay chronically ill. Those that *also* muster a strong cellular immunity commonly prevent the parasite from gaining a toehold. As proof of this theory, if antibody-producing animals are encouraged to develop cellular immunity, they eliminate the sleeping sickness parasites effectively and survive unscathed.[6]

Findings such as these suggest that sometimes reorienting the immune system toward its more evolutionarily recent, cell-dominated form by providing an extra boost with critical cytokines, may offer promise for control of parasitic disease and perhaps even AIDS.[7] These observations reinforce the importance of a deep understanding of the long and complex evolutionary history of the immune apparatus. Appreciation of this history is reflected in our awareness of the increase in number and classes of antibodies or immunoglobulins in more recent life forms. The details of these constituents have been ably described, but the fundamental question of how and why such a complex, multipronged immune system evolved remains largely a mystery.

FOUR

⌒*HE HEART OF DARKNESS*

Why Did the Immune System Evolve?

Despite a century of speculation, the original raison d'être of the immune system has remained obscure. As discussed earlier, the last decade has seen a veritable explosion of data on just how this complex system operates. But *why* it carries out such diverse functions is still a matter of great controversy and conjecture. For a long time, researchers believed that the immune system's sole function was to set up a biological margin between the host and a potentially harmful outside world.

In the beginning, the immune system was visualized as being akin to an early warning system that picked up invasive threats before they actually damaged the body, much as the 1960s DEW (Distant Early Warning) line north of the Arctic Circle was designed to pick up penetrating Soviet missiles. But in the 1970s, the old view that the immune system's surveillance function was primarily outward directed began to be replaced with the notion that it was directed inwardly, to the body itself. With Burnet's theory of self-surveillance in the late 1960s, researchers began to accept the idea that the immune system was designed to distinguish between "self" and "not self." At the core of this view was the conviction that the immune system was designed to ensure any aberrant tissue types within the body would be recognized and destroyed. Such a system could be critically important, for instance, in the control of cancer cells. This new way of thinking had the immune system moving away from an outwardly directed surveillance system, on the lookout for viruses, bacteria, or parasites, to one that looked within for evidence of cellular deviants, virally infected or dying cells, or just plain damaged tissue that needed removal.

But this dichotomy between inside and outside is largely an artificial one. It is more likely, in my view, that the immune system operates a surveillance continuum that responds to both internal *and* external threats, thereby ensuring the harmonious functioning of the body as a whole. To understand the critical importance of having such a watchdog system within us, it is critical to understand just how precarious our existence is.

THE INTERNAL MILIEU

All organisms live in a state of continuous struggle for their existence. When Alfred Wallace and his contemporary Charles Darwin first realized this fundamental truth in the 1840s and 1850s, they pictured a struggle where organisms were constantly pitched against a hostile external environment. Given the contemporary Victorian worldview, such a vision made sense. Nature was seen as "red in tooth and nail." The most intense battles took place *between* living things, not within them.

Neither Wallace nor Darwin could fully appreciate how much evolution was driven by microscopic battles. We now know that many of the most critical struggles for survival take place within the body. The real wars of evolution are not pitted against nature at large so much as against a universe of microscopic entities. The elements that make the body able to withstand the rigors of a hostile outside world—e.g., hair, fat, blood proteins—are in fact the very things that make it so attractive to other smaller living things to feast on. Body and head lice, bloodsucking insects, bacteria, and internal parasites are all drawn to us as inestimably (in their microscopic perspective) rich energy resources.

Every living organism from the single-celled protozoa to the weighty elephant expends a significant amount of its metabolic energy protecting itself against exploitation from the resulting microscopic hordes. The major vehicle for this protection is the immune system. For all living things above the size of a simple virus, the struggle for survival entails holding oneself apart from other living things, be it a bacterium infected by a bacteriophage, a paramecium infected by a bacterium or kappa particle, or a human parasitized by a malarial organism. The immune system helps approach this goal by maintaining a reasonable degree of sterility of the true internal environment. (Keep in mind that the orifices of the body and their connecting tubes, namely, the tract extending from mouth to anus, are strictly speaking "outside" the body.) At the level of "higher" organisms, its task is to exclude or kill viruses, bacteria, or parasites without compromising the body's own tissues. Such selective killing requires a level of chemical sophistication unachievable by the earliest multicellular organisms.

EVOLUTIONARY END POINTS

As shown in Figure Two, at least two forms of defenses evolved in the last 460 million years. The first, carried by primitive invertebrates like sponges, starfish, and tunicates in their body cavities, centered on wandering phagocytes (literally "eating cells") that served as a nonspecific, innate defense against a broad cross section of potential invaders. The second defense, which appeared at about the time of the emergence of heavily armored primitive fish known as placoderms, was a highly specific one directed against antigenically defined targets. Over evolutionary time, these systems appeared in sequence, as more primitive systems were supplanted by more specific and complex ones. The earliest systems, like those found in hydra and other early multicellular animals, relied almost entirely on preformed, chemical neutralizing poisons or aggressive macrophagelike phagocytes or coelomocytes to achieve a modicum of defense. Then invertebrates like insects, crabs, and worms emerged with special chemical toxins inside their body cavities and circulation systems that enabled them to coagulate and kill invading bacteria.[1] About 450 million years ago, cartilaginous fish (sharks) evolved with specialized lymphocytes that had the ability to hone their cellular skills in recognizing and destroying potential pathogens. It is this latter system, stacked on top of all of its more primitive adaptations, on which we humans rely today. The end point of all such systems is the same: the maintenance of an autonomous host, free—to the extent possible—of exotic interlopers.

HOMEOSTASIS

If, as Churchill once said, the price of freedom is eternal vigilance, the price of an autonomous organism's survival is a never-ending battle to ensure the integrity of this internal milieu. The necessity to maintain this state of autonomous existence puts tremendous evolutionary pressures on the organism. Constant vigilance is costly in terms of energy, putting the immune system under pressure to create ever more efficient means to ensure the safety of its host. These mechanisms were first directed at protecting the organism as a whole from microscopic invaders and only later at neutralizing potentially offending substances or toxins. Once organisms achieved an independent existence as stand-alone entities, they had to provide for this bodily integrity through effective isolation from all but their sexual partners. And even then, sexual contact became a major portal of entry for a host of opportunistic, sexually transmitted organisms requiring its own form of protection—namely, mucosal immunity.

EVOLUTIONARY ROOTS

The "long view" of the immune system suggests that it embodies features that are valuable to the group and not just the individual. Rather than reinventing itself with each new life, the immune system carries features from one generation to the next that underscore its evolutionary significance. With increasing diversity of life on earth, it became ever more important to hold members of one species separate from those of others. Even within a species, special isolating mechanisms evolved to maximize genetic integrity by prohibiting the introduction of foreign DNA. This is why members of one species such as lions cannot normally mate with even closely related ones such as tigers, or when they do, the resulting cross (the "liger") is a sterile hybrid like the mule. Indeed, recognition of non-self may have become an essential adjunct function of the immune system to ensure that organisms with genetic agendas different from their own would not prevail.

This autonomous biological isolation is as necessary for full-sized competitors in related species as it is for tiny ones. If individual microorganisms that bear no genetic resemblance to their hosts were allowed to survive, they could in theory "hitchhike" their own DNA onto that of their victims. Some viruses, like feline leukemia virus, have learned how to do just that. The feline leukemia agent, like several other viruses, usurp the host's vital functions for their own survival. Other viral genomes have become integrated into the DNA of many mammals, although the rarity of these events suggests that the immune system has acquired effective ways to thwart or abort internal viral infection.

As we have seen, the immune system normally does this by distinguishing new antigenic patterns of invading microorganisms or their protein products and elaborating a systemwide response. The ability of the immune system to distinguish "self" from "not self" may thus be an artifact of its ongoing internal evolution. As it continues to eliminate self-reactive clones that might attack the body and generate new variants in response to viral or bacterial assaults, it will become "self" defining, but only by default. That is, it will behave as if it distinguishes the outside world and "accepts" the inside one, but only because its self-reacting cell lines have been temporarily quashed or eliminated. In this model, vertically integrated viruses that establish their hegemony before the acceptance process remain a perpetual threat.

Another view has been championed by 1996 Nobel laureate Rolf Zinkernagel of the Institute for Experimental Immunology in Zurich, Switzerland. According to Zinkernagel, the immune system has no built-in "intention" of distinguishing self from non-self but has evolved self-recognition as a secondary consequence of recognizing and eliminating evolving parasites (especially viruses) while continuing to vouchsafe the survival of the organism.[2] Ultimately, the immune system becomes what it is as a result of a constant evolutionary endgame with alien genetic material. In maintaining an overall balance between infectious agents and the integrity of the host, the immune system does not so much distinguish self from non-self as it "learns" how to respond to harmful threats to the body.[3]

As we saw with the powerful immune reaction to the virus that infects the lining of the brain, it is sometimes just such a misplaced effort to dislodge a microorganism that causes disease rather than any direct damage done by the virus itself. As discussed in the Introduction, without an immune assault, viruses like the choriomeningitis virus merely survive as relatively benign inhabitants of tissue cells. Conversely, in some circumstances the immune system may simply give out and exhaust itself from attempts to respond to wave after wave of assault, such as that from mutant RNA viruses. This observation suggests that the immune system's success or failure does not necessarily turn solely on maintaining its ability to distinguish self from non-self but also on its own regenerative powers.

CELL SURFACE RECOGNITION AND CONTROL

It is now evident to most researchers that the immune system exerts *both* internal and external surveillance. A novel, as yet unrecognized, function for the immune system may be to regulate the expression of the special cellular characteristics that identify cells as adult or embryonic in form. This hypothesized "policing function" is tied to the fact that cells typically display surface configurations that signal their state of differentiation. That is, embryonic skin cells will have certain proteins on their surface that disappear when the cells become keratin producing. An analogy to the immune system's projected function would be a police force that was directed to identify and stop adolescents who wore certain age-related clothing (e.g., gang colors), while being told to ignore "more appropriately" attired adults. The likelihood that the immune system is similarly attuned to the surface markers that flag embryonic cells is reinforced by certain lines of evidence that show embryo cells to have special immune-provoking characteristics not found in adult cells.

Researchers have found that suspensions of embryonic tissue stimulate a strong, albeit nonspecific, immune reaction that can actually control the growth of certain tumors. Findings such as these suggest the immune system can recognize many tumor cells that reexpress antigens on their cell surfaces that appeared once before during embryogenesis. Some, like the so-called carcinoembryonic antigen (CEA), are produced in such high amounts by certain tumors (here, colon cancer) that their presence in the serum flags the presence of the tumor's growth in the body. Another piece of evidence for a link between embryonic antigens and tumor growth is the fact that tumors that are successfully "cured" by the body may simply "grow up," that is, they spontaneously redifferentiate into adult-type tissues. For example, I have found certain early skin tumors can regress and appear to incorporate their cells into normal-appearing skin. Whether or not this redifferentiation is linked to an immune response is still being studied.

Nonetheless, this idea that the immune system is intimately tied to recognition of adult cell surfaces is underscored by the fact that progression toward malignancy is keyed in part to the immune strength of the host. Malignancy, i.e., the degree to which a tumor deviates from normal, is often scored or graded by how closely the tumor cells resemble embryonic tissue. The more it resembles embryonic tissue, the more dangerous and out of control ("anaplastic") it tends to be.

The possibility exists that embryo-recognition by the immune system plays some role in this process of progression toward malignant growth. Immune recognition of embryonic antigens is linked to successful control of some tumors. A classic example is the ability to cause the regression of tumors induced by a monkey virus known as SV40. In this instance, the immune system can attack and control SV40 tumors if the host animal is preimmunized with virus-free *embryonic* (but not adult) tissue extracts.

In 1972[4] I postulated that the immune system's primary role is to keep cells at an appropriate level of differentiation. The utility and urgency of this function is underscored by the observation that certain embryonic cells themselves pose real risks to us over a lifetime. For instance, a choriocarcinoma can develop from fetal placenta cells, and certain tumors may arise from embryonic cells, namely, those of the germ cell line in the testis (teratocarcinoma).

Although this hypothesis is still just that, new data suggest that some type of recognition of the state of differentiation of tumor cell surface type by the immune system may be critical for tumor progression. Professor W. G. Hammond at the University of California Davis has discovered that the state of differentiation of tumor cells is directly linked to the immune status of the host animal into which a tumor is placed.[5] In the presence of intact immunity, tumors appear to progress toward more undifferentiated and hence more malignant types, whereas the same tumors implanted into animals with lesser immune strength remain highly differentiated. These findings are consistent with an immune *stimulation* of embryonic cell types with recognizable antigenic surfaces, a phenomenon discussed at more length in the chapter on cancer.

IMMUNITY UNDER SIEGE

Today, the immune system may be under unprecedented selection pressure. As population densities of human hosts expand and ecosystems are disrupted, the probability of novel biological threats correspondingly increases.[6] As I have argued in my book *Evolutionary Medicine*,[7] epidemics like AIDS and the resulting new stresses on populations of immunologically intact individuals are brought about by the much increased opportunity for human exploitation by genetically unique microorganisms. In time, if enough people are infected and their reproduction curtailed by disability or early death, disproportionately more persons with intrinsic resistance will survive and spread their genes. Over many generations, resistance genes will increase in frequency. Such a rise may have occurred with genes for TB resistance (notably those for Tay Sachs disease) and can be expected for the newly discovered HIV receptor genes that limit cellular access by viruses. (See Chapter Thirteen on HIV.)

The current sporadic epidemics of newly emerging diseases like Ebola may represent the first forays of new microorganisms into immunologically naive hosts. Additionally, the recent increase in cases of squamous cell skin cancer, melanoma, non-Hodgkin's lymphoma, and brain tumors in the United States and other developed countries may represent the failure of environmentally stressed immune systems to respond effectively to tumors with novel antigens. In these examples, the immune system's "effective" surveillance may be thwarted by the sheer numbers of new microorganisms or in the instance of novel tumor types, by the immune-impairing impacts of agents like pesticides or UV light, a topic discussed in the chapter on immunotoxicity.

FIVE

EMERGENCE OF AN AUTONOMOUS IMMUNE SYSTEM

By now we can appreciate that the integrity of the internal environment depends on its near-perfect isolation from other living things. As we have seen, to protect the body the immune system is encased in a genetically unique host that it "accepts" as self. By thwarting the entry and survival of anything that is not self, the immune system maintains and helps perpetuate the host species's and its own genetic integrity.

A more subtle point is that this integrity not only means being able to identify new pathogens and denying them a biological beachhead to the nutrient-rich confines of the host, but also the ability to recognize foreign immune systems and deny *them* a foothold. When this latter, self-protecting system fails, one immune system may attack another, as it does with disturbing regularity during bone marrow grafts. Under some circumstances, the immune cells carried into the graft recipient attack the host, and graft-versus-host disease (GVH) ensues. GVH is normally the result of the body becoming colonized through the intentional or unintentional injection of immunologically competent cells from an unrelated organism. These cells carry the capacity to attack and ultimately colonize the host. Ideally, engrafted cells merely take up residence and do no visible damage.

While most GVH arises as an unwanted complication of medical procedures such as bone marrow transplantation, such a circumstance can occur during pregnancy, when stem cells from the fetus enter the mother's circulation. It is also possible for GVH, in a mild form, to occur when cells from an organ graft grow indefinitely outside the grafted organ. These circumstances occur with sufficient regularity in both medical and natural experiments, like pregnancy, to warrant some reflection.

For instance, is it conceivable that at one time in evolution, immune system cells themselves were parasites? Wandering phagocytes could in theory survive in the early ocean, invading and taking up residence in new hosts, much as some amoebas still do today. Once inside the body, a phagocyte could in theory establish its DNA in the germ line that generates sperm and even the eggs. To do so, immunological stem cells would enter the cells that make sperm and integrate their DNA and perpetuate some of the genes that determine their own lineage.

Even more plausible, as evidenced by the "foreign" DNA found in cellular organelles known as mitochondria, in eons past, an invading amoebalike organism could have integrated its DNA into a primordial oöcyte or egg cell. Such a reality, should it prove true, would be revolutionary. If DNA arising from immune cells once actually entered and became encoded in the germ line, the immune system might have evolved to perpetuate *itself* from generation to generation. Any surveillance or protective function that gave the appearance of defending the body might in fact be evidence of an immune cell lineage defending itself as a vigilant "self-interested" system. In this radical and admittedly speculative view, the body may be seen as the vehicle for the immune system, rather than vice versa.

The roots of such a system could have evolved in the face of intense pressures to protect the body against the incursions of parasites, pathogens, or other energy-usurping invaders. We have already seen how primitive organisms appear to have relied almost entirely on a kind of cellular police system for such protection. Marshaling the cellular defenders against invasive organisms meant creating a highly specialized line capable of recognizing and ingesting foreign organisms and neutralizing or destroying them.

SLEEPING WITH THE ENEMY

The first cells to do this probably resembled Metchnikoff's macrophages. The first macrophages were probably amoebalike cells that either arose within the organism or, as I suggest, arrived as new interlopers that sought out refuge in the interior of fully formed, multicellular hosts. In the latter instance, it would be only a short step for macrophages to take up residence in their new hosts as permanent parasites or symbionts, in a cellular equivalent of the extremely ingratiating con man in the play *Six Degrees of Separation*. Of course, for sexually mating organisms, perpetuation of this state of colonization would eventually require the incorporation of macrophage DNA into that of the host, as I discussed earlier.

The likelihood that something like this actually happened early in the evolution of multicellular organisms (e.g., at the level of the sponges or tunicates shown in Figure Two) is reinforced by a unique feature of macrophages. Of all cell types outside the immune system, only macrophages (and related polymorphonuclear leukocytes) have the ability to recognize, ingest, and digest foreign particles or whole microorganisms within their cellular bodies. Like Wimpy's unlimited consumption of hamburgers in the Popeye cartoons, only the macrophage ingests the amount and kind of food provided in the never-ending stream of hostile organisms.

But the macrophage takes this process a step further. Under extreme pressures, such as those posed by organisms that have nearly indigestible coats like the TB bacterium, the macrophage undergoes a process unique to cells in the body. It produces first several and then hundreds of new nuclei, all contained within the same cellular membrane. So specialized is this ability that it invites speculation about the macrophages' potentially alien origins.

Once the macrophage produces this multinucleated "giant" cell, it makes a modern version of a cellular syncytium (sin-sish'-ēum). A syncytium is a colony of genetically related cells all descended from a common ancestor contained within a single cell membrane. Much like the teeming hordes of shoppers in a closed mall, the cell nuclei form a bizarre-looking, teeming mass of 100 or more discrete bodies, moving about within a single large containment system. Should the macrophage ingest and fuse with a host's body cell, the opportunity for genetic exchange would increase dramatically.

My own view is that this bizarre and unique cellular behavior provides a singular clue for the origins of the primitive immune system: The first "immune" cells were in fact amoebalike organisms from outside the host that were conscripted for their ability to eat other cellular organisms. The process by which such a state of cellular affairs came about is hypothetical, but it may be approximated through some evolutionary sleuthing.

A HYPOTHETICAL SCENARIO

The hypothetical "site of origin" of a parasite-derived immune system would likely be at the level of the earliest organisms that developed a body cavity and internal fluids. At this evolutionary moment, the need to police the internal milieu became an urgent necessity. With a body walled off from the sea, the need arose to ensure stability, and cellular integrity inside the most primitive body cavity became paramount. A likely candidate is the precursor of the modern-day descendants of the spongelike coelenterates (see Figure Three).

One model organism is the hydra, named after its mythical predecessor. The hydra has a three-cell-thick body wall and a number of tentacles and stinging cells that surround a "mouth" and body cavity. Instead of simply bathing the body with defensive chemicals that were inimical to potential invaders, the hydra carries in it an advance guard of cellular marauders that patrol against invading parasites. It is here, in the origin of these primitive protectors, that we must search for the primordial immune cell. Invading phagocytic cells could in theory take up residence in a host as a permanent symbiont, much as algae cells do in coral-forming organisms.

Today, amoebas still invade vertebrate hosts—such as those in the intestinal illness amoebiasis, caused by *Entamoeba histolytica*—still invade host tissues, and are among the most intractable of infections should they take hold within the body. *Entamoeba histolytica* and related amoebic forms like *Acanthamoeba*, *Naeglaria*, and *Hart-*

manella are all free-living species of amoebas found in aqueous, and sometimes marine, environments that could be relatives of the candidate immunocyte.

It is tempting to speculate that among our invertebrate ancestors were organisms that were invaded by similar amoebalike cells. Once inside the host, their propensity to form giant cells may have permitted host tissue to incorporate the amoeba nucleus into one of the cell lines that found its way into the germ line, and from there to be perpetuated through the generations.

PHAGOCYTOSIS AND EARLY IMMUNITY

However they arose, once the body acquired macrophagelike cells, it was prepared to meet invading parasites and bacteria with a potent defense: engulfment. The process of phagocytosis or cell ingestion involves at least three steps, each tightly coordinated by chemical messengers outside and inside the cell. The first phase involves cell surface recognition, recruitment of more macrophages, and initial contact with the invading organism, much as a very careful eater tentatively tastes his food. The second involves the actual engulfment of the invading pathogen by enveloping it with a bleb of the cellular membrane, making a tiny chamber (phagosome) for the microorganism. The third and final stage entails digestion of the offending organism, by employing a highly specialized enzyme-rich unit called a lysosome, just like the larger unit of digestion, the stomach, uses enzymes to break down proteins.

Because evolution is always a two-sided process, some of the ingested microorganisms, and perhaps parasites too, acquired the ability to withstand this intense enzymatic digestion. Some bacteria, especially those that cause upper respiratory infections by invading mucous membranes that line the lungs' passages, have evolved ways to do this by making special waxy or carbohydrate capsules around themselves. These capsular barriers, like the covering on a Jordan almond, prevent the body's first line of immune defense from entering or breaking the bacterial cells. This same strategy also works to protect bacteria against antibodies or complement that might otherwise attach to their surfaces, and shields them against being ingested by macrophages.

By forming heavily waxed coats and stiff cell walls, microbes like the tubercle bacterium have acquired the ability to persist and even divide inside macrophages, thwarting the macrophages' ability to neutralize them. Part of this survival strategy appears to rely on a mechanism that prevents the enzymes carried inside the cell within the lysosomes from digesting the ingested bacterium much as modern-day "fat-free fats" like olestra® prevent the body from breaking them down.

This mechanism is simple and eminently reasonable from an evolutionary viewpoint. Most of the lysosomal enzymes only work effectively when they find themselves in an acidified environment. Bacteria in the tuberculosis family of *Mycobacterium* prevent the host's lysosomal package from taking in the hydrogen ions needed to create an acidic environment, much like the "enteric" coating around a pill prevents it from breaking down in the stomach. Still other bacteria avoid phagocytosis altogether by neutralizing the binding proteins that macrophages use to adhere to microbial cells, much the way downy feathers prevent water from sticking to a bird's body. And some bacteria can veil themselves in host proteins like fibronectin, effectively hiding their own bacteria-specific coat proteins from immunological view.

A remarkable further adaptation may have emerged from this primitive process of phagocytosis. Through a process of trial and error over millennia of digestion of

microbes and their parts, the macrophage-type cells have
evolved into a processing system for microbes and small
molecules. In partially digesting and then disgorging the
complex mixture of proteins and sugars that commonly
make up bacterial cell walls, macrophages may inadvertently have "learned" how to present antigens at their cell
surface. Like a 10-year-old who is first taught how to catch
a ball with two hands and then learns how to "one-hand"
it, bacteria-processing macrophages may have acquired
the ability to hold antigen "balls" aloft for all other cells
around to see. As mentioned in our discussion of the
basics of immunology, this antigen-presenting function
has proven to be a vital first step in almost all effective
immune reactions, as it serves to flag new antigens in a
way that attracts specialized immune cells. On contact
with an appropriate antigenic target held out by such an
antigen-presenting cell, T cells are activated and B cells
begin the process to make antibody.

CELL SURFACE RECOGNITION

The reaction of macrophages to foreign-appearing
cell surfaces provides a clue to the origins of immunity
itself. The existence of self-awareness in multicellular organisms suggests that the recognition of cell surfaces was
among the earliest forms of adaptation to ensure survival.
Even the most primitive multicellular organisms carry an
intrinsic ability to distinguish one cell surface from another. This capacity exists in sponges, hydra, and other
primitive organisms with body cavities and appears to
help them organize their cellular layers and to keep their
own species identity. Embryologist Edward Zwilling
showed that cell surface recognition occurred even at this
primitive phylogenetic level. Using a blender to create a
highly dispersed cell admixture from two different spe-

cies of sponges, Zwilling showed that once recombined, the individual cell types will rapidly resegregate into their original genetic origins, reconstituting two different whole sponges, each made up of discrete cells of the original organism. Later work showed that even greater refinement of this sorting in higher invertebrates is also possible, as cell types of a given primordial organ system will also aggregate selectively into their characteristic layers. It is as if a video showing a layer cake being tossed onto the floor were shown in reverse, the cake seeming to regain its original form from thousands of crumbs.

It is tempting to speculate that later in evolutionary time, this simple sorting system gave rise to a mechanism for recognition of self from non-self. Anemones will touch and "feel" each other's presence, often appearing to draw back. And primitive algae will grow along a surface but recoil when they contact a separate species of the same order. On rocks along the ocean's tidal zone, a rock-clinging species of coelenterate that occupies one niche will commonly repel an encroaching species by creating a kind of no-man's land between them. The result is often a clear "battle zone" between rock-bound sponges, demarcating each organism's territory.

What is actually happening is at the same time much more complicated and much more profound than this appearance of mutual cellular dislike. A closer inspection shows that cells of many primitive organisms respond by *proliferating* when they encounter an unlike but alive cell surface of a related species. Apparently, something in the cell-to-cell contact triggers rapid cell division in one or both touching parties. This simple but profoundly important response is known as "contact hyperplasia"[1] and may be one of the earliest manifestations of immunity: a proliferative response in the face of difference. This reaction may be at the root of many of the later spectrum of attributes we find in the immune system of higher vertebrates. It can explain, for instance, the observation, discussed below, whereby tissues targeted by the immune system undergo a proliferative response rather than dying off. Contact hyperplasia can also explain the initial burst of cell divisions that occurs within cells of the immune system itself after contact with foreign antigens.

In this simple cellular reaction, we are probably witnessing a tremendously adaptive response. When one sponge or alga on a rock surface detects another, its proliferative response serves to increase its "claim" on ecological space. What may in fact be the threat of an actual invasion by a competing animal is met by a natural and clearly adaptive response: expand and extend the territory that can be claimed by occupying it with more tissue.

This primitive proliferative response has been coined the "hyperplastic contact reaction." It is mirrored in the response of actual cells of our own immune systems that first recruit other cells and then divide rapidly after contact with a "matching" cell or antigen surface. The related aversion response is a cellular equivalent to the reactions provoked by nonconsensual touching in people: It is annoying and provocative, and if it goes on long enough, we will often notify others.

It is conceivable that all vertebrate immunological mechanisms evolved out of such nonimmunological surface recognition phenomena.[2] This behavior, where a lymphocyte divides after binding with an antigen or "mitogen," is of inestimable value in expanding the number of genetically identical cells or "clones" that can respond to further incursions or assaults by invading microbes that display the same antigen. By initially proliferating nonspecifically after receiving a stimulus, the immune system maximizes its chances of catching an incoming microbe or other invader by surprise. It does this by throwing out a screen of activated lymphocytes or NK cells, much as flak was used by the British to hit unseen airplane attackers. The very breadth of the response is counted on to thwart an invader.

Conversely, the capacity for a proliferative response following contact with aggressive immune cells may help explain why cells under immune attack often respond by dividing rapidly themselves. From an evolutionary standpoint, making more of yourself available as targets can minimize damage to the group of cells as a whole. Such proliferation in response to contact with a marauding lymphocyte may be distinctly beneficial to a parasite or other cellular type, as it increases the number of cells that have to be killed to thwart the invasion. Rather than dying off from contact with an immune cell, target tissues of a range of types have been observed to proliferate, a phenomenon of increasing importance in appreciating the dynamic nature of the immune reaction. This little-recognized and only recently appreciated phenomenon is termed "immunostimulation" and was developed by Dr. Richmond T. Prehn and, to a lesser extent, myself.

DIVIDE AND CONQUER

The proliferative response of the immune system to certain antigenic provocations is so consistent and powerful that it has served as an assay for immune capacity generally. For instance, blood lymphocytes can be exposed to antigens like those from the keyhole limpet or plant extracts to see how quickly they divide, and hence to measure the strength of any future immune reactions.

This proliferative approach to immunity—"if there's more of us, there will be fewer of them"—probably represented the earliest evolutionary adaptation. In time, it gave way to the more refined apparatus characteristic of most advanced immune systems today, from the shark upwards. Typically, when the immune system of a higher vertebrate "sees" a foreign antigen, say on the surface of an invading parasite, it limits its cell proliferation response to just a few (perhaps 1 in 50,000) of the many thousands of cells in the regional outposts scattered throughout our bodies known as draining lymph nodes. The responding cell is most often the one with the closest fit to the attacking organism's surface configuration.

THE SUPERANTIGEN STORY

In addition to this measured, limited response, the immune system has evolved a mysterious but potent reaction to the class of substances known as "superantigens." These substances have the capacity of provoking not the 1 in 50,000 or so lymphocytes with a "good fit" to the provoking antigen, but as many as 1 in every *50* potentially responsive lymphocytes! Superantigens can do this by serving as a molecular bridge between antigen-presenting cells and special binding sites on responsive lymphocytes. Unlike standard antigens, which bind to a single surface marker, superantigens bind simultaneously to *two* of the variable regions displayed on the surface of lymphocytes, thereby conscripting not only the ones closely matched to the antigen's configuration, but a host of other lymphocytes that have only a loose "fit." A near analogy would be the general call-up of troops that produces a large but generally untrained cadre of future combatants in contrast to a call-up of specialized, Green Beret-like teams.

The superantigens that can incite this wholesale activation are found widely in nature. They are concentrated on the surface of certain bacteria or their toxins, such as staphylococcus, and are found in stressed cells within the human body itself. Originally, the most potent inducer of superantigens was found to be heat stress. When subjected to heat or other stressful environmental stimuli, cells derived from a broad array of organisms from bacteria to bats produce so-called "heat shock proteins." These proteins help the endangered cell by carrying essential molecules to the cell's nucleus and generally aiding repair mechanisms. Like the parents escorting teenagers to the prom, heat shock proteins that carry and protect cell proteins are called "chaperons."

What is less evident from an evolutionary viewpoint is why heat shock proteins are such potent immune stimulants. To understand, we need to know more about how heat shock proteins work. Recall that the immune system distinguishes among antigens that come from the body's own cells and those that pose a threat from outside the body. Internal threats arise from cells whose metabolic machinery has been subverted by viruses or distorted through the process of genetic changes that leads to cancer. External threats often take the form of invading bacteria or parasites. Infected cells may give off heat shock proteins as a kind of alarm substance.

To give it the best chance of surviving an invasion by a fast replicating virus or a burgeoning outgrowth of tumor cells, the body often tunes in to these markers of cellular distress. Heat shock proteins complexed with tumor or virus-related peptides provoke a powerful and highly specific immune reaction. Phagocytes in the immune system readily respond to these complexes, providing a rapid and full-bore immune reaction. Under ideal circumstances, this superantigen reaction leads to protective immunity that destroys some or all of the parasite or virally infected cells and ideally the invaders themselves.

We now know that a superantigen works by providing certain protein signals to trigger a broadside immunological attack. This wholesale response has clear adaptive value because a quick reaction to an influx of viruses or parasites can, in theory, stop the invasion in its tracks. Such a response is akin to the D-Day Battle of Normandy in World War II: Had the Germans mustered all of their strength superantigen-style and held the Allies at bay, the invasion of Europe might have failed. Instead of having to fine-tune a defensive reaction as did the Germans, superantigens link together many thousands of defensive actors, all bent on a single mission: Stop the enemy at the beachhead.

When superantigens conscript a T cell, each one is committed to repel the enemy with a blind counterattack. The resulting immunological assault is simultaneously broadly based but also a highly mobilized attack on a host of antigenic targets. From an adaptive vantage point, this type of response may buy time for a specific immune response some days later.

The superantigen reaction draws on a considerable amount of the immune response and focuses it on a nonspecific target. Perhaps for this reason, many bacteria and viruses have "welcomed" the preemptive commitment of immune troops on the part of the host and have evolved mechanisms to evade the broadly attacking immune system. An additional undesirable feature of superantigen activation is that it is so widely directed that it can threaten the body's *own* constituents. In some instances, as when heat-shock proteins are expressed by distressed cells, the resulting elimination is desirable. But in others, as when the attack homes in on inflamed or damaged tissue for which there is no replacement, the resulting self-inflicted damage can be severe. Many researchers believe that some of the joint damage following bacterial infections from salmonella or yersinia comes from such an abortive immune attack. Here the body focuses on routing out the few bacterial survivors that have found refuge in the lining of the joints. In this instance, the body may be guilty of "bombing the village in order to save it," as the assault on the joint spaces where *Yersinia* strains are found can damage the lining so badly that severe arthritis ensues.

The superantigen reaction can also be injurious when it leads to the release of secondary factors, like the cytokines generated in the toxic shock reaction to staphylococcus toxin.[3] In this case, the alarm reaction of the body can do more harm than good. Many of these cytokines are themselves distinctly "unhealthy" in the sense that they cause generalized malaise, fever, muscle aches, and fatigue even as they try to help the immune system muster the proper response to an invading pathogen.

These reactions help to explain the plethora of symptoms that accompany rheumatoid diseases. And for some of the cytokines released during toxic shock, such as tumor necrosis factor, the damage to capillaries, kidneys, and other organs can be downright fatal. As with the joint damage after a salmonella or yersinia infection, researchers now recognize that many diseases involve an initial immune reaction to a bacterium followed by massive activation of reactive T cells and accompanying cytokines.

Some bacterial toxins, notably the enterotoxin produced by staphylococcus, work much like an *agent provocateur*, setting off the body's T cells in a vain overreaction that turns back on the body itself. In the instance of one staph toxin, activated T cells inadvertently destroy islets of Langerhans in the pancreas and thereby generate all of the symptoms of autoimmune diabetes.[4] The resulting disease can be lifelong if the islets cannot regenerate their insulin-producing abilities.

These and related studies demonstrate that naturally occurring bacterial by-products can activate quiescent, self-reactive T cells and provoke autoimmune disease. The evolutionary significance of this response means that natural selection has permitted an extraordinary Faustian bargain to be struck within the immune system. The short-term survival advantage offered by the quick response provoked by superantigens appears to be partially offset by the possibility of long-term damage from unleashed autoimmune reactions. Here again, a military metaphor is useful: Commanders in the field faced with urgent military exigencies may make short-term decisions that compromise long-term battlefield objectives.

Paradoxically, carrying superantigens may also confer survival advantages on bacteria or even viruses. By provoking a wild, scattershot response that futilely tries to hunt down every possible invader, some inciting bacteria may avoid a direct, highly specific assault that might otherwise cripple *them*. It is also tempting to speculate that this form of response may ultimately restrict the ability of the immune system to mount its most effective weapon—a hand-tailored immune response—as its resources are pulled inexorably into the nonspecific haze of battle against superantigens. Similar strategies are used by antiterrorist squads who commonly set off shock grenades to create diversionary actions away from their own operations.

A still more clever way to evade the body's immune response is for an invading organism to keep shifting its surface components much like a disguise artist. In this way an initial immune response comes back to find a different target organism. The phenomenon of antigenic variation, as this process is called, can lead to a bewildering array of different antigenic types. In the instance of the influenza virus responsible for the "flu," a variant that produces immunity one year may be supplanted with a totally different antigenic kind the next, confounding otherwise adaptive immunological memory. Even more disconcerting is the ability of HIV to keep shifting its antigenic markers, even within the body of its primary victim. In both instances, any unilateral immune response generated by the founding organism is likely to fail because it will mistakenly go after an earlier antigenic variant that may no longer be present.

AN EVOLUTIONARY PERSPECTIVE

If the immune system is the *sine qua non* of an adaptive system that evolved to protect us, why does it so often fail—or worse, turn on the body in a paroxysm of self-destruction? This paradox is not so readily explained as one would think. For instance, some forms of autoimmunity that result from the immune system mistaking shared antigens on bacteria and human cells may simply be a recurring accident of nature. Such an accident could reflect the perpetuation of antigens from our common evolutionary heritage with the microbial world. This interpretation partially explains the maladaptive response that sometimes accompanies the reaction to superantigens. In this case, molecules closely resembling heat shock proteins are remarkably ancient, having been found in every species examined, from bacteria to fruit fly to humans. Hence, a reaction elicited by a bacterium's heat shock protein may be identical to that produced by the human body, tricking us into thinking our *own* cells need rescuing.

According to this "ancient mimicry" model, some reactions are simply the result of an otherwise effective immune response that is mistakenly mounted against an evolutionarily primitive invading organism that still resembles us. Proponents of ancient memory posit that autoimmunity is an unfortunate but coincidental reaction against a bacterium that just happens to express an evolutionarily old protein that we still express on our own cells.

Evolution does not occur in a vacuum. Both humans and their enemies have evolved in concert giving credence to the coincidental antigen model.

A much more plausible explanation is that the human immune system, like antibiotics, works as a powerful force to cull from hordes of bacteria those that are susceptible to immune attack. Those that are left behind are likely to include variants that evoke the weakest responses. The most adaptive bacteria express the antigens most like those of the body. Over time, bacteria that "look like" the body are best able to evade an immune reaction. By garbing themselves in a version of the body's own proteins, an antigen-mimicking bacterium can express surface features that are less likely to set off an immune response than would those that are totally bacteria specific. In a sense, some bacteria play Halloween all the time, hiding their true appearance behind a mask of distracting humanlike antigenic protrusions.

Those bacteria that look most like us are likely to be the most successful in evading attack. This subterfuge to avoid setting off an immune reaction may have untoward consequences for the body, especially after it effectively unmasks the offender and learns how to attack it. Under normal circumstances the body will not fight a look-alike bacterium as vigorously as it will a foreign-looking one. On those few accounts where a bacterium shares a common antigen with the body and the body does decide to fight, for instance against strep A, the resulting immune response goes after bacterium *and* normal body tissue alike. Autoimmunity may be the result.

Ironically, holding back an immune response against a molecular mimic—say a bacterium garbed in self-proteins—may itself be more injurious than going after it full bore. After a salmonella infection, those patients who mount only a weak immune response against this common food poisoning bacterium tend to be the ones who develop an autoimmune condition that leads to joint pain and eye problems known as Reiter's disease. Based on animal studies, only those who come closest to eradicating the salmonella infection and hence stopping the smoldering immune reaction are likely to remain arthritis-free.[5] How long, you may ask, has this Damocles state of affairs existed?

According to Professor Gian Franco Bottazzo, Chair of the Department of Immunology at the London Hospital Medical College, not very long. In Bottazzo's view, only since the advent of civilization and its concomitant population densities have disease-causing microbes and accompanying autoimmune reactions predominated. Just as modern forms of intensive warfare only developed after citadels and cities fortified themselves, it may be that autoimmune-inducing forms of bacteria only evolved *after* the body developed strong immune defenses. According to Bottazzo, the resulting overtaxed immune response only recently overstepped its natural constraints, making the advent of autoimmunity a modern phenomenon. This hypothesis is consistent with the paucity of reports of anything resembling autoimmune disease before the eighteenth century.

A further explanation for self-reactive disorders that affect multiple organs in the body after bacterial assaults is that there is only a finite number of proteins that will work as cellular membranes or scaffolding. The common structure of many tissues explains why the immune system commonly targets multiple organ sites in autoimmune diseases.

This model still leaves unexplained why the body reacts to so many self-antigens. This maladaptive response is best seen as a result of the spontaneous breakdown of the unspoken code of nonaggression against the self. Aberrant immune reactions may be the result both of intense disease processes that lead to cross-reacting immunity and to the immune system forgetting what the rest of the body looks like as a result of the spontaneous loss of self-tolerance. In a perverse form of self-hate, over time many of us literally become intolerant of our biological selves. I will try to explain this paradox in the chapter that follows.

SIX

*A*UTOIMMUNITY: THE CURSE OF IMMUNOLOGICAL INTOLERANCE

By now we recognize the immune system's multifarious functions sometimes turn it into an enemy as well as a benefactor. Natural constraints on how we defend ourselves normally stop the immune system far short of damaging the body. But German physician and scientist Paul Ehrlich (1854–1915) recognized early in the 1900s that the immune system's very sharpness in discerning minute differences between self and non-self made an attack against the body not only possible but inevitable. Knowing the potency of a full-fledged immune attack, Ehrlich visualized the devastating consequences of an immune system attacking its own body as a *"horror autotoxicus."*

For decades after Ehrlich postulated the terrible consequences of an immune system running amuck, most immunologists resisted the concept of autoimmunity. At best they believed that self-directed immune attacks were rare aberrations brought on by poisonous plants or allergens, poorly matched blood transfusions, or mismatched organ grafts. Occasionally, as with serum sickness (from blood transfusions) or graft-versus-host disease (where, as we have seen, immune cells in mismatched bone marrow attack the recipient), clinicians acknowledged the consequences as serious or fatal. Indeed, many of the symptoms of AIDS resemble the clinical pattern of graft-versus-host disease's impact on the host's immune system.

Sometimes, even this misdirected attack can prove salubrious. It is precisely this graft-versus-host reaction that contributes to survival of leukemic bone marrow recipients because the grafted cells attack the tumor as well as the host. In most instances of autoimmunity, early 1900s immunologists and clinicians believed that simple improvements in blood typing and tissue matching would obviate the problem. Then in the 1940s and 1950s, textbooks of medicine recognized some forms of anemia as having an autoimmune component. But it was not until the 1960s that many clinicians recognized that autoimmunity itself was a serious generalized problem.*

Most clinicians now suspect that the immune system may engage in silent wars more often than previously believed. Many diseases once thought to be stress related or nutritional in origin, like hypertension or diabetes, are now recognized as having subgroups (like juvenile diabetes) with an autoimmune component. As we have seen in many instances, these reactions ensue where tolerance to self-antigens breaks down or when the body mounts a

---

*The traditional view is that for a disease process to be autoimmune, it must arise after an immune attack against self-antigens. Such an attack can be mediated by self-directed antibodies or T cells—or both. The resulting tissue damage may be direct or indirect, as when adjacent tissues are injured by chronic inflammation.

misdirected attack on a virus or microbe that is ensconced in or near a body cell that shares antigens with that pathogen. In juvenile onset diabetes, autoimmune attacks can, in some instances, be unleashed by a prior bout with a coxsackievirus. In allergies and asthma, the immune system's usually well-directed attacks on an outside source most clearly rebound against the host in distressing ways.

I explored the evolutionary explanation for such aberrant attacks in my previous book.[1] In that book, I asked the question, "Why would a system that has evolved to protect the body have retained the capacity to engineer its destruction?" All of the answers are not in, but it may simply be that autoimmunity is the price we pay for sustained vigilance against the microbial world and its associated toxins. In the instance of asthma, it may well be that an initially beneficial response became maladaptive. An immune-mediated reaction causing an abrupt constriction of the air passages may once have ensured that no potentially fatal fungi invade the lungs. Over several thousand years, the same reaction could have paved the way to an overly reactive airway system. As partial support for this novel hypothesis, recent work has confirmed that about one in five asthmatics are allergic to spores of the fungus *Aspergillus*, an agent capable of producing a sometimes fatal lung disease known as aspergillosis.

Why the body would actually attack its own tissues raises deeper questions. This is particularly so because, as we have seen, many autoimmune diseases appear to target women (and less often men) of reproductive age, a circumstance that evolution would ordinarily abhor because it would eliminate a generation of susceptible people. If any autoimmune disease routinely compromised women of childbearing age, it is axiomatic that any genetic predilection for that disease would likely not be passed on to future generations. Because of resulting impairments to their health, such women would likely have fewer offspring than their non-autoimmune-inclined peers. Hence, the predilection for many autoimmune diseases would simply disappear as susceptible parents died before passing on their genes. Given the relatively high prevalence of autoimmune diseases like lupus erythematosus and multiple sclerosis in young women aged 25–40 in the United States (5–20 per 100,000), the persistence of these autoreactive diseases is troubling.

The body has designed a dramatically effective system to ensure that such potentially damaging autoimmune reactions happen only rarely, or ideally not at all. Under most of the circumstances encountered in a lifetime, the normal checks and balances of the immune system ensure that the body will remain "self-conscious" and not autoreactive. The mechanism that nips incipient autoreactive cells in the bud is remarkable for its simplicity and efficiency. To avoid self-directed immune attacks, the immune system undergoes a process of internal housekeeping by which it culls cells that are potentially self-reactive from the lymphatic circulation. This process, elegant in its simplicity, involves the previously described "clonal deletion" of autoreactive lymphocytes in the thymus. The details of this event are described below.

THE HISTOCOMPATIBILITY COMPLEX

Contrary to its name, the major histocompatibility complex (MHC) described earlier does not denote a psychological state but rather a closely linked group of genes on human chromosome 6 that regulates immune activity throughout the body. MHC genetic by-products are antigens and fit into two classes. To recap what we learned in the Introduction: Class I MHC molecules are involved in *cellular* immunity and recognize antigens that arise from trouble *inside* the cell, such as from infecting viruses, internal parasites, or aberrant tumor cell types. These MHC genes are listed under alphabetical headings A, B, C, and so on. Class II MHC genes assist the body in recognizing threats that come from *outside* the body, e.g., from bacteria, and generally regulate B cells and antibody production.

Each of us has four major genes that determine our MHC specificities and several minor ones that shape the special strengths and weaknesses of each individual's immune response. As discussed previously, the importance of *variety* between individuals may be to ensure that the human species as a whole is not overwhelmed by a new virus. With multiple markers that anticipate all sorts of virus surface types, at least some individuals in the population will be equipped to handle any new viral infection.

Some MHC determinants (notably the one designated HLA DR53) greatly facilitate the processing of certain bacterial or parasitic antigens, such as those from the malarial parasite, and thereby improve our ability to ward off such serious infectious threats. Others (notably HLA A1) permit recognition of specific tumor antigens (in this case, one from melanomas). But a few HLA markers predispose us to overreact to certain bacterial and/or self-antigens and as a result put us at heightened risk for developing potentially debilitating autoimmune reactions. I have one of these latter markers known cryptically as "HLA B27." Having B27 improves my antibacterial skills and apparently even lessens the severity of an HIV infection, but it puts me at risk for developing ankylosing spondylitis, an arthritic condition of the spine.

How does this happen? Many researchers believe that when the immune response to the bacteria fails to eradicate an infection, T-cell clones reactive to HLA B27-carried antigens begin to attack body tissues carrying persistent bacteria. Unfortunately as we saw, a favored hiding place for bacteria such as yersinia (*Yersinia entero-colitica*) are the synovial tissues in the joints. A smoldering, chronic immune response aimed at yersinia or HLA B27-positive cells nearby can thus produce enormous collateral damage to surrounding tissues.

The increasingly wide acceptance of the triggering role of bacterial infection for autoimmunity[2] has some modern-day twists. I have hypothesized that hypersensitivity to persistent bacterial infections could explain some of the autoimmune symptomatology seen with breast implants and perhaps other silicone-based implants.[3] Such implants can serve as seeding points for chronic, often "silent" infections, as many bacteria have been shown to adhere to the implant surfaces. In such circumstances, the formation of capsules around the implant can create a protected environment for the growth of bacteria. Because some forms of silicone enhance the immune response, silicone implants may exacerbate any immune attack on the bacteria. In such circumstances, removing the source of silicone and eliminating the offending organism with appropriate antibiotics may be a better approach than the draconian immune suppressants such as prednisone currently used to treat silicone-associated inflammation.[4]

AN OVERVIEW OF AUTOIMMUNE DISEASE

Whatever its pluses and minuses, it is obviously important to factor in the immune system's strengths and weaknesses into an overarching theory of health and well-being. By providing a model of disease in which the immune system itself plays the pivotal role, autoimmunity provides a window of opportunity both to understand the immune system better and to fathom how it causes illness. The number of different diseases that have an autoimmune component is surprisingly large. Table One lists the major diseases and their target tissues.

SCLERODERMA

Of all of the autoimmune diseases, scleroderma is the most perturbing because it can ultimately affect almost all of the organs of the body, leading to progressive disease and death. Scleroderma begins with a phase characterized by a mysterious blanching of the fingertips that can be triggered by cold. Called Raynaud's phenomenon after the Frenchman Claude Raynaud who first reported it in the early 1900s, this reaction appears to result from hyperreactivity of blood vessels in the fingers. Scleroderma is also reflected in a characteristic dilation of vessels in the capillary bed of the fingernail. Later, in the progression of the disease, the skin is affected, becoming puffy and ultimately severely contracted. The afflicted patient is often uncompassionately described as "hidebound" because the skin feels as if it is literally stuck to the muscles.

These pathognomonic signs of scleroderma are the first changes that result from a variety of autoimmune activities in the body. The breadth of reactions can include antibodies directed against the centromere (a critical component of the cell nucleus), antibodies directed against collagen or a small molecular weight protein known as P-100, and others directed against specific proteins in the nucleolus or nucleus. One of these, the scl70 protein, is particularly diagnostic of diffuse scleroderma.

Although the exact immunological triggers for scleroderma remain unknown, exposure to a number of different substances has been associated with the onset of the later stages of the disease. Among these are inhalation

Table One. Major Autoimmune Diseases and Their Targets

Disease	Target tissues	Description
Rheumatological conditions		
Rheumatoid arthritis	Joints, connective tissue	Immune attacks directed at connective tissue at multiple sites
Mixed connective tissue disease	Collagen, joints	
Scleroderma	Skin, heart, lungs, kidney	
CREST syndrome	Blood vessels, skin, esophagus	
Sjögren's syndrome	Liver, kidney, brain, salivary gland, thyroid	
Polymyositis	Muscle tissue	
Dermatomyositis	Skin, muscle	
Systemic lupus erythematosus	DNA, platelets, kidney, skin	
Endocrine disorders		
Graves' disease	Thyroid	T-cell-mediated attacks on endocrine organs
Hashimoto's thyroiditis	Thyroid	
Insulin-dependent diabetes	Pancreas	
Addison's disease	Adrenal gland	
Polyglandular endocrine disease	Multiple glands	
Dermatologic diseases		
Pemphigus vulgaris	Epithelium	Autoimmune reactions against the skin and its components
Alopecia areata	Hair follicles	

and skin absorption of solvents like trichloroethylene, oral ingestion of toxic components of rape seed oil, and systemic exposure to vinyl chloride, silica, and possibly the silicone found in breast implants. Some of these dangerous products, notably trichloroethylene and vinyl chloride, have been largely eliminated from household products, but others, like silica, have not. Some women who developed the unfortunate habit of sniffing silica-rich scouring powders have developed scleroderma.

With later progression, scleroderma can become systemic, leading to an interstitial lung disease in which the connective tissue thickens and impedes breathing, renal failure, a diffuse hardening of the stomach lining and intestinal tract, and eventually heart damage in which muscle is replaced by scar tissue. These latter changes are life-threatening. Once scleroderma has spread to the body's organs (diffuse disease), the 5-year mortality has an incidence of nearly 40 to 50 percent.[5]

The pathogenesis of this disease is clearly complex but involves the vascular and immune system at virtually every step. Some of the causative agents can injure blood vessel walls and activate T cells. T cells and monocytes in turn, and particularly the cytokines they release (e.g., IL-2), may then push fibroblasts, the cells that form connective and scar tissue, into overdrive. The resulting fibrotic lesion that characterizes the more progressive forms of the disease results from the overgrowth of these fibroblasts into normal tissue.

The key to understanding scleroderma turns on this singular cell, the fibroblast. Normally, the skin fibroblast is a quiescent cell that divides slowly if at all. With inflammation secondary to tissue damage, fibroblasts receive a series of chemical signals that lead to a limited phase of growth and repair. As they participate in bridging damaged tissue sites and forming the scar tissue that serves as a scaffolding for normal healing, they proliferate—in scleroderma they appear never to stop.

This reaction clearly has something to do with T-cell activation and cytokine release. When monocytes including macrophages and lymphocytes gather at a wound site, they release cytokines like IL-1 and IL-4 in addition to IL-2. These chemical mediators stimulate fibroblast proliferation and the synthesis of excess collagen. Macrophages may release other cytokines, like IL-6, that stimulate the production of enzymes involved in the synthesis of collagen. Many other substances are triggered, and if inflammation persists, these hormonelike instigators prod the body into uncontrolled fibroblastic growth.

Scleroderma involves unrestrained growth and expansion of clones of tissue fibroblasts. As they proliferate, the fibroblasts lay down progressively thicker layers of collagen and elastin. The resulting scarlike tissue eventually replaces otherwise functional organs with a mass of nonfunctional cells. Eventually, the fibroblasts that are at the hub of immune assaults in late-stage scleroderma begin to divide on their own, outside the bounds of normal growth control. Indeed, it is reasonable to think of scleroderma as another instance where the immune system provokes rather than constrains cell growth. Fortunately it is rare, affecting only about 6–9 per 1,000,000 persons.

The chaotic, out-of-control fibroblast provides a clue to scleroderma's etiology. On close inspection, this disease process resembles a classic disorder in which proliferating tissue blocks, replaces, or destroys normal cells. To recap: scleroderma involves at least three stages: (1) activation of the immune system, leading to the influx of lymphocytes and monocytes into connective tissue; (2) release of cytokines that trigger and activate fibroblasts to proliferate and produce more of the nonfunctional biological matrices like collagen that incapacitate tissue and organ function; and (3) extensive fibrosis that ultimately replaces normal tissue with scarlike tissue.

Once activated, fibroblasts then appear to retain the tumorlike ability to proliferate. If, like tumor cells, the fibroblasts have been genetically "released" to express their growth potential in an unlimited fashion, it may explain why simply knocking down the immune system has not proven effective in halting or reversing scleroderma.

THE IMMUNE SYSTEM AS AGENT PROVOCATEUR

A credible but long-ignored explanation for the paradoxical role of immunity in scleroderma was offered by a team of researchers writing in 1982. This team proposed that immune cells home in on an initially deviant clone of fibroblasts that are already programmed for high-level collagen production and *provoke* their outgrowth.[6] In this view, scleroderma results from an abortive immune attack that stimulates the targeted cell rather than suppressing it. Such provocation is analogous to the effect picadors have on a bull: The barbed batons enrage and stimulate the bull even as they try to achieve their intended purpose of weakening it.

The concept of immunity as an inciter of cell growth has attracted little attention even though it helps explain why some tissues proliferate in autoimmune disease and sometimes—as in autoimmune thyroid disease—an autoimmune attack favors cancerous growth. This is unfortunate because the similarities between unfettered growth of fibroblasts and tumor cells under an immune attack are more similar than different.

IMMUNE STIMULATION

The fact that so little attention has been given to this alternative model of immunity suggests we are still constrained by unidimensional ideas about immunity as routinely destructive. Immune stimulation is an especially counterintuitive idea because most of us have been encouraged to think of immunity as suppressing growth or killing it altogether. The orthodox model of immunity as a defense system may be keeping many clinicians from appreciating potentially viable therapeutic strategies.

Clearly, some new approach is needed to rein in scleroderma. In keeping with the old paradigm, almost all of the therapies developed for this disease concentrate on suppressing the immune response. And, as one would expect from an inappropriate model, they have proven largely ineffectual. A more subtle approach that recognized the disease's weaknesses might prove more beneficial than an all-out assault.

Immunosuppressive agents like cyclosporin A and photophoresis (a process in which the blood is treated outside the body with light and a chemical known as psoralen) can knock down the immune response but have proven of limited value in stemming the progression of scleroderma. Some clinicians have even suggested completely destroying the autoimmune patient's immune system and starting over with a bone marrow transplant.[7]

If the true culprit in scleroderma is the fibroblast, new therapeutic approaches that dampen T cells and target this cell line may offer better hope for specific disease control. Among the more promising alternative therapies are antifibrotic agents that include D-penicillamine and cytokine agents like alpha and gamma interferon that depress the immune response's stimulation of fibroblast growth.

AN ALTERNATIVE VIEW OF SCLERODERMA

Consider scleroderma as a localized process in which a new variant or variant connective tissue cell (e.g., an endothelial cell in a blood vessel) provokes an immune response. The ensuing T-cell response attempts to control the embryonic forms of cells that begin to proliferate. But the immune attack provokes the outgrowth of still more aberrant cells. Then the immune system begins to release cytokines to encourage the final stages of repair, encouraging fibroblast growth. The resulting overgrowth of fibroblasts and overproduction of collagen eventually encase the scleroderma patient in a hardening cloak of scar tissue. This model explains why immune-suppressing drugs have proven useful only in the disease's early stages, whereas antifibrotic agents remain the therapy of last recourse at its end.[8]

If true, this immune stimulation hypothesis suggests the best avenues of therapy may be those that suppress cytokines rather than impede the immune cells themselves. This model is consistent with what is known about many of scleroderma's chemical initiators. The common denominator of many of the provocative agents like vinyl chloride and trichloroethylene is that they injure blood vessel endothelium and can incite new cell variants by their gene-damaging activity.

But still another factor may be afoot in the etiology of this perplexing disease. Scleroderma patients with whom I have spoken have often voiced concern that the medical community is neglecting psychogenic factors that may play a powerful but underappreciated role in the development of this disease. It is ironic that the psychology community speaks freely about body-armoring and walling oneself off as modes of coping, but when the medical profession stumbles on people who are *literally* trapped inside their bodies, they neglect the mind altogether. The possible linkage between the mind and the body has only been accepted grudgingly into modern thinking about the immune system.

As with so many other diseases, autoimmunity may have a psychological component, especially if the mind can be shown to upset the delicate balance between self-acceptance and rejection on a tissue as well as a psychic level. As extreme as such a radical notion sounds, new data associating stress with disease suggest it is not so far off.

SEVEN

$\mathcal{I}$MMUNITY UNDER STRESS

Stress provides a unique vantage point for understanding how the mind and body interact to affect immunity and ultimately disease itself. Stress occurs when the body's physical, emotional, or psychic coping mechanisms are pushed beyond normal limits by external events or forces. All of us have some rudimentary understanding that too much stress, be it physical or psychogenic, is not good for us. Indeed, a linkage between stress and illness has been made since the time of Hippocrates in ancient Greece. From anecdote or personal experience, we know (or think we know) that "stress" can make us sick. For many, this belief turns on popular wisdom, the folklore of our grandmothers' urgent direction to stay out of the rain, avoid cold, or minimize our long nights out. Some of us have since learned that grandma's adages about stress were surprisingly apt: When we were stressed, we often *did* get sick.

Until recently much of the scientific evidence for these common anecdotal observations was far off. But now we know that many children who face their first days at school with trepidation show measurable increases in stress hormones. More critically, a striking correlation between these immunosuppressive hormone levels and subsequent illness suggests that such increases contribute to an otherwise inexplicable wave of respiratory illness in those first trying weeks. In a recent study conducted on 236 three- to five-year-olds in child-care centers, researchers at University of California at San Francisco's Departments of Medicine and Pediatrics found that children who responded to challenging developmental tasks or familial stress with elevated blood pressures were more likely to get sick at school than were their nonresponsive peers.[1] The illness measured was childhood respiratory disease, a common and sometimes serious affliction in young children. The researchers also found a seemingly paradoxical effect: Children who were stress "reactive" (as measured by blood pressure readings) fared *better* than their peers when subjected to low-level stressful events.

Now there is even more compelling evidence that the stresses associated with the first weeks of school do contribute to the observed increase in the rate of childhood illnesses. By measuring key cellular and hormonal stress factors (e.g., the level of cortisol secreted in saliva), researchers have shown that kids who were stressed by entering kindergarten experienced deleterious changes in their capacity to make antibodies.[2]

Other examples of the impact of stressors on bodily functions provide clear evidence for a directly harmful effect of stress on the body. For those who developed acute inflammation of the stomach (gastritis), irritable bowel syndrome, or even ulcers, stress has a particular resonance. For ulcers and intestinal hyperactivity, it has almost become dogma that stress produces illness, albeit indirectly (ulcers most often result from an overgrowth of the bacterium *Helicobacter pylori* in an acid environment). In reality, even these commonly held beliefs have proven more complex than previously thought. Many conditions of the gastrointestinal tract have been shown to be linked to related germs like *Campylobacter jejuni* as well as the stressors that create conditions favorable to their growth. These and related observations open the door for immunity to play a role in systemic illnesses of the gastrointestinal tract, as control of intestinal infection is preeminently immunological. Stress can also trigger the release of many of the chemical mediators of inflammation, suggesting that many forms of chronic inflammation can also be powerfully influenced by stress.[3]

THE STRESS RESPONSE

The key to understanding the vital role of the stress response and its paradoxical anti-immunity effect lies in understanding why the body can trade-off long-term losses in immune efficiency with short-term improvements in adaptation. In the 1940s and 1950s, Canadian researcher Hans Selye (1907–1982) studied intensively the general features of this stress response.[4] Selye found that under conditions of long-term, chronic stress, animals undergo profound degenerative changes. Strangely, the organs that show the most immediate adverse impact are not muscles or body tissues but those of the immune system.[5] In the classic chronic stress response, the thymus begins to atrophy, shrinking to a fraction of its normal size. At the same time, the lymph nodes lose their cellularity. And the ability of the spleen to respond to immune challenges plummets.

With repeated bouts of stress, the animal may undergo a wasting syndrome remarkably similar to that experienced by patients with AIDS. The animal loses body mass and hair, develops diarrhea, and commonly succumbs to devastating sepsis or bacterial infection. In rodents, the chronic stress reaction culminates in a fatal reaction that includes the massive deposition of calcium in the skin and body organs in a process known as calciphylaxis. A calciphylactic rat looks grotesque: Its fur is matted and its skin becomes rock-hard.

Selye beautifully documented these and other components of the body's stress response over 40 years ago. He linked the observed involution of the thymus and other organs in the lymph system in restrained animals to the effects of chronic psychogenic stress, a phenomenon duplicated by other "no escape" situations. In such situations, an animal is typically placed in a cage where the bars on the floor are sequentially electrified. Because the pattern of shocks is delivered randomly, the animal cannot learn how to escape and is therefore subjected to repeated stressful events.

Despite efforts to link stress and immune depression to cancer in the late 1960s, few commentators appreciated the pervasiveness of stress-mediated immune depression or how it might work to produce tissue damage in people until the 1990s. By about 1991, researchers had worked out the details of how stress-inducing or stress-mimicking chemicals could depress the immune system. Many were found to work through the hormonal interplay that links the brain and pituitary gland with the endocrine system of the body.

STRESS DEFINED

In its simplest sense, stress is a state of disharmony that upsets the normal balancing mechanisms of the body.

If the stress is mild, the body may return to normal. If protracted and severe, stress threatens to disrupt this homeostasis by resetting critical hormonal relationships that favor a few critical organs involved in short-term reactions at the expense of long-term functioning.

Thoughts and emotions triggered by stressful events can activate the hypothalamus in the brain to produce critical "releasing factors" that act on the pituitary gland, lodged securely just below it. As shown in Figure Four, during severely stressful events, the hypothalamus receives signals from the brain that provoke it almost immediately to release a barrage of such chemicals. These chemicals are secondary "triggers" or releasing factors that incite the release of key hormones from the pituitary gland. These pituitary hormones, in turn, activate genes in target organs like the adrenal gland that control the synthesis or release of still other critical hormones. The adrenal hormones set in train a series of physiological reactions leading directly to effects on the immune system itself. Cortisol, one of the so-called glucocorticoid hormones from the adrenal gland, boosts the number of quick-acting, phagocytosing white blood cells available while depressing circulating lymphocytes and macrophages.

During the stress response, the body increases its heart rate, blood pressure, and respiration. Oxygen and nutrients are shunted to organs that may require additional energy to cope with the stressful circumstances. (Selye termed this reaction the "general adaptational syndrome.)" At the core of this stress response is a factor from the hypothalamus known as corticotropin-releasing factor, a small polypeptide that triggers the cascade of chemical reactions that follow a stressful event.

One way of visualizing this system is to picture the stress response building from a stacked array of organs (see Figure Four). At the top is the *hypothalamus*, closest to the brain, which responds to nerves and emotional

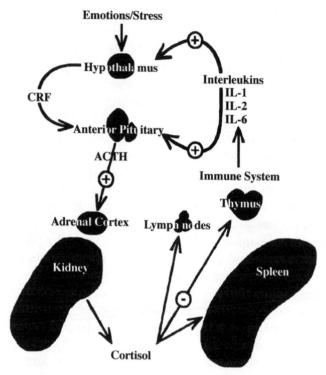

Four.   Stress and immunity. Illustration of how emotions or stress working through higher centers in the brain can dampen immune reactivity via cortisol production (⊖) and, conversely, how some immune cytokines (IL-1, IL-2, and IL-6) work to stimulate (⊕) the hypothalamus and pituitary into regulating the hormonal control of immune responses. Adapted from an illustration copyright © Marc Lappé, 1997. ACTH, adrenocorticotropic hormone; CRF, corticotropin releasing factor; IL, interleukin.

events. Beneath that is the *pituitary,* which responds to the hypothalamus. And under that is the *adrenal gland,* which responds to the pituitary. Finally, there are all of the end organs in the immune system like the thymus and lymph nodes, which respond to the adrenal hormones.

The hypothalamic hormone corticotropin-releasing factor (CRF) has the most powerful impact on the immune system. CRF acts on the pituitary and causes the release of the adrenal-activating hormone known as ACTH, which in turn provokes release of the cortico-steroids that have the most profound immune-inhibiting effects.

Among the other chemicals released by the adrenal gland are norepinephrine, epinephrine, endorphins, opiates, and dopamine, all of which directly or indirectly contribute to immune suppression in as yet unknown ways. The ultimate actors in the immune system, the lymphocytes and macrophages, carry receptors for many of these molecules, increasing the likelihood that they actually impact on immune functions. To keep the system under control, the immune system itself releases chemical feedback to the hypothalamus in the form of cytokines to let it know that it has received the signals from the endocrine system.[6] Normally, this feedback loop serves to dampen the suppressive effects of adrenal corticosteroids and thereby reduce their deleterious impact on the immune system's mediators.

The final evidence for an intimate link between the brain and the immune system is the existence of nerve endings terminating directly in organs of the immune system like the lymph nodes and spleen. This innervation appears to be essential for the normal functioning of the immune system. If the major source of these nerves, the spinal cord's sympathetic nervous system, is impaired or severed, the effects can be astonishing and dramatic. In spinal cord-damaged mice, certain autoimmune diseases that normally lie silent will flare up and normal bodily functions, such as metabolism, will be disrupted. These events are consequences of T-cell attacks on tissues and glands like the thyroid.[7] Inexplicably, drugs designed to block the sympathetic nervous system activity actually exacerbate certain autoimmune diseases like experimental allergic encephalitis. These findings suggest activities that tone the sympathetic nervous system, like exercise, may assist the immune system's normal functioning.

We also know that animals that are subjected to physical stresses by being restrained or given mild electric shock undergo immune depression that puts them at risk for viral and bacterial infections. Some of this damage appears to be mediated by a new class of recently discovered natural opiates known as endorphins. Evidence for a direct role of such opiates is now in. When rats are subjected to inescapable, random electric footshocks (we will put aside our ethical concerns here), their immune system's NK cell activity plummets. If their reaction to opiates is blocked with receptor-blocking drugs prior to being shocked, no such depression occurs.[8]

CENTRAL CONTROL OF IMMUNITY

All of this evidence points to a vital dependency of the immune system on the integrity of the brain. If the central governing gland of the brain, the hypothalamus, is damaged (e.g., by passing an electric current through it), the immune system will be similarly impaired. Following hypothalamic injury, the immune system loses much of its reactivity and strength. In turn, if the pituitary gland, the mediator of the hypothalamus's instructions, is removed after hypothalamic damage, no immediate effects on the immune system are observed. But if the pituitary is removed altogether, in time the treated animals die of overwhelming infection as a result of immunological breakdown.

The key role of the pituitary in mediating immune strength is revealed in a natural experiment. Pituitary-deficient, dwarf mice are naturally immune suppressed. If treated with the growth hormone normally produced by the pituitary, their immunologically compromised state disappears! Indeed, human growth hormone (HGH) itself will augment the immune system's activities, particularly those that are central to protecting the body against infection. Thus, one of the factors in immunological decline during aging and stress may be the known depletion of growth hormone that accompanies aging. Recent Veterans' Administration-sponsored studies in San Francisco in which elderly men have been given HGH offer a first experimental test of this linkage. Some men undergoing treatment showed an increase in body mass and modest strengthening of immune parameters. But final proof of these effects could not be confirmed because HGH-treated men failed to show other predicted benefits, and some experienced adverse side effects such as liver dysfunction.

DAILY STRESS AND IMMUNITY

Workers and family members subjected to repetitive stressful situations or conflict know firsthand what social stress means. A thick volume of new research has illuminated the linkage between these stressful events and disease.[9] Psychological stress clearly impairs wound healing and the ability to mount an effective antibody response. From an evolutionary viewpoint, such a reaction appears dysfunctional at best. Why would someone in a life-threatening situation be better off if he healed less quickly?

At one level it is quite simple. Evolution has provided almost all higher vertebrates with what is initially an adaptive reaction to stress. When faced with a life-threatening situation, every animal has the capacity for an immediate "adrenaline surge" that puts all of the body's quick response systems in high gear. This reaction, first described in the 1920s by Walter Cannon (1871–1945) of

Harvard University, has been dubbed the "flight or fight reaction."[10] Following a stressful environmental or psychological event, the body releases a cascade of chemicals that enhances certain neural pathways and leads to a heightened state of arousal and alertness. Attention span increases, vigilance improves, and the threshold for aggression goes way down. Concurrently, relatively nonessential bodily functions, notably appetite, sexual arousal, and other factors associated with growth or reproduction, are held in abeyance until the emergency is over.

Released adrenaline (literally, from the organ above the renal gland or kidney) constricts blood vessels at the periphery of the body, increases blood pressure, and starts a high rate of metabolism of glucose reserves, depleting the sugar stored in the liver. Glucocorticoids, special corticosteroid hormones that mobilize glucose into the blood, go into action. The amount of glucocorticoid released by the body is directly correlated with the extent of resulting depression of the immune system. At very low levels of glucocorticoids, the proliferative responsiveness of lymphocytes is actually enhanced, whereas at the higher levels produced by chronic stress, depression of immune activities is the rule. Glucocorticoids also depress the rate of metabolism and inhibit immunological and inflammatory reactions and wound healing alike. Under stressful conditions, glucocorticoids shift the body away from long-term cellular immunity in favor of short-term antibody production.

By activating those glucocorticoids that impinge on its activities, any number of stressful external stimuli can depress the immune system. These include physical factors such as heat, cold, noise, as well as excessive exercise and the heavy "G" loads from gravitational forces experienced in military jet travel. Each such stressor can evoke a common immune-damaging effect by indirectly activating the body's internal, hormonally mediated stress response.

IMMUNOSUPPRESSION

Ultimately, it is cortisol, the main adrenal cortex-produced glucocorticoid, that has the most profound depressant effect on the normal activities of the immune system. Many different components of the immune system may be adversely affected by cortisol, including the lymphocytes, macrophages, and leukocytes. Cortisol depresses the amount of certain cytokines like IL-2 and other inflammatory chemicals, and can even block the ability of some of them to lock onto their target tissues. By so doing, they prevent the normal chemical boost such cytokines give to the immune response and dampen inflammation generally. This is how, in part, certain over-the-counter hydrocortisone creams work to soothe irritation and reduce inflammation.

Cortisol is the most powerful anti-inflammatory precursor that the body eventually converts into the slightly (20 percent) less potent chemical known as cortisone. When cortisol levels are high, muscles are suffused with oxygen-rich blood while digestive organs and those involved in intestinal transport like other systems relatively nonessential for short-term survival are put on hold.

At times of high cortisol secretion (i.e., above 20 mg/100 ml of blood), otherwise active lymphocytic cell lines lose their ability to proliferate in response to antigens and mitogens that normally provoke rapid cell division. Cortisol also greatly increases the resilience of the lining of the small blood vessels to minimize bleeds during stress-related high blood pressure. This increases the integrity of microvascular endothelium but cuts down appreciably on the migration of leukocytes through blood vessel walls, a process vitally needed to ensure optimal inflammatory responses.

Coincidentally, cortisol production is greatly elevated in the manic phase of manic–depressive illness but reduced appreciably during the depressive phase. The linkage between such mental states and the immune system is underscored by the fact that a synthetic corticoid, methyl prednisone, also produces mania and euphoria. The converse reaction can occur during withdrawal of this drug. It is also significant that depressive patients are prone to illness, suggesting their immune systems may be depressed as well.

FLIGHT OR FIGHT

In its simplest sense, the stress reaction can best be seen as a trade-off between the urgent, immediate needs of an organism to avoid noxious stimuli and its long-term needs to sustain life. But one key property that cannot be overemphasized is the fact that it is a short-term solution. If animals are repeatedly put into classic stressful situations or are prevented from moving or escaping, they commonly undergo the profound changes of the stress response. With repeated exposure to high-intensity sound, forced exercise, restraint, or low temperatures, stressed animals contract a variety of bacterial and viral infections not normally acquired by nonstressed ones.

In light of these seemingly detrimental properties, it may come as a surprise that the ability of the adrenal gland to release stress hormones in general and glucocorticoids in particular is essential for survival. In syndromes where glucocorticoids are virtually absent, such as Addison's disease (which afflicted John Kennedy), otherwise noninjurious stressful events such as repetitive exposure to cold can be potentially life-threatening. For this reason Addison's disease patients must replace missing adrenal hormones. Paradoxically, Addison's patients have a superabundance of lymphoid tissue, in keeping with the idea that adrenal hormones are needed to balance the immune system. Without them, lymphoid tissue may overcompensate.

Overall, glucocorticoids protect the body against the deleterious effects of nutritional stresses (fasting), permitting the body to conserve its internal organ systems while allowing the body to break down or catabolize fats and organ systems more "peripheral" to survival. As we have seen, lymphoid organs and other components of the immune system's long-term response are deemed expendable under times of duress.

THE ROLE OF PSYCHOGENIC FACTORS

The stress response can originate in the higher centers of the brain, or it may be entrained at a lower, conditioned level, much as Pavlov did when he used the ring of a bell to provoke salivation in his conditioned dogs. A stress response may also be released by a general unconditioned stimulus to which an animal becomes habituated. Indeed, it is actually possible to train animals to cut down their antibody production by linking lower production to a reward stimulus. Findings such as these suggest that the brain may work at a subconscious level during stressful events to modify the immune system. Given the existence of a linkage between emotionality and stress, it becomes understandable why certain people routinely "become sick" after visiting their parents or attending social functions in which they feel trapped. And, as we have seen, stressed children—particularly those from highly emotionally charged family situations—fall prey to immune depression and get sick more often than do their nonstressed peers.

DIFFERENTIAL EFFECTS

In animals some stressors appear to affect one arm of the immune system over the other. For instance, when mice are stressed by physical restraint, their capacity to make antibodies remains intact, but their cellular immune strength plummets.[11] The excess glucocorticoids produced by physical stress make it more difficult for the immune system to get antigens to the proper cells. Glucocorticoids do this by knocking down key cytokines needed by cells engaged in immune responses.

Such immunosuppressive effects of normally released glucocorticoids on T cells encouraged a generation of transplant surgeons to look to corticoids for immunosuppression. A drug once commonly used in transplant patients is prednisone, a relative of cortisone. Prednisone's list of adverse effects includes moonlike facial features, destruction of the thymus, susceptibility to infection, as well as calcium depletion and vulnerability to decay of bones, particularly the head of the femur that fits the hip socket.

Corticoid drugs in general knock down the T and T helper cell count, while sparing the key white blood cells needed for short-term defense against bacterial invasion. During periods when natural glucocorticoids are being released, red blood cells and platelets go up, further reinforcing the belief that the stress response plays a supportive role in short-term protection of the body.

IMMUNOTOXICITY AND STRESS

It is not surprising that many chemicals such as prednisone depress immunity by mimicking the natural hormonal changes of the stress response. Other immunosuppressive drugs artificially raise the levels of glucocorticoids that circulate in the blood, thereby indirectly simulating the heightened levels of suppressants produced naturally during the body's stress response. If such immunosuppressants are simply mimicking a natural state, why should we be concerned about their expanded use?

First, clinical judgments about why and where it is desirable to depress the immune system are not always sound. Clinicians who use corticosteroids to control inflammation, such as in sinus infections, may be unaware they risk a host of secondary unintended effects including bony changes, viral infections, and runaway infection. Others may not know how altering the body's glucocorticoid levels can produce unpredictable effects on immune function.[12] For instance, slightly increasing the level of circulating glucocorticoids through modest exercise may lead to a general toning of the immune system, whereas more extreme elevation from overtraining can lead to immune depression. It is also clear that glucocorticoids, although a major chemical involved in producing immune suppression during the stress response, are not the only chemicals produced by the body that modify the immune response. Other brain-released hormones like thyroxin can participate in immune depression, and sex hormones, as we have seen, play a powerful role as well.

A third point is that corticosteroids can increase the toxicity of potentially harmful chemicals. Stress hormones increase the vulnerability of the body to specific toxic substances that may then damage the immune system further. A case in point is the widely used pesticide DDT. When birds are stressed by reducing their daily food intake by as little as 10 percent, the amount of DDE—a chemical produced by the breakdown of DDT in the body—needed to interfere with immune responses and reproductive success drops precipitously.[13] The immunotoxic effects of other chemicals could likewise be augmented by stressors in the environment. An example is the pesticide malathion. The technical grade of this chemical contains highly immunosuppressive by-products that are rendered much more toxic when given to overstressed, crowded chickens than to nonstressed ones.[14]

REFLECTIONS ON STRESS AND ADAPTATION

The big question is of course why evolutionary forces have permitted stress to jeopardize the body's immune system in the first place. The old adage, that an animal who neither fights nor flees from a stressful circumstance is not around to need an immune response, is cute but ultimately unsatisfying. So many of the stresses of everyday life are by their nature intense, including crowding, competition for mates (for instance during the rut or mating season in deer and other ungulates), and the tensions of family strife that explanation is needed.

It may be that the immune system is simply an unfortunate bystander that gets swept up by more urgent physiological exigencies. But it is much more appealing to postulate that some dampening or modulation of the immune response, such as routinely occurs during everyday stressful life situations, may in fact have some beneficial effects. For instance, the childhood stress work cited earlier, which showed stress-reactive children doing better on antibody tests, has since been extended to monkeys. Paradoxically, stress-reactive monkeys explore more, learn better, and become the "alpha," or leaders, of their social group.[15]

Another clue for the adaptive value of low-level stress is that many of the cells of the immune system themselves actually carry receptors on their surfaces that bind with the key endocrine mediators of the immune response. Not all of these binding interactions are immunosuppressive. Some actually serve to focus the immune reaction toward making highly specific subsets of immune cells.[16] It is only after stress becomes chronic and thereby life-threatening itself that the immune system is sacrificed.[17] Thus, mild or moderately stressful events do not usually impair immunity.

A LITTLE STRESS MAY BE GOOD FOR YOU

These examples suggest that the body may actually benefit at some stage in the stress response. A simple syllogism suggests that if strong maladaptive stresses knock down the immune system, weaker, positive ones may improve it. Recent studies have shown that something like this does indeed occur, both during the "stress" of modest exercise and from the neural stimuli of a sensorially enriched environment, both of which tone the immune system's responsiveness. Researchers have linked general health and a diminution of colds and illness in fit individuals to their consistent activity level. Such an effect may be explained by the ability of low-level stress to stimulate antibody production and maintain modest levels of NK cell activity.

TRAINING AND IMMUNITY

But generalizations here can be dangerous. A common misperception about the immune system is that its fitness goes hand and glove with fitness in the more traditional sense. Extremely well-trained, fit athletes are simply presumed to be immunologically fit as well. Now new evidence suggests that this belief is misplaced, at least for the most heavily conditioned athletes. Overtraining is associated with a plethora of newly recognized maladies.

Among high-endurance athletes and Olympic runners, it has been commonplace to hear whispered rumors of an abnormally high prevalence of colds and influenza. This originally anecdotal information has since been confirmed with genuine data. Researchers at the University of Queensland, Australia, have found that antibody levels in saliva are dramatically reduced (by as much as

70 percent) after just 2 hours of cycling at a racing pace. A parallel study at the University of Cape Town, South Africa, has shown that the best marathon runners experience a profound drop in white blood cell counts in the days immediately following their races.[18]

Other researchers at the Copenhagen Muscle Research Center have found that with protracted exercise the levels of T lymphocytes and NK cells are depleted for as long as 20 hours after cessation of extensive training sessions. As further evidence for the debilitating effects of endurance training, at least two internationally known track stars from Great Britain, Diane Edwards and Sebastian Coe, have had to drop out of international competition after contracting toxoplasmosis, a rare protozoan parasitic disease to which they would normally have innate resistance. This disease is typically carried by cats, and full-blown, disseminated toxoplasmosis usually afflicts only those who are immunologically depressed. The vast majority of immunologically competent adults who are infected with the causative organism remain symptom free. So what accounts for two superathletes contracting the disease?

What appears to be happening with prolonged endurance training is that the stress hormones normally associated with short-term stressful events become turned on chronically, leading to a syndrome of chronic fatigue and malaise that appears to be intimately linked to the immune system's decline. These effects, I should emphasize, are seen only at the extremes of exercise. At present, most researchers believe that suppression of the immune system by such protracted stresses on the body is short lived and may not impair health over the long run. But it is far from evident that this is true, as data from marathon runners demonstrate shorter than expected life spans and more illness than among less heavily trained individuals. Indeed, chronic overtraining appears to lead to a syndrome of its own, one that is strikingly similar to chronic fatigue syndrome, and its associated symptoms may persist for years.

Extreme exercise, thus, can be maladaptive. Under the strain of high-level training, NK cell levels and their activity may rise initially, only to fall precipitously a few hours after cessation of exercise. The resulting period of depressed NK cell activity, often lasting 6 hours or longer, produces an open window for new infections. This paradoxical effect of immunosuppression is supported by studies showing that elite athletes often experience an increased incidence of upper respiratory tract infections compared with individuals who undergo regular, moderate exercise.[19]

Findings such as these underscore the tightrope we walk in maintaining an adaptive level of immunological fitness. Clearly, the immune system is like a finely tuned engine in a luxury sports car—overtuning can produce as much of a deficit in performance as can be found in an untuned car. All of this suggests that the body has an incredibly delicate and complex system for homeostasis of the immune system, one that is remarkably akin to the traditional notions of balance in Chinese medicine where health is always seen as a state of dynamic equilibrium between opposing forces.

The mystery of the stress response, and the theme that intrigues most people today, is how the mind can set loose this stream of chemical mediators that begins in the brain's hypothalamus and ends at the adrenal gland. The resultant field of study of the linkages between emotions, the brain, and the immune system is known as psychoneuroendocrinology.

EIGHT

$\mathcal{M}$IND, BRAIN, AND BODY

A new field of biology opened up, or more accurately reopened, in the late 1970s with the creation of the discipline of psychoneuroimmunology (PNI). This new field blended principles gleaned from neurobiology and immunology into a common discipline that emphasized how human emotions and psychological factors could affect immunity. In its earliest manifestation, PNI picked up from the stress research we have just reviewed. As we saw, stress can have systemic impacts on the ability of the body to ward off infection or heal wounds. In animals, researchers have firmly established that both physical and psychic stress can suppress many of the functions of the immune system.

PNI researchers pushed these studies into the human arena by asking if psychological forces, short of the extremes of stress, might not also modulate the immune response. If the immune system could be controlled by psychological forces, then a host of social and mental interventions, including biofeedback, stress reduction, and peer group support systems, could be called on to modify the course of diseases. Indeed, early data are quite compelling that diseases *are* amenable to psychological interventions. Breast cancer patients survive significantly longer with social reinforcement than without; genital herpes sufferers report longer remissions when their emotional lives are balanced; and patients with lupus—and some of their doctors—swear that they experience longer remissions when their emotional health is restored. But many traditional practitioners are skeptical about such reports, alleging they are merely the result of suggestion or a placebo (literally, "I will please") effect. Before we dismiss these early but dramatic findings, perhaps we should reflect on what we do know.

Certainly we now know that the mind and body are integrated in highly coordinated and complex ways. We understand that the immune system is not only potentially controlled by factors that originate in the brain but that once activated, the immune system can in turn influence the brain itself.

The likelihood that the brain does play an intimate role in shaping immune responses is underscored by a substantial body of independent evidence. We have already seen how stress, much of it psychogenic in origin, clearly affects the immune system's capacity to fight disease. Until recently, the more subtle interactions between mind and body have eluded successful investigation. Although to many it appears only logical that the brain and body are connected, proving that "reality" remains fraught with confounding factors.

Not least among these is the uncertainty of the direction of any causal influence: The causal arrow may point from the mind to the body or from the body to the mind or some combination of both. Many patients with depression may have impaired immunity (some do): But is it the depression that depresses the immune system or the impaired immune system that causes the depression? It is even possible that *both* are caused by a common third factor. The mind and the immune system may each respond similarly to common events, creating a misimpression of a causal relationship between one reaction and the other. Consider the observation that depression is linked to susceptibility to infection or vulnerability to cancer.[1] But many forms of cancer may be the result of a common factor, like alcohol addiction or immunosuppressive chemicals or drugs that also produce depression. Conversely, the euphoria experienced at times of good health may be produced by the cytokines released by a healthy immune system; or euphoria may release opiatelike endorphins that improve immune function.

At the primary level of bodily repair, researchers have shown that inflammation and normal wound healing can be dramatically slowed by emotional stresses. Women who have to care for demented relatives for a protracted period—and presumably suffer the psychic stresses of watching loved ones decline—show much slower healing of simple wounds than do age-matched controls. Specific immune responses to challenge antigens also appear to be depressed in the same women.[2] And heart disease and its recurrence are more likely in depressed patients than in more balanced patients.

Until recently, interpretation of the causal arrow in such findings went in polarized directions. Clinicians generally considered that people were depressed because of their illness rather than vice versa. Natural healers and other alternative practitioners often had the arrow in the opposite direction. They perceived illness as the result of depression. In a sense, both groups are right. We now know that depression is a two-way street: Immunological reactions can affect the mind and the mind can affect the immune system, often profoundly so. A case in point provides suggestive medical evidence for such an effect.

A CASE STUDY

In 1994, a 59-year-old white woman was admitted into the neurology department of a Paris hospital.[3] Her provisional diagnosis was Creutzfeldt–Jakob disease, a normally unrelenting, progressively deteriorating neurological condition. Her history was significant for the development of a disorder in her walking and muscular control. She also experienced psychological problems severe enough for her to be treated for 6 months in a psychiatric ward with a diagnosis of depression and hysteria. In fact, she alternated between periods of acute psychosis and general improvement, trends that her treating doctors related to her treatment with antidepressants and neuroleptic (antipsychotic) medication. By the time she was admitted to the Paris hospital, she was confused and disoriented, with amnesia, impaired ability to speak, and numerous other signs of severe central nervous system damage.

A full workup revealed the surprising finding that although her thyroid appeared anatomically normal, it was filled with solid and cystlike nodules. Her physicians believed that she might have an immunological problem: an underlying thyroid disorder known as Hashimoto's thyroiditis, which results from an autoimmune attack on this central metabolic gland.

In an attempt to resolve her physiological problem, doctors began a course of immunosuppressive therapy with prednisone, a powerful immunodepressant. To their surprise, her mental status improved remarkably over the next month with dramatic resolution of virtually all of her cognitive disturbances. Within a year of her admission, the patient had made a spectacular and complete recovery from all of her psychiatric problems, including those of her (misdiagnosed) Creutzfeldt–Jakob disease. Apparently, by suppressing her immune system's overreactive production of antibodies against her thyroid tissue, her physicians were able to stem the tide of an unrelenting autoimmune process *and* bring her mentation and psychic functioning back to normal. Alternatively, the corticosteroid might have directly enhanced her mood and mental functioning, an effect seen in prednisone-treated Addison's disease patients.

With hindsight, we may relate her psychiatric problems to her thyroid condition, but a direct contributing role of autoimmunity to her mental state cannot be discounted. For instance, it is as plausible that the same autoimmunity that damaged her thyroid gland produced psychosis as it is that her psychosis disrupted her immune system. Although one can make too much of a single case report, a growing body of literature suggests that the mind can exert remarkable control over the body and, by inference, the immune system may exert considerable control over the mind.

INDIRECT DATA

The suggestion that the brain and immune systems are inextricably linked is reinforced by indirect evidence of this sort, much of it very recent. Although it is by now incontrovertible that major psychogenic stressors can disrupt immune functions,[4] it is less clear that minor shifts in mood or emotionality can also affect the immune system.

Suggestive evidence for such effects has been available for at least three decades, notably from findings that widowed survivors are more likely than their married peers to die in the first 2 years following the death of their spouses. And the general observation, popularized by Norman Cousins, who apocryphally laughed his way out of a severe bout of autoimmune disease (ankylosing spondylitis), that an upbeat mood can reinforce a balanced immune system appears to have some general support. But proof positive is lacking for establishing the causal net between positive emotions and healthy immunity. Some believe it is more likely that elevated mood simply reduces predilection for self-injurious activity and enhances general improvement in personal care and hygiene than it cures any illness.

But the adverse proposition is well established. Careful, case-controlled research has now shown that negative, stressful life events are intimately linked to an increased occurrence and downward course of breast cancer.[5] Based on questionnaires administered *before* the results of a biopsy were available, researchers discovered that women who were given a diagnosis of breast cancer were more likely to have experienced a severe life stress in the preceding 8 years than were women who were found to have benign breast disease.[6]

This study was recently reexamined in a larger cohort involving 119 women who were seen consecutively in a surgical outpatient clinic at King's College Hospital in London.[7] The British study examined women aged 20–70 to determine if life events that were particularly threatening to psychic well-being affected breast cancer diagnosis. Importantly, no events were scored that might themselves have an independent, hormonal impact on breast cancer, such as stillbirth or an abortion. The dramatic findings showed that women who had experienced severe life events and attendant stresses were more likely to develop breast cancer than were their relatively stress-free peers. The significance of this risk level was extremely high, reinforcing the likely reliability of the findings.

But how any increased cancer risk is linked to an effect on the immune system remains unknown. It is equally plausible that secondary hormonal changes that accompanied these life events themselves contributed to an increased likelihood a woman would be diagnosed with cancer. The authors believed that the severe life events increased the growth and multiplication of cancer cells through alteration of the natural immune surveillance process. In keeping with this view, they cite studies demonstrating that stressful effects on the endocrine system can produce immunological depression. But as we will see in the chapter on cancer and immunity, it is not always clear that an improvement in immune strength translates to a better outcome. In fact, some women (Finnish flight attendants) with mild immune depression as a result of radiation from flying at high altitudes have *less* breast cancer than expected.

MOOD AND IMMUNITY

Other lines of evidence offer strong, albeit indirect, proof for a mind–immune system connection. People who use certain psychoactive medications have shown shifts in immune system indicators. Such an effect is consistent with the idea that mood change can alter the immune system.

For instance, patients who take therapeutic dosages of antidepressants such as imipramine, amitriptyline, and nortriptyline show a dramatic and significant decline in their levels of natural killer cell populations.[8] It is unclear if this effect can be translated to one affecting the body as a whole. Perhaps the depressive effect is chemically mediated directly via drug effects on the immune system, bypassing the brain altogether. It is tempting to speculate that human neurons and NK cells may share common pathways that allow antidepressants to act on the same receptors. If so, this would suggest that both brain and immune cell types are linked, a possibility supported by their common origins in a common layer of the early embryo.

Perhaps most interestingly, evidence of mood swings can be discerned *during* an immune response. In the midst of a strong antibody response, many people insist that they feel a sense of well-being. This otherwise quasi-mystical assertion is actually quite reasonable: An ongoing immune response is heralded by an elevation in the circulating levels of endogenously produced chemicals known to affect mood, including catecholamines like adrenaline, opiates like endorphins, and corticosteroids themselves. Again, the direction of the causal arrow here is at issue, as many people naturally feel better at the end of an illness. But it is tempting to speculate that the sense of well-being that comes when we "get well" reflects the mind-altering chemical mix released by a successful immune response.

Activated immune cells themselves release a number of potentially psychoactive chemicals, including those that participate in nerve transmission or the stimulation of the activity of several glands, like the thyroid, pituitary, and hypothalamus. It is well to remember that each of these organs can also indirectly affect our psychic sense of well-being. Some of these chemicals, notably the corticotropin-releasing hormone discussed earlier, play back to the immune system indirectly by decreasing the secretion of growth hormone and prolactin and thereby depress or "downregulate" the immune system even as they affect mood.

Such checks and balances may be critical if the immune system is going to avoid going out of control in the face of major emotional upheavals. Lacking such controls, the body may be prone to enter a state of constant exhaustion like that found in the chronic fatigue syndrome during times of great emotional distress. When the body overproduces corticotropin releasing factors during such events, it may influence the immune system profoundly. Approximately 40–50 percent of patients with a major depression have been found to overproduce corticotropin and corticosteroids,[9] consistent with the previously cited work. Depression in mood may go hand and glove with depression in immunity.

PSYCHOGENIC STRESS

The key question in all of these events is whether or not stressful events that produce chemical imbalances can affect overall health via an immune mechanism. The best answer to this query is to be found in studies on psychogenic stress and disease. As we have discussed, the psychological stresses from major life-disturbing events clearly have a major effect on bacterial infections, especially those that cause upper respiratory disease. They also can affect the course of certain viral infections, notably those caused by herpesvirus. Under major psychological and emotional stresses, recurrence of diseases like TB has been reported to occur, especially in institutionalized patients. Stress also can exacerbate group A streptococcal disease and even such obscure conditions as trenchmouth (also known as Vincent's disease) in which the lining of the mouth becomes inflamed from viral infection. Viral upper respiratory diseases are also more common following stressful events, as are episodes of mononucleosis. Following a severely emotional, stressful event, such as separation, latent herpesvirus infections can flare, leading to painful recrudescences of old lesions.

Among the conditions that have been shown to lead to such reactivation are divorce, caregiving of a sick relative, depression, and even medical examinations themselves. Each of these events has been shown to lead to reactivation of various herpesviruses, including the cytomegalovirus and the herpes zoster responsible for shingles.

The exact mechanism by which stress contributes to recrudescence of disease is largely unknown, but it is reasonable to consider the immune system as the key intermediary. Such disease flareups after putative immune depression are also consistent with the idea that many viral infections are not so much cured as put into remission by immune reactions. Even a transient depression of antibody production may allow a latent virus to recur.

The observation that many serious diseases also appear to progress more rapidly in stressed patients provides further, albeit anecdotal, evidence of a connection between mental state and longevity. Stress also seems to plays a role in permitting the more rapid progression of tumor cells. Several complementary studies show that women who have widely metastasized breast cancer will succumb much sooner to their malignant disease if they have had recently stressful events, even where those events are unrelated to their underlying illness. Conversely, as noted earlier, support groups that provide a social network of compassionate friends appear to prolong the lives of women with advanced metastatic breast cancer.

At the opposite end of the spectrum from the impact of emotion or other amorphous forces on immunity are a concrete list of immune-damaging chemicals. Because of the growing realization that many potentially immunotoxic chemicals permeate our environment, it is critical to review just how much (or little) is known about their prevalence and impact.

$\mathscr{C}$HEMICALS THAT POISON IMMUNITY

It is one of the profound ironies of modern science that many of the deleterious factors that threaten survival have come under scrutiny only at the eleventh hour. Only belatedly have we learned that many of the chemicals that threaten the immune system threaten species as well. Such chemicals include PCBs, DDT, stabilizers, and certain pesticides. The physical impact of ultraviolet radiation is also a threat. It may not be too late to examine these previously underappreciated threats to immune system integrity.

The importance of such an inquiry is underscored by one of the more ominous developments in the last decade: From 1987 through 1994, over 700 bottlenose dolphins died off the mid-Atlantic U.S. coast; another 220 died near Texas. Many marine biologists are especially concerned that these die-offs result indirectly from high contaminant levels of chemical toxicants that are poisoning the immune system. A recent dolphin die-off is a case in point. This and related die-offs have been attributed to immune depression and a concomitant increase in infections.

Scientists who examined body tissues of 19 bottlenose dolphins found beached along the Florida coast between 1991 and 1994 found extraordinary high levels of tributyltin, a plastic stabilizer and marine paint additive. This tin compound was suspected of being an immunotoxicant,[1] but few studies could be found.

A LOOK BACK

Ironically, despite the obvious importance of such studies, the effort to fuse immunology and toxicology is just now getting under way. As with other disciplines that require a melding of two different paradigms, neither toxicologists nor immunologists appeared to pay much attention to each other until the data were too obvious to ignore. In the 1970s, the first evidence of profound immune suppression from exposure to chemicals like dioxin began to be reported independently by toxicologists and immunologists. Prior to this period, most immunological suppression work involved studying radiation's responsibility for immune depression. These studies showed that x-irradiated animals could be expected to recover their immune strength after sublethal radiation, but only if they had an intact thymus gland. The fact that the thymus was necessary for an experimental animal to recover from radiation-produced damage proved to be one of the clues for understanding chemical immune toxicity. Many of the first chemicals studied systematically for their immunotoxic effects, notably dioxins and PCBs, home in on the thymus gland, destroying its tissue architecture and generally rendering the thymus nonfunctional.

PRIORITIES

Given the central role of the thymus in the immune system, the systematic study of how these and other chemicals might damage it would appear to have been a high priority. Unfortunately, even today, immunotoxicology, the study of the toxic properties of chemicals on the immune system, generally is being given short shrift. Although the field of toxicology expanded greatly in the 1970s and 1980s, particularly in the area of genetic toxicity and cancer studies, immunological effects of chemical toxicants were rarely examined. During this period, virtually no attention was paid to the impact of environmental chemicals on the immune system. This neglect is all the more noteworthy, given the long history of studies that showed the immune system to be exquisitely vulnerable to environmentally prevalent, cancer-producing chemicals such as benzo[a]pyrene, a common contaminant of fossil fuels, and other so-called aryl aromatic hydrocarbons.

CANCER IMMUNOTOXICITY

With hindsight, we can identify the pioneering works in immunotoxicology as studies that began in the early 1950s. This research was designed to examine the possible link between cancer and an intact immune system. At the time, a few prescient researchers wondered if cancer-causing chemicals might not also be immunosuppressive in their own right. In a remarkably short period between

1960 and 1970, many investigators in Great Britain and the United States showed that at cancer-producing doses, virtually all chemical carcinogens are dramatically immuno-suppressive. Many of the most potent carcinogens, including coal-tar-derived chemicals like methylcholan-threne, benzo[*a*]pyrene, and dibenzanthracene (all found in cigarette smoke), proved to be such powerful immuno-suppressants that animals treated with them in cancer-causing doses readily accepted foreign tissue grafts.

In experimental studies in rodents, these and related chemicals routinely depressed the body's ability to make antibodies or fend off pathogenic viruses. Given the hope of these researchers that immune responses could control or eventually destroy cancer in the human body, it is astonishing how many pharmacology-oriented research-ers were nonplussed by the discovery that most cancer chemo*therapeutic* agents were also immunosuppressive.[2] If cancer control needed some immune response, then kill-ing cancer cells *and* immune cells was potentially counter-productive. To this day, too little attention is paid to this unfortunate linkage, leaving an indeterminate number of chemotherapy patients unnecessarily immune depressed, at risk for opportunistic infections and, possibly, cancer recurrences.

CASE STUDIES OF IMMUNOTOXICITY

We now know that a host of chemicals involved in industrial practices have dramatic immunotoxicity. Yet, virtually all remain in commerce even as their toxic prop-erties become better understood. A case in point is iso-phorone diisocyanate, one of the chemicals used exten-sively in the plastics industry. The isocyanates as a group have been known for at least three decades to have the ability to produce a florid contact hypersensitivity and to sensitize an exposed worker's lungs for asthmalike reactions for years after exposure. A disproportionate number of such workers develop asthma, an often permanent affliction that causes airway narrowing and difficulty in breathing. Despite this known adverse property, researchers chose isophorone diisocyanate as a chemical that could be added to polyurethanes to prevent the finished product from discoloring and to help prevent it from succumbing to chemical attack.

In 1992, the National Toxicology Program (NTP) selected this diisocyanate for testing in its budding immunotoxicity program because of its widespread use in paints, varnishes, and elastomers. To hardly anyone's surprise, isophorone diisocyanate proved to be able to produce the same poison ivy/poison oak-like reaction of skin sensitization in mice that it had already been shown to produce in people.

These studies raise the question of why chemicals with potent sensitizing ability continue to be used in such volume throughout the United States. Although workers can find a "skin notation" on the Material Safety Data Sheet for one isocyanate (toluene diisocyanate) and are required to wear protective clothing when working with it, they will not find a similar entry for isophorone. Warning labels to alert the user of the presence and particular dangers of this chemical in paints and varnishes used by consumers would clearly be useful, yet for inexplicable reasons, none is required.

Another chemical in widespread industrial use that raises immunological concern is gallium arsenide. Gallium arsenide is extensively used by the semiconductor industry in the manufacture of many electronic components, including light-emitting diodes. Like isophorone diisocyanate, it was already known that the class of compounds under study was likely to show immunotoxicity. Many arsenic-containing compounds are well known immunotoxicants. Gallium arsenide suppressed the ability of test mice to produce antibodies and depressed various

parameters of the immune response to classic test antigens that normally provoke cell divisions in lymphocytes.
The NTP's terse summary of these studies was simply
that gallium arsenide produced "multiple immunotoxic
effects." No recommendations for limiting its use or im-
posing special exposure precautions appear in NTP's literature, much less a plea for reduced reliance on this
highly immunotoxic chemical.

ENVIRONMENTAL IMMUNOTOXICANTS

Given the climate of environmental concern about
toxic chemicals generally, it would be logical for the NTP
to concentrate on those that interact with living systems,
the so-called xenobiotic chemicals.[3] For many, there is a
gnawing fear that many new and subtle environmental
threats to our immunological well-being exist in such
exposures. Even trace levels of dioxins or polychlorinated
biphenyls (PCBs) that bioaccumulate in the body can depress the immune system and put animals at high risk of
disease.[4] Disturbingly large numbers of human populations now have these chemicals in their bodies at or near
the same concentrations capable of depressing immune
parameters in animals. People who consume two or more
portions of Great Lakes salmon or whitefish and Eskimos
who eat high on the food chain are two such groups.

Health and environmental agencies have been equally
derelict in recognizing the critical importance of identify-
ing and reducing certain chemical hazards to the immune
system. Although immune suppression by chemicals like
benzene, a common component of gasoline and other
petroleum products, had been recognized for over 30
years—and by new ones like diethylstilbestrol (DES) only
more recently—no immunological testing requirements
were imposed on manufacturers of chemical or pharmaceutical products until 1990. In addition to standard

toxicity testing, a new battery of "immunotoxicity" tests is now required by the EPA as part of the registration of new products.

IMMUNOTOXICITY TESTING

In 1988, the NTP instituted a formal Immunotoxicity Testing Program to ferret out the chemicals that carry the greatest danger to our immune systems.[5] This is a bit like closing the barn door after the horse has bolted, as virtually all of the first battery of tested chemicals were already loose in our environment. But even in an environmental-friendly administration, this immunotoxicity program languishes with a small staff (only six professionals). Of the 2257 chemicals that the NTP singled out for toxicological evaluation, only 58 were selected as warranting immunotoxic evaluation. Of these 58 chemical studies undertaken, only 41 were completed as of mid-1996, and the program has been reduced to two Ph.D.-level professionals and support staff.

When queried by mail, Michael Luster, currently Chief of the Toxicology and Molecular Biology Branch at the CDC and NIOSH and formerly a member of the research team at the NTP Immunotoxicity Testing Program, indicated in writing that he was unaware that only 58 chemicals had been tested. Luster believes that more work is needed on agency collaboration, proper design of testing, and interpretation of data for the program to be valuable. He also advocates the more systematic development of a battery of test chemicals for both wildlife and occupational exposures. More critically, Luster is skeptical about the adequacy of the present level of data interpretation.[6] All of these findings point to a less than ideal program in this most critical area of research.

The absence of a more intensive effort leaves a substantial number of at-risk chemicals unstudied and unregulated for immunotoxic effects. The Agency for Toxic Substance Disease Registry has promulgated a priority list of the 275 most hazardous chemicals facing the U.S. public. By my own count, fully half of the listed chemicals have evidence of some adverse consequences to immune competence, especially after protracted exposure. At the top 25 of the list are chemicals like lead, arsenic, benzene, cadmium, PCBs, benzo[*a*]pyrene, trichloroethylene, DDT, dibenzanthracene, and chlordane, all of which have been shown to have some immunosuppressive properties. Inexplicably, the NTP's efforts in immunotoxicity exempted *all* of the top 25 high-risk chemicals from further study because they were not nominated by any of the review teams. Considering that this unit was charged with the responsibility of screening chemicals of human significance for potential immunotoxicity, this omission would be laughable if not for the seriousness of the potential exposures.

Some of the chemicals, like trichloroethylene (TCE), a widely used (*and dumped*) solvent, have become widespread trace contaminants of over 70,00 drinking water systems in the United States. TCE has been assigned a number (#IMM96007) and selected for immunotoxicity testing. But the actual testing has barely begun. Through 1996, NTP released no data implicating or exculpating this chemical in a host of immune-related disorders reported by residents in thousands of communities with low-level water contamination of TCE. This yawning data gulf leaves a significant portion of the exposed population in limbo.

SCOPE OF INQUIRY

A case in point illustrates the rift that exists between the exigencies of testing and the practical, often economic, considerations that drive the choice of chemicals to be tested. A listing of the chemicals tested by the NTP's immunotoxicity program is given in Table Two. Note that this list concentrates almost exclusively on pharmaceutical chemicals, with only a handful of occupational chemicals and virtually none of environmental concern. Excluded are tributyltin, PCBs, dioxins, and other chemicals with substantial immunotoxic potential.

Note also that only four chemicals are pesticides (alachlor, aldicarb, atrazine, and chlorpyrifos) whereas at least half are pharmaceutical chemicals or drugs like AZT, and the remainder miscellaneous industrial chemicals. A few highly sensitive chemicals like patulin and poly-dimethylsiloxane are listed for scientific *and* political reasons. Patulin is a naturally occurring contaminant of apple juice and claimed by some researchers to be a potential human carcinogen. And silicone has never been alleged to be an immunotoxic (i.e., immune depressing) chemical. Not unexpectedly, both were found to lack immunotoxic properties. How, you might ask, could politics appear to drive choices in what is ostensibly a purely scientific body?

A call to the NTP revealed that the chemical selection committee for the Immunotoxicity Testing Program works as an ad hoc group that makes its choices based on "nominations" by interested parties, most often industry or university scientists with a pet chemical that they would like tested—and in industry's case, exonerated. This is exactly what took place in the testing for silicone. Extensive tests to establish its toxic properties failed to show any significant suppressant properties. But silicone was never suspected to be an immuno*suppressive* substance. Instead, it was thought to be an immuno*stimulant*. It was only after prodding by the FDA to study *something* about silicone's properties that it was added to the high-priority list. Although the government's ITP testing protocols were not designed to pick up such effects, at least three different parameters of immune stimulation were indeed

Table Two. Immunotoxicity Testing Status as of June 1, 1996[a]

Alachlor	C	2-Mercaptobenzothiazole	C
Aldicarb oxime	Inc	Methadone hydrochloride	C
Atrazine	C	Morphine sulfate	Inc
3'-Azido-3'-deoxythymidine/2',3'-dideoxycytidine	Inc	Nitrobenzene	Inc
		Nitroforazone	C
		m-Nitrotuluene	C
AZT and pyrimethamine	Inc	p-Nitrotoluene	C
Benzethonium chloride	C	Oleic acid diethanolamine	Inc
o-Benzyl-p-chlorophenol	C	Oxymetholone	C
n-butyl-acrylate	C	Patulin	C
t-Butylhydroquinone	C	Pentaerythritol triacrylate	Inc
Carbon tetrachloride	C	Pentamidine isetisonate	C
4-Chloro-o-phenylene-diamine	C	Phenolphthalein	Inc
		Polydimethylsiloxane (silicone)	C
Chlorpyrifos (Dursban)	Inc		
Crotonaldehyde	C	Ribavirin	Inc
2,4-Diaminotoluene	C	Sodium arsenite	C
2',3'-Didehydro-3'-deoxythymidine	C	Succinyl concanavalin A	C
		4,4'-Sulfonyldianiline (dapsone)	C
2',3'-Dideoxyadenosine	Inc		
2',3'-Dideoxyanosine	C	2,3,7,8-Tetrachloro-dibenzo-p-dioxin	C
Diisopropylcarbodiimide	C		
Ethyl acrylate	C	Thalidomide	Inc
Ethylenediamine	C	4,4,-Thiobis (6-tert-butyl-m-cresol)	Inc
Ethylene glycol monomethyl ether	C		
		Transgenic model evaluation (cyclosporin A)	Inc
Ethylene triourea (ETU)	C		
Fluconazole	C		
Gallium arsenide	C	Trichloroethylene	Inc
Glyadol	C	Triethanolamine	C
Indium arsenide	C	Trimethylolpropane/triacrylate	Inc
Isobutyraldehyde	C		
Isoniazid	C	2,4,7-Trinitro-fluoren-9-one	C
Isophorone diisocyanate	C	Vanadium pentoxide	C
Lead (2+) acetate	C		

[a]C, complete; Inc, incomplete.

found, suggesting a modest provocative effect of silicone on immunity, especially on macrophage activity.[7]*

This belated testing has an almost tragic overtone as the immune system is currently under increasing attack from both chemical and infectious agents. Physical forces that affect the immune system are also more prevalent in contemporary environments, from the powerful immune-suppressing effect of radon's alpha radiation from certain soils to that of ultraviolet light. In the last few years, we have learned that particular immune cells that make up our first bastion of defense in the skin are exquisitely vulnerable to damage from ultraviolet light. The so-called "helper" immune cell is devastated by HIV. Macrophages, which are responsible for processing foreign materials, are rendered helpless by certain chemicals and minerals such as silica. And dioxin, the most toxic environmental contaminant of all (with the possible exception of plutonium), has a particular penchant for destroying the immune system's home base, the thymus gland. Presumably, all would have been detected had the testing program instituted by the NTP been in place in 1970 when concern for immune depressants peaked in the cancer community.

The new battery of tests puts chemicals into mice for a pilot test for exposure periods of 14–30 days (and sometimes longer) with an eye to finding dosages of chemicals without overt toxicity that may nonetheless produce immune damage. Typically, the testing includes one level that measures direct indices of immune reactivity (ability to make certain antibodies, measurements of white blood cells, lymphoid organs, standard blood work, and so forth) and another that looks for functional evidence of damage.

I have represented that silicone can stimulate the immune system as an expert witness for plantiffs in breast implant litigation.

The second tier includes more specific tests of immunological damage, such as a reduced ability to survive a bacterial challenge. A promising test to measure the ability of chemicals to trigger autoimmune disease is also being developed. Called the popliteal lymph node assay (based on the location of this node just above the ankle), this simple test measures the response of the draining lymph node after a challenge by a test substance is administered in the footpad of a test animal. An increase in lymph node weight reflects expanded clones of antibody-producing cells within the node and serves an (arguably) indirect measure of autoimmune potential or immune stimulation.

Of course, the ultimate test for an effect on humans is one that is done on humans themselves. A classic non-invasive measurement of NK cell activity could be performed in otherwise asymptomatic adults with prior industrial chemical exposures and measurable body burdens of the chemical in question or by the newly found "biomarkers" that flag its presence. Such a test would be particularly valuable, because low NK activity is widely associated with vulnerability to infection.[8]

With some luck, this vanguard of new tests will anticipate environmental and pharmaceutical immune suppressants or sensitizers before they wreak additional havoc on an already compromised population. Without such foreknowledge, substantial damage to the immune systems of a diverse group of organisms on the planet, as well as ourselves, has probably already occurred. Among the physical and chemical agents that deserve immediate and sustained investigation are dioxins, PCBs, and ultraviolet light; specific subgroups of chemicals, such as the organophosphorous compounds used in pesticides; and components of plastic and resin manufacture.

Repeated pleas from the environmentalists and the research community generally to expand testing to include PCBs fell on deaf ears in the United States but not in other countries. In 1994, the Health Protection Branch of Health Canada's Bureau of Chemical Safety called for a "considerable" expansion of the investigation of PCB-induced immunotoxicity to establish a critical data base for evaluating the potential risk PCBs pose to human health.[9]

This policy call appears well-founded: As we will explore below, PCBs are still ubiquitous contaminants, and their effects on the immune system are multifarious.[10] PCBs can destroy bone marrow, thymus, and spleen cells; suppress both humoral and cellular immunity; decrease resistance to microbial infection; and interfere with immune surveillance against cancer. Its devastating effect on animals in the wild, especially in polar regions, is still being measured.

The full impact of immune suppression on organisms in the environment is only now becoming evident: Die-offs of marine mammals, such as harbor seals that have died from canine distemper virus, are increasingly linked to high body burdens of DDT's breakdown product, DDE, dioxins, and/or PCBs. Data from WHO and other scientific groups suggest that a veritable epidemic of ultraviolet light-linked skin cancer and attendant immune depression is in full swing throughout tropical and subtropical areas of the world.

Overreliance and misuse of pesticides have also been associated with immune suppression and concurrent outbreaks of infectious disease in Third World countries.[11] And bisphenol A, a slightly water-soluble ingredient of plastics and resins including those used to make the polycarbonate water bottles now in wide circulation, is also suspected of being an immunosuppressive chemical.

Further data on the almost 80 different pharmaceutical chemicals that appear to produce aberrant immunological responses are also desperately needed. Some of these pharmaceuticals may be contributing to an upsurge in drug-associated diseases like asthma and lupus erythematosus. And allergies have risen in incidence annually, as novel biological and chemical substances flood our environment. The contemporary increases in skin, lymphatic, and brain cancer in aging populations as well as a near epidemic of melanoma in middle-aged persons deserve close scrutiny to determine if one or more have their roots in chemically mediated immune system damage.

MECHANISMS

The manner by which a substance "damages" the immune system may be quite subtle. In addition to the obvious direct damage brought about by killing white blood cells or their supporting tissues (e.g., the bone marrow, spleen, or thymus gland), some xenobiotic chemicals may cause damage indirectly. This can occur by an interaction with a host antigen that culminates in a destructive autoimmune reaction directed against the body's tissues or by binding with hormones or enzyme receptors that indirectly affect immune strength.

When direct damage occurs, the consequence can be a diminished resistance to infection by viruses or bacteria or the appearance of certain forms of cancer intimately tied to the immune system. A case in point is multiple myeloma, a tumor of the cells of the antibody arm of the immune system. (Myelomas actually make antibody chains.) Multiple myelomas have been linked to overexposure to chemicals like benzene (a potent immunosuppressive agent) and, with less certainty, to silicone (a probable immune stimulant).

A few researchers, notably Richmond T. Prehn and Michael Potter of the National Cancer Institute, believe these and other tumors may arise from chronic overstimulation of the immune system. The recent evidence that implicates silicone is worth reviewing. Direct injection of silicone gel into the body cavity of genetically susceptible mice has been shown by Michael Potter to produce a tumor of the antibody-producing cell lines (plasma cells).[12] New data suggest that some of the women who have been exposed to similar materials following breast implantation have an increased prevalence of clones of antibody-making cells, an early sign of possible tumor formation in the immune system.[13]

Allergies are still another form of immune dysfunction induced by chemicals in the environment. Although generally dismissed as bothersome but not too serious disorders, some forms of allergy, particularly asthma, can be life-threatening. We have already reviewed the lung sensitization caused by various forms of isocyanates used in manufacturing polyurethane, but other chemicals and potent natural allergens such as fungal spores are responsible for lung sensitization in increasing numbers of people.

CHLORINATED COMPOUNDS

Many chemicals that were passed off as "safe" years ago because their acute toxic effects were minimal have since proved to have hidden immunotoxic properties. Some of this immune-directed toxicity renders them among the most dangerous chemicals that can affect human health. Among these chemicals are the previously mentioned PCBs and their related compounds, the polychlorinated dibenzofurans (PCDFs) and polychlorinated dibenzodioxins (PCDDs) that include dioxin. As their names imply, these compounds have multiple chlorine atoms placed at different positions between two benzene ring structures. The biphenyls are linked benzene to benzene, while the furans have a nitrogen atom in between and the dioxins an oxygen atom.

In the case of PCBs, these compounds were originally developed as virtually fireproof oils in transformers and capacitors or as ink and dye additives that would improve their staying power. The PCDFs and PCDDs are generally unwanted by-products of the synthesis (or incineration) of still other compounds of our chemical age, including certain herbicides like 2,4,5-trichlorophenoxyacetic acid or vinyl chloride plastics.

All of these chemicals have found their way into the human body in modern times, primarily through incineration of chlorine-containing chemicals combined with organic chemical waste. In spite of manufacturers' insistence that dioxins are perennial hazards produced by forest fires and human fire-making, studies of ancient Peruvian mummies show that virtually *no* dioxin or related products were present before the modern era. Very recently researchers have uncovered evidence that "normal" concentrations of these chemicals in body tissues are sufficient or nearly so to alter immunological parameters. Previous work had been largely limited to experimental animals receiving doses that were greater than those reached in nature.[14] However, a recent study suggests that people who ingest foodstuffs "high" on the food chain, such as fatty meats, may receive a dosage of dioxins and furans sufficient to put them at risk for immunological damage. A recent test of this proposition produced highly provocative findings.

Norwegians, by virtue of their proximity to the sea and their dependence on fish for a protein source, are at especially high risk for the accumulation of the fat soluble chemicals such as dioxins or PCBs that concentrate in the food chain. Because of their molecular structure, such chemicals dissolve readily in fat but are virtually insoluble in water. Recognizing this fact, a group of researchers at the National Institute of Public Health in Oslo decided to study a group of "hobby" fishermen who ingested a diet particularly rich in potentially contaminated marine animals, especially crustaceans.

The group under investigation fished in a fjord that received discharges of organochlorine compounds from a magnesium production plant. The researchers studied the diet, tissue levels of organochlorines, and immunological parameters of 24 otherwise healthy male hobby fishermen who consumed locally caught crabs.

Although their work is still incomplete, the study team found evidence for the predicted immune-suppressing effects of the chemicals, specifically a dose-related depression of lymphocytes in the case of dietary PCDDs and PCDFs.[15] They also found evidence for immune sensitization. The crab-eaters' lymphocytes responded powerfully to a provocative cell-division stimulus, suggesting that the immune system of these fishermen may be in a chronically activated state that could put them at risk for autoimmune disease.

All of these complex polychlorinated biphenyl chemicals have some immunotoxicity, with the dioxins as a class being of greatest human health concern. The most toxic is the dioxin found in Agent Orange, namely, 2,3,7,8-tetrachlorodibenzodioxin (TCDD). In every species tested, microgram quantities per kilogram (measured in parts per billion) and less of TCDD caused the thymus to atrophy and impaired immune competence.

As with so many other immunotoxicants, it turns out that the younger the test animal, the more profound is the immune damage caused by any given dose of TCDD. Another disturbing finding is that immunological impairment may be passed vertically, from mother to child, following contamination of the mother during or before pregnancy. This has proven particularly true with endocrine-disturbing substances like DES or dioxin. Some studies even suggest that immune damage may be mediated through the father, where the harmful effects would likely be the result of genetic damage carried by the sperm.

POLYCHLORINATED BIPHENYLS

PCBs include 209 related chemicals that were widely used as a nonconducting, flame-resistant oil-like fluid in the 1960s and early 1970s in transformers and capacitors, leading to their global distribution. Pioneering environmental toxicologist Robert Rieseborough found PCBs in both Antarctica and the Arctic Ocean as early as the mid-1960s, even though their use was almost entirely confined to the Northern Hemisphere. As mentioned earlier, the greatest concern is the fact that PCBs enter the food chain and bioconcentrate into animals situated at higher and higher "trophic," or feeding, levels. This means that organisms like the polar bear or the bald eagle, which are at the top of Arctic food chains, accumulate extraordinary amounts of PCBs. PCB levels of 70 μg/kg have been found in the fat of polar bears (*Ursus maritimus*), about 6–15 times higher than those found at the next trophic level down, i.e., in ringed seals (*Phoca hispida*).[16]

Concern exists even at this lower level of contamination. Several researchers believe that the amount of PCBs found in seals is immunotoxic and is related to outbreaks of the previously mentioned serious and sometimes fatal epidemics of viral diseases in seal populations seen over the last two decades.

PCBs were also the dominant biological compound found in a recent survey of chlorinated hydrocarbon contaminants in polar bears.[17] High concentrations of PCBs—more than sufficient to depress immunity—have been uncovered among mammals like these in the upper trophic levels throughout the Arctic region, suggesting that

PCBs are a ubiquitous and biologically active contaminant in the circumpolar food chain.[18]

HUMAN EXPOSURE

The first human episode involving PCB exposure occurred in the early 1960s in Kyushu province in northern Japan. Some 1600 people became ill after they consumed food prepared in PCB-contaminated rice oil. The oil became contaminated when a heat transfer pipe containing the PCB Kenechlor 400 leaked directly into the rice oil. Levels as high as 1000 ppm of PCBs ended up in the finished oil. Although no medical data were taken early in this epidemic, crude mortality data suggest an effect of exposure. Among 1200 of the mostly middle-aged oil-ingesting patients who were followed prospectively, 22 died within 5 years and stillbirths exceeded population norms by over tenfold. Many PCB-exposed adults later developed severe acne and liver damage as well as subtle impairments of their immune systems that made them vulnerable to a higher rate of infectious disease.

The most dramatic effect of consumption of PCB-contaminated oil was seen in the offspring of women who ingested the oil during pregnancy.[19] The resulting disease process, called "Yusho" or rice oil disease, was grossly characterized by growth retardation, excessive skin pigmentation, prematurely erupted teeth, and liver disease. As with PCB-exposed adults, many infants later showed evidence of immune depression, the most insidious legacy of PCB poisoning.

In 1968 a repeat occurrence in Japan was reported, where once again rice oil was contaminated. The resulting Yusho disease led to the birth of children with prematurely erupted teeth and hyperpigmented gums, chloracne like that seen in Taiwan, and a pervasive and persistent susceptibility to respiratory infections that plagued the population for a decade or longer after the initial exposure.[20]

Despite this devastating chemical epidemic, still another episode of rice oil contamination occurred a decade later in 1979 when Taiwanese residents were poisoned by rice bran oil heavily contaminated by PCBs and their structurally related breakdown products. This second incident eerily mirrored the first epidemic. In May 1979, first 122 pupils and staff at a school for the blind and later 85 workers at a nearby shoe factory developed florid skin eruptions and chloracne that signaled PCB poisoning. Ultimately, 2060 people were poisoned. In late 1979 and 1980, a new cohort of infants were born with the Yusho syndrome. Twenty-one percent of the affected offspring subsequently died as a result of perinatal infections facilitated by the immune depression caused by PCBs.[21]

In the 1980s, lingering immunological and reproductive sequelae were still found in the victims who survived these two episodes. Although exposure to the contaminated rice oil produced only minor visible evidence of toxicity, notably the acnelike lesions of the skin and hyperpigmentation of the skin and mucosa, deep within the body more subtle effects were evident. Results of liver function tests were abnormal and immune function was severely altered. Many of the affected Taiwanese could not pass a standard skin test challenge that measured their immune strength.[22] This so-called Yu-Cheng episode left a tragic legacy. An indeterminate portion of the exposed population were immunologically crippled and especially vulnerable to infectious and parasitic diseases.

It is important to note that rarely, some ostensibly immunotoxic exposures can lead to a paradoxical stimulation of the immune system, a point taken up in detail in the next chapter. A case in point is the discovery made 2 years ago that residents in the highly polluted city of Cologne, Germany, had an unexpected *elevation* in all of their tested immune parameters compared with the citizens of the relatively pristine city of Borken.[23]

MECHANISMS

PCBs exert their immunotoxic effects in part by binding to cell surface molecules known as the aromatic hydrocarbon hydroxylase receptors. These receptors control several different proteins, including those involved in detoxifying PCBs themselves. Without such binding, no immunotoxicity is observed.[24] Through their chemical interactions, PCBs may affect only a selected subpopulation of T lymphocytes, particularly the cells in the lineage that gives rise to macrophages.[25] This observation is crucial because, as we have seen, macrophages are critical for the phagocytosis and clearance of disease-causing bacteria in the spleen and liver.

Further studies of PCB exposure indicate that other critical components of the immune system can be crippled following poisoning. The resulting damage can include reduced resistance to viruses, heightened sensitivity of the body to cell-damaging bacterial endotoxins, and depression of NK cell activity, putting the body at risk for new tumor formation.[26] Most ominously, early data from some industrial studies conducted at the University of Illinois School of Public Health suggest that non-Hodgkin's lymphoma and possibly multiple myeloma are elevated in PCB-exposed workers.

POLITICS OF LATENT EFFECTS

Aside from the suggestion of slightly increased cancer risks, a pattern of latent and often invisible damage from long-lived compounds like PCBs explains in part how corporate executives can assert that PCBs and dioxins are virtually harmless to workers or citizens generally. By citing the fact that few workers experience more than chloracne and occasionally porphyria, PCB manufacturers and dioxin producers have diverted attention away from their more insidious properties, including those on the immune system. In fact, the ubiquity and projected toxicity of PCBs inspired the 1976 Toxic Substances Control Act (TSCA).

I personally have been involved in these disputes on three different occasions: once, as health advisor to the State of California in 1976–1978 when I urged the dismantling of the energy industry's reliance of PCBs in transformers; again as a health official with the California Department of Industrial Relations where I successfully urged California's Occupational Safety and Health Agency (CalOSHA) to lower permissible occupational exposure levels (from 100 to 25 ppm); and finally as a technical advisor to the CBS television film, *Natural Causes*, a film starring John Ritter about the tragedies inflicted on Vietnam veterans by Agent Orange.[27]

In each case I encountered adamant opposition to more protective standards or to candid statements about risk. Industry-related officials or corporate lawyers often downplayed the toxicity of PCBs or dioxins. The relative success of their claims, repeated over decades of regulatory efforts to control these ultrahazardous compounds, points to a fundamental flaw in public policy. Regulations designed to protect workers have traditionally focused on short-term effects rather than long-term damage. And population protective efforts have similarly been blinded by minimal and shortsighted studies hampered by inadequate dose estimations and crude end points limited to only the most evident, gross signs of toxic effects.

As we will see, toxicological damage to the immune system is the epitome of such chronic bodily injury. After a PCB or comparable dioxin exposure, damage within may take years or decades to become manifest, and by then, immunological injury to the body may have become irreparable, often because of thymic atrophy. Even today, evidence of delayed illness is still accumulating from the Seveso, Italy, catastrophe where dioxin-contaminated smoke from a Swiss pharmaceutical plant drifted over the community. High dioxin levels there have been linked to poor birth outcomes (especially miscarriages) and, provisionally, with increased lymphatic cancer and leukemia.

Behind much of this hidden damage lies the fact that chemically induced immune toxicity is often secondary to organ-specific destruction elsewhere in the body. For example, dioxin in its TCDD form appears to produce its profound immunotoxic effects almost exclusively via damage to the thymus gland, the major mediator of cellular immunity capacity. Many other chemicals that damage the thymus do so by virtue of their ability to mimic the body's own stress response. Dioxin appears to do so as well: By causing the release of glucocorticoids, many chemicals force the body into depressing the immune system by thinking that it is under an acutely stressful chemical attack.

PESTICIDES

It is a truism that chemicals that can affect biological systems in one species are likely to have similar effects on the same or related systems in other species. Pesticides are no exception. Even though the majority of the major pesticides in commerce work by inhibiting insect-specific enzymes that are involved in the regeneration of key nerve conduction enzymes, related systems in humans are also potentially affected.

The fact that many pesticides are neurotoxic obviously should have given pause to researchers who were looking at the potential interface between chemicals and the immune system. We have already seen how intimately linked are the nervous and endocrine-linked immune systems. Depression in one can lead to depression in the other. Researchers should not have been surprised to have found that pesticides as a class, especially organophosphate pesticides, are broadly toxic to the immune system. At least three independent lines of evidence support this broad contention: laboratory tests conducted in tissue culture; human assays of peripheral lymphocytes and immune reactivity; and direct studies on the well-being of wildlife exposed to pesticides. Almost every major chemical class of pesticides has been found to contain some compounds that are immunotoxic in these assays.[28]

CHEMICAL AIDS

The fact that so many different chemicals can damage the immune system makes it difficult to ascertain when and if any single chemical or group may be contributing to an ongoing or new public health problem. A classic case in point is the AIDS epidemic. In 1987 molecular biologist Peter Duesberg of the University of California, Berkeley, suggested that drug-induced immune suppression was responsible for the symptom complex that led to multiple opportunistic infections.[29] Although this hypothesis is now widely discredited, the underlying reality that many abused drugs, like HIV itself, can adversely affect immune competence made it difficult initially to test this idea critically. Some researchers still believe the occurrence of Kaposi's sarcoma in some HIV-positive subgroups now linked to a new herpesvirus variant can be attributed in part to drug-induced immune depression. But this idea too, that immunosuppression automatically leads to a heightened cancer risk, needs careful examination.

TEN

CANCER AND THE IMMUNE SYSTEM

The concept of the immune system as a surveillance system against aberrant tumor cell types is widely attributed to the late Lewis Thomas, long the head of the prestigious Sloan Kettering Cancer Institute in New York.[1] His ideas were based in part on the pioneering work of two researchers, Richmond T. Prehn and Joan M. Main, who in 1957 codiscovered that tumor cells could be detected by the body's own immune system.[2] For at least a decade thereafter, the language of tumor biology itself proved an obstacle to accepting that the host could detect and destroy incipient tumor cells. Until about 1970, tumor biologists who saw tumors disappear on animals described such reactions in passive terms, using phrases like "tumor regression." Although some early tumors do in fact regress spontaneously, the idea that the elimination of incipient tumor cells was an *active* process, involving immune identification and rejection, simply did not take hold in the tumor biology community until about 1972. Then, the idea of immunological surveillance was embraced wholesale, and a whole new field of tumor immunology blossomed.

But once again, a conceptual error may have been made in shifting paradigms too rapidly. In a matter of a few years researchers adopted a model from one where the immune system was a passive bystander to the tumor process to one where it was engaged in constant battle to suppress hordes of incipient tumors. As with other aspects of immunity, the truth lies somewhere between these polar extremes. Early in my career, I staked my work and reputation on the surveillance theory, proving in 1968 that chemically induced tumors could be "seen" by the immune system and eliminated. Although I was right about the immune system's often dramatic abilities to control some early chemically induced cancers, I was wrong about how generalizable the phenomenon might be.

Within 10 years from 1960 to 1970, an impressive body of knowledge had developed that seemingly clinched the vital role of the immune system to control cancer. As we saw in the previous chapter, carcinogens are notorious immunosuppressants. What gave additional credence to the surveillance model was the fact that the most potent carcinogens were found to also be the most potent immunosuppressants. Among the leaders was dimethylbenzanthracene (DMBA), a potent animal carcinogen and coal tar contaminant (it is also found in cigarettes) that produced profound immunosuppression in rats after only a single pulse dose.[3] Other polycyclic hydrocarbon chemicals that produced a great number of tumors when given to newborn animals were likewise found to produce protracted immunosuppression when administered shortly after birth.[4] With researcher David Steinmuller (now editor of the journal *Transplantation*), I found that other chemicals, such as the anesthetic urethane, routinely depressed the ability of the cellular arm of the immune system to identify foreign tissues when given in carcinogenic doses.[5]

The data linking depressed immunity with cancer formation were impressive but intrinsically flawed. Because almost every carcinogen simultaneously knocked out the immune system as it was producing cancer, it was virtually impossible to study a given animal's native ability to rein in incipient tumors: By the time the animal developed cancer, its immune system was in shards. The solution to this dilemma came to me in 1966 when I discovered that it was possible to treat one animal with a carcinogen, remove a field of chemically treated skin tissue, and graft it to another genetically identical animal. By systematically shifting the immune strength of the graft recipient and observing the progression of cancer on the chemically treated skin graft, it proved possible for the first time to test Lewis Thomas's surveillance theory.

The theory posited that by raising the immune strength of the recipient animals, I could control the development of incipient tumors on the skin grafts. Conversely, lowering immunity in the graft recipients should increase tumor yield. To my delight, the system worked flawlessly—up to a point. Every group of animals whose immune systems were impaired developed more skin tumors that lasted longer and progressed more readily to malignancy than did tumors in the immunologically normal control animals. A small, annoying result was that when I *boosted* the immune strength of the animal graft recipients, the recipients initially allowed a flood of early tumors to arise. Although most of them later regressed, this discovery was duly reported as an "aberration."

Unbeknown to me at the time, the data on tumor excess provided the first inkling that a hyperreactive immune system might actually *stimulate* rather than impede tumor development. Within the next 4 years, this finding was confirmed independently by several research teams. In time, immune stimulation was to prove instrumental in understanding the troubling dynamics of the immune response to tumor cells.

In 1968, I reported evidence that some incipient tumors were actually detectable by the immune system, and that in some instances, this reaction could cause their rejection or regression.[6] Although others have found that not all early tumor regressions were immunologically mediated (indeed, some early tumors simply disappear on their own as a result of reconforming to local growth control), these studies suggested that the immune system could ferret out early tumor cells in the skin and kill them.

One of the predictions of the immunological surveillance theory was that cancer should be much more common among persons whose immune systems were damaged, either naturally because of genetic defects or acquired from the immune-suppressing regimens used in transplant patients. For many of us who in the 1970s believed that there was a direct link between damage to the immune system and the freeing up of aberrant tumor cells to proliferate in the body, the results of the survival patterns of the first organ transplant recipients were awaited with bated breath.

Kidney transplant patients who are intentionally subjected to immune depression to permit a foreign graft to take in their bodies are reasonable subjects to test the proposition that immune depression permits tumors to grow. Many such patients did develop more tumors—but only of a limited variety. In fact, skin and other epithelial cancers (exclusive of melanoma) arose in immunosuppressed patients at much higher than expected numbers. However, with the exception of some tumors of the lymphoid tissues themselves (which were directly impacted by immunosuppressive agents), *no* additional tumors of the breast, lungs, cervix, bowel, or elsewhere were seen. Indeed, the most recent data show that heart and kidney transplant patients actually have *less* breast cancer than expected.[7]

The logical extension of this prediction, that improvement of immune function would lead to the restraint of incipient tumors, has similarly proven surprisingly elusive. Virtually no studies have shown that spontaneously arising tumor cells can be effectively restrained by the immune system in *non-chemical* carcinogen treated hosts. In fact, the Hammond studies discussed in Chapter Four actually show that in the face of strong immunity, the body of a test animal may actually encourage the progression of early tumors to become much more aggressive and ultimately fatal.[8] These data fly in the face of the current dogma that touts the immune system as a ceaseless bastion of defense against cancer. Clearly, reexamination of this theory is long overdue.

AN IMMUNE STIMULATION THEORY OF CARCINOGENESIS

Despite what appeared to be overwhelming support for the concept of immunological surveillance that emerged in the 1970s and 1980s, increasing numbers of studies presented contradictory data that immune reactions could *encourage* rather than inhibit the process of tumor formation. But for years, these data—along with my own—were largely ignored. Probably because of the powerful heuristic appeal of the idea that the body can defend itself against all assaults, to this day few researchers have been willing to reconsider the universal applicability of the immune surveillance hypothesis. But such reconsideration, in my view, is long overdue.

A RECONSIDERATION

First, the theory of immunological surveillance postulates that most tumors are caught at their inception and rejected by a highly specific and individual tumor-directed response. The fact that transplants of chemically induced tumors were found to be inhibited by a specifically engendered immune reaction initially gave credence to this theory. In fact, most chemically induced tumors were found to carry highly tumor-specific, unique antigens that flagged them, individually, for destruction. In practice, the enormous variety of new antigenic variants among chemically induced tumors dampened the prospects for a single cancer vaccine.

In contrast, virally induced tumors express common antigens, making all tumors induced by the same virus vulnerable to a wholesale immune response. These findings initially promised substantial hope for immunological control of cancer, at least for virally induced tumors. But these hopes have yet to be realized.

An additional source of pessimism is that many tumors appeared to escape from immunological surveillance on a routine basis. Coupled with the Hammond work showing that some animals that had partially intact immune systems appeared more rather than less vulnerable to cancer, the prospect for a simple immune solution to cancer appears unlikely. With the exception of lymphomas arising from cells in the lymphatic tissue itself, even the most immunologically crippled mice failed to show an increase in tumor incidence.[9] And as I had shown, animals whose immune systems were seemingly prepared to react against antigenic tumors paradoxically had *more* tumors initially than did their normal counterparts.

These data have direct bearing on the human predicament. Recall that people whose immune systems were heavily suppressed in preparation for organ transplantation were *not* overwhelmed by the rash of new malignancies that the theory of immune surveillance predicted. The final blow to the idea of universal immune control of cancer came from data on the ability of spontaneous tumors in animals (the nearest analogue of human cancers) to provoke an immune response: Such tumors appeared to lack immune-provoking capacity altogether!

These data were at first perplexing. If the immune system were designed to control cancer, why was it that genetically defective animals, such as a strain of hairless "nude" mice that lack a functional thymus-based immune system, fail to develop tumors in great excess? Why did some animals get more cancer when their immune systems were *over*stimulated than did those animals whose immunity was just on par? And why was it that spontaneous tumors that arise in old age (in contrast to early, chemically induced cancer) fail to produce an immune reaction in all but a few assay systems?

One explanation for this latter finding is that by the time a tumor appears in an immunologically competent host, it has run the gauntlet of immune responses. To slip through these defenses, the theory goes, only the least antigenic—and hence least vulnerable cells—would survive. But this explanation fails to account for the fact that many chemically induced tumors that arise in immunologically depressed animals are no more provocative to the immune system than are those that arise in competent hosts. In fact, the property of being antigenic appears to be linked to *how* the tumor is induced rather than *where* it is induced.

Virtually all chemically induced tumors where *high doses* of carcinogen are used are indeed highly antigenic, whereas those that are produced with very low doses or that arise in the complete absence of an immune response are not.[10] Thus, whether or not a tumor is "antigenic" appears to be relatively independent of the existence of an effective immune system during its origins.

Indeed, over the last two decades, no consistent evidence for the immune surveillance theory has been developed.[11] Despite this continued spate of negative data, many scientists have continued to promote the concept of an effective immune system well into the 1990s and to proffer immune regimens to control cancer that too often do not succeed.

This phenomenon by which scientists cling to an old model or paradigm in spite of mounting evidence to the contrary has been described by Thomas Kuhn in his short (172 page) but provocative book *A Theory of Scientific Revolutions*.[12] There, Kuhn discusses the difficulties that the scientific establishment has in shifting from one paradigm (e.g., immune surveillance) to another (e.g., immune stimulation). Reluctance to give up a heuristically appealing idea, vague and often conflicting data, and an entrenched expectation that nature will always behave rationally, often stand in the way of making a shift to a new model.

This is no more true than in the evolution of thinking about the immune system and cancer. Although this theme was in fact my doctoral thesis topic, I have had to rethink if not relinquish the idea of a fixed entity known as immune surveillance.

Evidence for immune stimulation of tumors was actually available in the late 1960s and showed that direct mixes of tumor cells with immune cells primed to attack them actually led to enhanced survival rather than death of the tumor. These studies provided some of the most perplexing pieces of data. If true, these data (based on what was called the "Winn test" after its founder, Professor Winn of the Jackson Laboratory) appeared to turn the model of the immune system as an efficient cancer killer on its head. Much had been reported about how antibodies could sometimes mask the target sites on tissues under immunological attack (a process known as "enhancement"), but no one was able to explain why or how the immune system could apparently *stimulate* its targeted cells. This phenomenon, which my mentor Professor Richmond T. Prehn and I described in detail in a paper we cowrote in 1971,[13] still remains to be accepted by all tumor immunologists. Yet, the existence of immune stimulation plagues the current efforts to develop cancer vaccines.

CANCER VACCINES

Currently available data provide only a scant basis for enthusiasm that tumor vaccines will work.[14] Although the almost universal appearance of tumors able to elicit immunity provides the scaffolding for an anticancer immune response, in my view the prevalence of weakly antigenic tumors in most human situations opens the door to stimulatory rather than inhibitory immune effects.

The latent danger is that increasing the intensity of the immune reaction in cancer-bearing adults may promote rather than inhibit tumor growth. Ironically, under such circumstances, the well-known immunosuppressive effects of many of the chemotherapeutic agents used against human tumors may prove to be a blessing in disguise.[15] Some of the "success" of chemotherapy may be incidental to knocking back immunostimulatory effects. By the same token, the existence of immune stimulation will likely confound early attempts at immunotherapy.

Part of the reason for this pessimistic outlook is that spontaneous or radiation-induced tumors typically have antigenic properties that are intermediate or substantially less than those of the chemically induced type. As we have seen, under most tests, spontaneous tumors elicit little if any immune response. Because the bulk of spontaneous, nonviral tumors are likely to be of this type, immune stimulation after cancer vaccination remains a perplexing threat to the success of immune control.

The consensus to date is that a weak immune reaction against antigenic surface features stimulates tumor development, whereas a stronger reaction inhibits it.[16] The most extensive of these works demonstrates that tumor types that elicit a weak immune reaction grow more vigorously rather than being slowed following an immune assault.[17] These data suggest that an immune reaction from a vaccine under some circumstances might encourage tumor growth and provoke a faster progression of the tumor to malignancy. Conversely, the *less* the immune reaction, the more likely it would be for the tumor to differentiate and lose its growth potential. These are exactly the findings reported by the University of California Davis scientific team headed by W. G. Hammond.

IMMUNE ACCOMMODATION

Should such an effect prove generally applicable to human tumors, the likelihood of a quick immunological fix of the cancer problem, the longstanding holy grail of tumor immunology, may prove elusive. An emerging view of the immune system, and the one espoused in this book, is that immunity most often evolves toward an *accommodation* of potentially foreign tissue, including some longstanding parasites, viruses, and perhaps the human fetus itself. Much of the newfound success in the field of organ transplantation may relate to this phenomenon, as overtly "foreign" grafts do surprisingly well once the immune system has adapted to their presence. If proven applicable to cancer (and I believe it will), immune accommodation may mean that some tumors come into a state of equilibrium or balance with an active immune response. If so, tumor immunologists will of necessity have to proceed with caution—and great wisdom—to control cancer.

IMMUNOLOGICAL DÉTENTE

The idea that the immune system may engage in a kind of biological détente was one that occurred to me early in my career. At the time (in 1968) I was a graduate student at the Jackson Laboratory working with George Snell and Ralph Graff. The "elementary" project I undertook was an attempt to find out why it took the immune system longer to reject a larger graft of skin or tissue compared with a smaller one. Although on the surface the answer to this simple question seemed self-evident, it was anything but.

In the biology of the immune system, the larger the amount of antigenic stimulus, the quicker the immune system normally mounts an effective "assault." In the case of typical skin grafts exchanged within a given species (so-called allografts) across a "major" tissue difference, it normally takes the immune system about 10 days to detect and destroy a foreign piece of skin. As the size of the graft increases, the time for recognition and rejection should in theory decrease as the larger antigenic "doses" provoke quicker and more aggressive immune responses. And this is in fact the case where graft and host tissue differ greatly. But I found that if the donor of the graft and the recipient were genetically closely matched, making for a weak antigenic difference, increases in graft size resulted in a *prolongation* of rejection times. In fact, if large and small grafts were put on opposite sides of the same animal, the smaller of the two would always be rejected before the bigger one.

What was most interesting to me was to watch the process from day to day. When a small *and* a large weakly antigenic graft (8 versus 16 mm) were positioned on the same mouse recipient, the circular fields of skin would typically heal in well by the second week, complete with a full growth of new hair. But by the beginning of the second week, I observed the tissue in the smaller graft became a bit moth-eaten. Hair would disappear in patches, and the perimeter of the graft would begin to shrink. By the end of the 17th day, most of the animals would have rejected their small grafts entirely. But the larger graft, which also initially lost small patches, would soon recover with even a thicker and more luxuriant coat of hair than the animals' own surrounding skin.

After the 21st day, the larger graft began to contract slightly. A day later, most of the animals had lost their transiently exuberant patch of hair on the graft and the graft was finally rejected. Given the fact that the only difference between the two grafts was size (by a surface area of approximately 4×), I concluded that with slight antigenic differences, sufficiently large and genetically closely matched target tissues actually underwent a kind of compensatory growth while under immune attack by the host.

In the paper in which these details were reported,[18] I concluded that a dynamic equilibrium had been established between destruction of target cells in the graft and replacement by new tissue. The validity of this conclusion has since been confirmed. In rabbits that also received skin grafts across "weak" histocompatibility lines, the grafts provoked an immune reaction. But instead of succumbing to the resulting influx of "assaulting" lymphocytes, the skin of these grafts actually *flourished*, undergoing a dramatic increase in cell division.[19] In fact, some large, weakly incompatible grafts survived indefinitely on the sides of their rabbit hosts, even in the face of an ongoing immunological response.

These data have profound implications for transplantation biology generally because they show that under some circumstances, foreign tissues can survive under immunological attack. If some consistent way could be found to steer the immune response toward its stimulatory mode, weakly incompatible grafts might be made to survive indefinitely, although highly incompatible grafts would likely be rejected. In fact, this is the hidden logic of transplantation biologists who have learned that weakly differing organs often have a good chance of survival even if the recipient mounts an immune "attack," especially if the organ grafts seed the body with some of their transplanted cells and establish a state of immune tolerance. But, of course, such reactions might prove to be counterproductive if the "foreign" tissue happens to be a clump of cancer cells.

The idea behind this radical thinking is that the immune system can establish a dynamic equilibrium between the destructive actions of its own cells and the survival of cells in a targeted graft, tumor, or even foreign organism. Such a view is still not widely held among immunologists, in part, I believe, because it conflicts so radically with the idea of the immune system as a unilaterally destructive agency.

But evidence for its coherence and plausibility are to be found in many areas of study, most notably transplantation biology. In fact, it is now widely recognized that after immunosuppressing the patient, organ graft survival can be routinely ensured despite a weak immune response if cells from the graft and the host colonize each other, and a strong rejection reaction is dampened with continued treatment.

In almost every "successful" organ transplant the body's immune response is not so much turned off to the foreign tissue as it is accommodating to it. In those instances where the graft sets up residence in the body, it creates a kind of chimerism (kī'-mer-izm) (from the three-bodied chimera of Greek myth)* in which the cells of the two different tissue types, graft and recipient, commingle. In pregnancy, many of the otherwise antigenically disparate cells of the fetus can commonly be found floating blithely in the maternal circulation during pregnancy. Even more remarkably, some of these cells can be found in the mother up to 17 years after the baby's birth.[20] Let us now explore the mystery of this phenomenon.

*In Greek myth, the offspring of Typhon and Echidna was composed of three parts: a lion's head, a female goat's body, and a snake's tail. Natural chimeras exist in freemartin cattle, which share the same placenta. Freemartins, though fraternal twins, are mutually tolerant and freely exchange tissue and organ grafts because their shared blood circulation mutually tolerizes each animal.

ELEVEN

MOTHERHOOD AND IMMUNITY

According to traditional immunological theory, every human pregnancy should end in a miscarriage because all fetuses express antigens that come from their father's genetic contribution and are thereby ostensibly foreign to their mother. These paternally derived antigens are routinely displayed on embryonic cells early during pregnancy, often shortly before implantation. Although such a display makes early rejection of the embryo plausible, this rarely occurs. When it does, it is the source of much concern on the part of obstetricians and mothers: It's not supposed to happen. Indeed, some pregnancies that end in spontaneous miscarriage (perhaps 5–10 percent) are in fact the result of maternal rejection of the fetus or its placenta. The existence of a routine maternal immune response directed against some paternal antigens, e.g., blood groups, further intensifies the mystery of why fetal *survival* occurs so often.

Fetal endangerment by a hyperactive maternal immune system would appear to be a constant potential threat during pregnancy. The fetus expresses histocompatibility antigens (MHC Class I) on many of the cells in intimate contact with its mother, including some placental cells. These antigens, which appear to be crucial for cell-to-cell interactions during embryogenesis,[1] are potential "flags" for a reaction from the maternal immune system. Given their demonstrable immunogenicity, these antigenic configurations would be predicted to serve as lightning rods for immune recognition by the mother. Why more pregnancies do not end prematurely from unbridled immunological assault is thus a major mystery.

BASICS

To understand the full dimensions of the various roles and features of the immune system during pregnancy, it is important to understand some basics of fetal/maternal anatomy and to track what actually happens to the immune system during pregnancy. As the embryo develops in the uterus, it forms a special layer between itself and the mother that is incorporated into the placenta. This layer is made up of fetal cells that form a special part of the placenta known as the trophoblast. It is the trophoblast that occupies the zone of separation between mother and fetus.

The paradoxical survival of the fetus across from this narrow "no man's land" is all the more remarkable in human beings. The human connection between mother and fetus is the most intimate among all mammals—only a single cell layer separates the two. During pregnancy, a few maternal lymphocytes actually traverse this fetal–maternal barrier, and fetal cells reciprocate by entering the mother's circulation in small numbers, heightening the risk of alerting the immune system to its presence. In fact, some trophoblast cells that go into the mother's bloodstream can lodge in her lungs where, under unusual circumstances occurring no more than once in every 8000–10,000 pregnancies, they can lead to a type of cancer known as choriocarcinoma. Choriocarcinoma becomes progressively more likely with subsequent pregnancies, perhaps because the mother's immune system becomes progressively more accepting of fetal cells. Remarkably, this often fatal tumor can sometimes be destroyed by reactivating the mother's quiescent immune system, sometimes with paternal vaccines, and thereby inviting an immune attack on the father's antigens expressed in the choriocarcinoma. This reality explains why the various forms of choriocarcinoma are the *only* metastatic human tumors that can be routinely cured (about 80 percent of the time).

VIVE LA DIFFÉRENCE

For a long time, the only explanation for the paradoxical survival of the antigenically dissimilar fetus was that it must not express the cell surface antigens that would otherwise be sensitizing; or that the mother underwent such a profound suppression of her immune system during pregnancy that it was all but impossible for her to mount an immunological assault on the fetus. Both of these models have some experimental support.

Whereas the fetus per se does express paternal antigens—and does so even as an embryo—the fetal cells that are in intimate contact with the mother do not. The trophoblast cells of the fetal placenta are remarkable for their absence of effective antigenicity. In the view of some knowledgeable immunologists, these cells appear to serve as a virtually impenetrable immunological barrier to the mother's access to fetal antigens that would otherwise "tip off" her immune system to a foreign tissue's presence.[2]

An additional feature of the trophoblast is that it, like the Stealth Bomber, uses both direct and indirect guises to hide itself from maternal recognition. It carries proteins that inhibit the action of complement, a critical molecule needed for cell killing. Trophoblast tissue also secretes factors into its cellular environment that prevent it from binding and interacting with the cells of the maternal immune system, and it releases IL-10, which knocks down cellular immune reactions. Finally, trophoblast cells swathe themselves in a special histocompatibility antigen, HLA-G, that is remarkable for its universal acceptance by maternal cells.[3] These facts diminish but do not preclude the likelihood of an effective maternal response to fetal surface proteins.

FETAL SURVIVAL

A related explanation for uterine survival is that the fetus somehow delays expression of its most immunologically provocative antigens until after birth. Some evidence for antigenic delay exists: The fetus does alter its display of antigens during embryonic development. But the waxing and waning of certain cell surface antigens appears to be less a ruse to prevent immune recognition than it is a process by which fetal cells pass through certain stages of differentiation. Based on animal studies, by the middle of gestation most of the key histocompatibility antigens *are* expressed in the fetal placenta. In fact, if the fetal placenta is removed and grafted under the skin of animals with the same genetic makeup as the mother, the placenta is roundly rejected and sensitizes the animal against paternal tissues.[4] So the anatomical site of the placenta is also critical.

Thus, the "problem" of an immunologically disparate fetus is a real one. It is underscored by reports of maternal rejection of the fetus, a problem that many believe undergirds the tragedy of habitual miscarriages experienced by some infertile couples. In some animal experiments, it has proven possible to "immunize" the mother against her fetus during pregnancy and thereby to cause fetal damage during embryogenesis and even well into postnatal development. Indeed, in humans, some women who have had more than two miscarriages have been shown to have become immunologically "sensitized" to their spouse's tissues. Sometimes, by judicious use of paternal antigens, this reaction can be reversed. For instance, oral administration of antigen or ultralow-dose "shots" similar to those used to break up allergies can be used. Some antipaternal immune reactions nonetheless contribute to abnormal immune responses during pregnancy, producing hypertension, preeclampsia, and rarely, fetal destruction. As mentioned earlier, a rare form of nonfetal immunity is linked with the production of antibodies to blood lipids. This disease, known as Hughes syndrome, is associated with repeated miscarriages, thickening of the arteries with atheroma formation, and antiphospholipid antibodies that can cause placental blood clots.

SURVIVAL IN THE FACE OF ADVERSITY

Several independent reasons may account for the paradoxical survival of the fetus: In addition to those already reviewed, the fetus may induce a temporary state of tolerance in the mother toward its own tissues. It is also possible the mother remains immunologically ignorant of the fetus until after birth, perhaps as a result of some modulation of immunity coupled with the insulating effect of the trophoblast cells in the placenta. Finally, the mother may just "shut down" part of her immune activity during pregnancy.

At least one experiment in mice seems to show that the mother may suspend immunological operations directed against her mate's antigens.[5] By mixing the mother's immune cells with cells from the father's tissue, the researchers showed that the mother's immune reactions relent dramatically during pregnancy. But a closer examination of the test system used in this key experiment reveals a potential flaw. The tissue chosen to analyze the mother's reactivity was a tumor that mimicked the paternal antigens. As discussed in the last chapter, a tumor may be able to provoke an immunostimulating reaction, so that continued tumor growth might have occurred despite an immune response. If so, the "transient state of acquired tolerance" proposed by the authors may reflect the fact that the mother's immune system recognized paternal antigens in the tumor cells, but stimulated them rather than merely tolerating them.

Researchers have also found that the fetus puts itself in potential jeopardy by displaying certain antigens from the *mother's* repository of protein types. Several of these products are the very antigens that, when attacked, lead to autoimmune disease. But during pregnancy, the mother's T cells appear to "decline to respond" to these antigens. This reality helps explain the fact that many autoimmune diseases like lupus erythematosus and rheumatoid arthritis undergo remission during pregnancy.[6]

The sometime invisibility of the fetus to the mother's immune system, her temporary suspension of some immunological reactions, and her reshaping of any reaction into a toleragenic or immunostimulating mode, may separately or together help explain the paradoxical survival of the fetus. These factors, coupled with the general dampening of the mother's immune response, may account for the otherwise paradoxical "favored status" of the developing fetus in most pregnancies.

AN EVOLUTIONARY VIEWPOINT

But the story is incomplete without considering the evolutionary features of immunity during pregnancy. Considering how powerfully the forces of natural selection operate to ensure survival, it is worth considering the counterintuitive notion that immune recognition of the fetus may be *beneficial*. This view is predicated on the assumption that evolutionary mechanisms have long driven and shaped the interplay between mother and fetus, even as they molded the immune system into a powerful force for insulating the body from inimical external factors. The fact that maternal and fetal tissues emerge as "incompatible" does not mean that they were selected to be so or that such differences are maladaptive. Instead, it is plausible that natural selection led to structural differences that permitted trophoblast cells to express some paternal antigens other than HLA-G because those foreign antigens have a beneficial function.

The first fact to consider is that a full-fledged immune system probably existed in higher vertebrates prior to the development of placental mammals. We find evidence of such systems in all surviving descendants of vertebrates from the shark on. This reality forced the whole process of sexual mating and pregnancy to accommodate the presence of potentially adverse immune reactivity from the female. Over time, the necessity of a long, intimate gestation period *in utero* gave the fetus a nutritive advantage, but at the expense of immunological peril.

The second fact is that the immune system is finely tuned to recognize an almost infinite range of genetic differences and to respond accordingly. Together these observations provide a powerful argument for evolutionary forces coming into play during pregnancy. If immunity predated the evolution of the close cellular-bonding and physical intimacy of the human placental contact zone, placentation itself could only come into existence by some accommodation by the immune system.

To put this in perspective, recall that the number of possible antigenic types among human beings is so vast that it is virtually impossible for any two unrelated persons of different sexes to share the same histocompatibility genes and antigens. As we have discussed, during pregnancy this state of affairs would otherwise pose insuperable problems for a fetus facing an immunological surveillance system. But what if an immune response directed at antigens from the male could prove *beneficial* instead of inimical to fetal survival?

KEEPING GENETIC DISTANCE

Consider for a moment the fundamental biological axiom: Genetic diversity is crucial to species survival. In simple terms, this translates into a powerful set of adaptations to guarantee every sexual mating is an "outcross." To ensure the widest diversity, the male's genetic repertoire of 160,000 or so genes must be far removed from the female genotype as possible. In simple terms, this means that the male should have as many *different* gene variants or alleles from his mate's genetic contribution as possible. This is achieved in plants by self-sterility genes and other mechanisms that prevent the bringing together of like alleles. Mammals use other means to ensure outcrossing by limiting the likelihood of fertilization bringing together closely related genes. Genetic diversity is reinforced in many animals by behavioral (or in human, cultural) prohibitions against inbreeding. Some species like elephants, lions, and wild dogs achieve this by forcing the out-migration of siblings. In the case of humans, the same effect is achieved by cultural prohibitions against intermarriage between first degree relatives. The taboo against incestuous mating evident in many human societies and culturally driven adaptations to marry "outside the clan" are further examples of devices to ensure maximal genetic distance between mates. The immunological contribution to this process may be more important than previously acknowledged.

One way in which immunity could contribute to genetic diversity is by making genetically distant matings *more* successful compared with close ones. If there were somehow a selective *advantage* to being immunologically "recognizable" during pregnancy, then fetuses that differed systematically from their mothers, and hence represented greater genetic variability, could be favored immunologically. In theory such a process would increase the likelihood of genetically dissimilar fetuses surviving over and against those that resembled their mothers. Such a state of affairs would be highly beneficial to maximizing genetic diversity. A pregnancy-immunity system where a maternal reaction against the fetus is beneficial would potentially aid both individual and species survival through the enrichment of genetic diversity.

In 1972 when I first proposed this idea as the raison d'être of immune stimulation, I postulated in some circumstances that reaction of the mother against her fetus would prove favorable rather than harmful. In one animal model designed to test this idea, I found some preliminary evidence for just such an effect. By vigorously im-

munizing female mice against the male-determining antigen (known as the Y antigen for the Y chromosome on
which it is expressed), it is possible to get female mice
eventually to reject male skin grafts within the time limit
posed by pregnancy. According to traditional immunological theory, if cell-mediated, Y-specific rejection were to
take place during pregnancy, and if the fetus were vulnerable to an immunological attack, male fetuses should be
at a *disadvantage* relative to female ones. By my way of
thinking, the opposite should prove true: Males would be
favored in "hostile" environments.

I put this prediction to the test in an experiment in
which female mice were intensively immunized against
their male mates' Y antigens. Instead of the anticipated
damage of the male fetuses, the results appeared to show
just the opposite trend. The most highly sensitized female
mice had the largest number of male offspring, reaching a
ratio of 2:1, male to female. This finding is consistent with
the favored survival of male embryos which normally die
in greater numbers than do females early in mouse pregnancies.

This finding, if replicable across species lines, suggests that an immune reaction to antigens expressed in
the fetus may sometimes enhance rather than compromise fetal survival. As we have seen, such favorable immune recognition of the fetus would be one means of
reinforcing genetic diversity because it would favor those
matings in which the father was most genetically distant
from the mother.

A few researchers now entertain this previously heretical idea: Fetal survival may not depend on always
dodging potentially "fatal" immune aggression on the
part of the mother. What was a contrarian, heretical view
in 1971–1972 appears to be gleaning some newfound re-
spect. A recent review article expressed the need to "keep
an open mind to other possibilities such as MHC genes

are expressed [in the embryo] intentionally to provoke attack to ... increase placental and fetal weight in mammals."[7]

To sum up what is known in 1997: The mother normally maintains a strong immune system during pregnancy, even as she modulates its expression to reduce the likelihood of inducing autoimmune disease during exposure to self- or fetal antigens. An efficient immune system during pregnancy increases the likelihood that cellular material that otherwise has a high growth potential is kept in check. A strong immune system may be needed to stem the outgrowth of trophoblast cells that constantly shower the maternal circulation, but new evidence suggests it may also be needed to limit endometriosis, an overgrowth in the body cavity of cells that normally line the uterine cavity.

When female rhesus monkeys' immune systems are weakened by radiation or immunotoxic chemicals such as PCBs, they characteristically develop endometriosis—often months to years after their immune suppression. Researchers from the Institute for the Study and Treatment of Endometriosis in Chicago, Illinois, have shown that endometrial cells that implant outside the human uterus in the peritoneal wall of the body cavity during menstruation (and thereby produce endometriosis) are more common in women whose immune systems are impaired.[8]

A ROLE FOR IMMUNE STRENGTH

Evolutionarily, it was also critical for the pregnant animal to be in a strong position to react against potentially life-threatening viruses or bacteria that might prove fatal if the fetus were to be infected. Examples include bacteria in the *Brucella* group that can induce miscarriage.

Where breaches in this defense have opened, as with the domestication of cattle and the appearance of abortion-inducing infections (*Bordetella* or *Brucella abortus*), the fault may lie with the breeders for inadvertently selecting immune-deficient cattle, coupled with poor hygienic stockyard conditions rather than with biology.

Another advantage to having a strong immune system operating during pregnancy would be to mitigate sexually transmitted diseases that might otherwise compromise fetal survival. Being able to mount an effective mucosal antibody response to chlamydia, gonococcus, or even HIV, even only transiently, would confer a strong evolutionary advantage to the mother and her genetically related offspring.

Although the obvious success of many sexually transmitted disease organisms militates against an effective mucosal immunity operating all of the time, the failure of routine sexual inoculation with these organisms to produce disease on each occasion where sexual exposure occurs suggests the operation of a modicum of resistance. Maternal immunity may, for instance, explain why historically only about 20 percent of HIV$^+$ mothers pass the infection to their infants. Today, such infection is minimized by treatment during pregnancy with AZT coupled with Cesarean section and by discouraging nursing.

Rather than being an experimental artifact (as originally thought), a functional immune system during pregnancy may be an essential element in the massive endocrine changes that accompany pregnancy. New research shows that having a strong immune system may be critical in protecting the fetus against birth defects caused by environmental teratogens.

Researchers recently studied the activity of two highly potent teratogens, one an immunosuppressant drug (cyclophosphamide) and the other a natural derivate (2,3-quinoxalinedimethanol 1,4-dioxide) under different immune conditions. Remarkably, the team found a dramatic adaptive advantage in those female mice that exhibited an immune response *against their own fetuses* after being exposed to the teratogens. Those females whose immune systems became naturally sensitized to their fetuses had offspring with far fewer birth defects than did those whose immune systems were unsensitized by fetal tissue, suggesting a protective effect akin to immunostimulation. Teratogen-exposed pregnant mice that were carrying antigenically dissimilar fetuses also had far fewer birth defects than did those that carried genetically identical offspring. Perhaps for similar reasons fetal mice that are genetically similar to their mothers appear to be more vulnerable to developing neural tube defects than are their dissimilar littermates. The protective effect of being immunologically different from the mother appears to be closely tied to an actual immune response because it is abolished if the mother's reactive lymph nodes are removed before pregnancy, leaving her without a cadre of immune cells.[9] In theory, an immune reaction that increased placenta size could improve the fetus's chance of fending off a teratogenic assault, perhaps by providing better blood circulation to damaged tissues.

As further evidence of the soundness of this theory, fetuses that differ from their mothers antigenically actually do have larger and hence more nurturing placentas than do those that are genetically similar. In conjunction with the birth defect data, these observations suggest that being different from your mother is an adaptive advantage that favors survival.

Taken as a whole, these data suggest that an active immune system during pregnancy participates in encouraging and shaping placental and perhaps even fetal development. Rather than being the harmful force associated with recurrent miscarriages and fetal damage, under normal circumstances the immune system may serve to

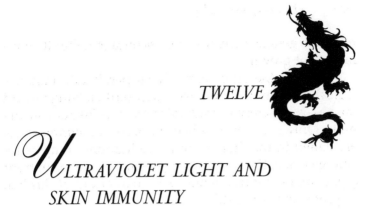

TWELVE

ULTRAVIOLET LIGHT AND SKIN IMMUNITY

It is almost an oxymoron to speak of the skin as part of the immune system. Until very recently skin was seen merely as a casement, an external garment that passively shielded the body from physical harm. To speak of the skin as having a sophisticated immune function is tantamount to saying a concrete wall works like an electronic barrier. But the skin has a remarkable degree of sophistication.

Beyond its role as a physical barrier to external threats like bacteria and certain viruses, anatomists of the eighteenth and nineteenth centuries were reluctant to consider it an organ. In part this limitation was dictated by the fact that it occupied largely two-dimensional spaces. Because all other organs in the body were "solid" objects that took up three dimensions, the idea that a flat sheet of cells could carry out special functions seemed unlikely. Until late in the 1960s, few dermatologists even imagined that the skin hid a nascent immune apparatus.

This limited view shifted in the 1950s with the discovery that the skin was the major organ of synthesis of the precursor to vitamin D. Then in the 1960s, the skin was recognized to have special metabolic activity: It could detoxify certain chemical threats and convert cortisone to its active form, hydrocortisone. By the 1970s, it became reasonable to conceive of the skin carrying out coordinated functions.

The first glimmerings of an immune component to this idea appeared in 1970. At that time, W. B. Streiland, a biologist who studied the skin's anatomical structure, predicted that it would have immune capabilities. For Streiland, such an observation comported well with what he observed: The skin is shot through with both afferent (outgoing) and efferent (incoming) lymphatic drainage, giving it an intimate connection with the scattered lymph nodes that drain all of the peripheral regions of the body. Streiland also noted that the skin is interpenetrated by cells that have immunological capability, including lymphocytes, dendritic epidermal cells similar in shape and function to macrophages, and a host of other white blood cells of various composition.

The discovery of an actual immune capability residing within the confines of the skin had a serendipitous beginning: It was only after Margaret Kripke, a researcher then at the National Institutes of Health, tried to see if exposure to ultraviolet (UV) light might reduce a mouse's ability to recognize foreign tissue that the central role of the skin in mounting tumor-controlling immunity was recognized. Kripke found that if mice were preexposed to UV light, skin tumors grew that normally would be rejected. Because UV light only penetrates the first few millimeters of tissue, Kripke correctly hypothesized that

UV's damaging effects resulted from local rather than systemic action. Years later, researchers learned that the skin lymphatics sooner or later carried most of the lymphocytes in the body. Under such conditions, UV light delivered to the skin could in theory affect the full complement of lymphocytes in the body.

Kripke and her co-workers directly demonstrated that the success of UV light in depressing immunity hinged on its ability to knock out lymphocytes that passed through as well as resided in the skin. In fact, if lymphocytes from UV-irradiated mice were taken from their treated hosts and injected into genetically identical peers, they carried over their immunosuppressant effects. Such transfusions permitted pigmented skin tumors called melanomas to grow unchecked by normally inhibiting immunity. This dramatic experiment suggested to the research team that UV-mediated suppression might in part be responsible for the spate of melanomas currently afflicting growing numbers of Caucasians in areas of high solar exposure such as the U.S. Southwest, Australia, and New Zealand. In other words, UV light appears to somehow "poison" lymphocytes, preventing them from carrying out their usual policing roles. For melanomas, a group of unusually antigenic tumors, this may mean letting some tumors escape surveillance.

Data supporting such a connection include the fact that UV irradiated and presumably immune-suppressed ear skin (in animals, of course) is much more likely to accept grafts of melanoma tumor cells than is the nonirradiated ear. The fact that the anatomical distribution of skin tumors generally is directly associated with regions of high solar exposure, particularly on the face and in the fold of the eye, is further evidence for a role of local immunity in controlling skin carcinogenesis.

Of even greater concern is the fact that at the most active wavelengths of UV, notably around 310 nm, as much as 10 percent of a given dose of UV penetrates the skin, making it plausible that high-intensity UV light can produce systemic immune depression by affecting the deeper lymphatics. Evidence that such a phenomenon may have an impact on the circulating white blood cells in the body is indirect but provocative. When exposed to UV light in tissue culture, white blood cells have impaired functional capacities.[1]

One of the more mysterious discoveries about UV light is that survival of foreign organ transplants can be enhanced by exposing the organ itself (and *not* the recipient) to UV light prior to transplantation.[2] This discovery points to the role of contained immune-active cells in organ grafts as a major contributing factor to the rejection phenomenon.

Skin UV exposure can depress the immune response to transplantation antigens[3] as well as to infectious agents.[4] A dramatic report from the Netherlands demonstrated that prior UV-B exposure impairs animal resistance to infection by the hookworm *Trichinella spiralis*.[5] When Wistar rats were orally infected with the larvae of *T. spiralis* and exposed to UV radiation daily for just 5 days, dramatic increases in parasite load were seen compared with rats that received their UV radiation 6 to 10 days after initial infection, i.e., after the immune system had a chance to limit infection. One mechanism for this effect is the release of regulatory cytokines like IL-10 from irradiated skin that then depress the T helper cell population.

Even more provocative data are available from studies that show that chemically induced tumors "take" and grow better—as do their metastases—in UV-exposed animals than in those that are not so exposed.[6] This UV-mediated immune suppression also has great significance for the outgrowth and continued presence of herpesviruses. The immune suppression that is now recognized to accompany solar exposure, even exposure that is insufficient to produce a sunburn, will suppress the immune response to herpes simplex.[7] This fact explains why so many children (and some adults) may experience flare-ups of their herpes-induced "cold sores" after a day in the sun.

Animal studies show that some parasites such as *Leishmania* responsible for African sleeping sickness, also gain a greater toehold if the body is first irradiated with UV light.[8] These data suggest that both local *and* systemic skin-mediated immunity are critical barriers to the ingress of many pathogens. UV-protective skin pigmentation may have evolved to maintain that immune barrier and thereby reduce the risk of blood-borne parasitic disease.

The full extent to which humans are impacted by UV-related effects on their immune systems remains to be determined. But it is clear that depression of resistance to infection following chronic exposure to UV light generally, and especially to short, high bursts of its higher-energy UV-B light, may be a serious public health problem. The fact that persons with heavily pigmented skin have greater resistance to such infection than do their paler counterparts may in part be related to the barrier function of heavily pigmented, melanotic skin in preventing the immune suppression produced by UV light. Mice infected with yeast cultures also live longer if they are not UV irradiated than if they are, suggesting a role of immunity in keeping these organisms at bay.[9]

Taken together, these findings have immediate and potentially profound importance to patients at risk for yeast and fungal infections, particularly those with AIDS, who may seek out the sun as a balm to their otherwise immunologically crippled bodies. Although still a hypothetical proposition for people, the animal data on UV suppression of immunity are particularly compelling. In a phrase, if you are prone to opportunistic disease, the sun is not likely to be your friend.

WHYS AND WHEREFORES

If all of these data on UV light can be extrapolated to the human condition, it makes sense to look for evolutionary explanations for what is otherwise a paradoxical occurrence: If immune suppression after outdoor exposure to sunlight is a regular phenomenon, it might reasonably be expected to have an adaptive function. One such function is in suppressing dermatitis. In fact, some experimental work has shown that skin-sensitizing antigens are rendered harmless in potential reactors if those persons are first subjected to UV light.[10] In other words, being pale-skinned, outdoors, and UV-exposed may provide some protection against severe skin reactions to plant irritants. This unusual response to sunlight has now been attributed to the presence in the skin of a special photoreceptor that converts UV-B radiation directly into a biochemical signal that activates the previously described suppressor cells.[11] When suppressor cells are present, they tend to dampen T-cell immunity.

This photoreceptor reaction has been hypothesized to work by allowing energetic wavelengths of UV light to perform a bit of chemical sleight of hand: When hit by UV rays, *trans*-urocanic acid, a naturally occurring substance found in the skin, is converted into a variant molecule that then sets in train a series of reactions leading to depressed immunity.[12] As part of the support for this idea, UV-altered *trans*-urocanic acid inhibits the antigen-processing cells of the spleen.[13] Of course, the key question is why the skin would have such an apparently complex and intricate *in situ* system for knocking *down* a vital defense system. Why would evolution be inviting adaptive disaster?

It *is* problematic that UV light is a powerful suppressor of just those reactions needed to keep tumor cells in check. But in fact, if solar immune suppression had beneficial effects, it might eclipse its negative attributes. One such activity is the minimization of the injury to sun-damaged skin brought about by solar radiation. After a severe sunburn, many skin cells die, and new sunlight-altered proteins called "photoantigens" appear on their surface.

An immune response to such antigens could spell even greater injury, as a blind-side attack against damaged and undamaged cells alike would be sure to wreak havoc on sun-injured skin. This likelihood is underscored by the severe photoactivated damage to sunburned skin experienced by patients with autoimmune diseases like lupus erythematosus. Sunlight-induced immune suppression may be but an inadvertent, secondary consequence of the more urgent need to suppress skin damage in autoimmunity.[14]

Another explanation for sunlight-mediated immune depression, and one that I have offered, is that such (initially) local and later full-blown suppression can help prevent skin contact sensitivity brought on by contact with plant immunogens like the rhus toxins of poison oak and ivy. According to this hypothesis, sun-induced depression during daylight hours may reduce the later dermal consequences of contact with noxious plants or other contact hypersensitivity-inducing agents. (Anyone who has had widespread poison oak or ivy knows the seriousness of what I am talking about!) These adverse effects are both more troublesome and potentially distracting than is the admittedly more serious but remote risk of sunlight-mediated cancer. Fortunately, the body carries internal repair mechanisms that can reverse some of the solar damage. And the immune system's intrinsic checks and balances are normally sufficient to restore homeostasis after a bout of poison oak.

Where immune suppression is more extensive, involving the body as a whole, internal damage control is hardly a viable alternative. The extraordinary havoc wrought by infection with immunosuppressive viruses like HIV points to the truly vital role of intact immunity in the body.

THIRTEEN

$\mathcal{H}_{IV}$

The Scourge of Immunity

Through the tragic loss of lives, AIDS provides a ghastly "natural experiment" demonstrating that an intact immune system is vital for survival. The disastrous vulnerability of patients infected with HIV to wave after wave of opportunistic infection is a clear demonstration of how important the immune system is in fighting infectious disease. After a variable latency period subsequent to being infected with the HIV type 1 (HIV-1), an AIDS patient's immunological bulwark against infectious disease commonly crumbles. Within months of the precipitous decline in immune strength that all but a few fortunate HIV+ patients experience, there is a progressive loss in numbers of CD4+ helper cells. Once below a critical cell count, the body falls prey to assault by a series of opportunistic organisms. The nature and severity of these infections are proportional to the degree of immune depression and indirectly to the "load" of circulating virus itself.

In developed countries like the United States, the first organisms to lay siege to the body are commonly bacteria like *Pneumocystis carinii*, which cause an often devastating pneumonia. Thereafter, other opportunistic organisms including cytomegalovirus (an RNA virus) and later yeast and fungi come to the fore until finally the host may be decimated by fungal cells. In Africa, AIDS patients are commonly overwhelmed by TB and malaria. In both places, organisms like *Candida albicans* form veritable mats of thick, throat-clogging white growths. Tumor cell types that might otherwise have been held in check by the immune system flare and invade. A simple basal cell carcinoma that normally limits its growth to the superficial layers of the skin will commonly invade deep into the body tissues of an AIDS patient.

Today women, who make up some 42 percent of people with AIDS, often first come to medical attention because of another invasive tumor, cervical cancer. But just how the immune system wanes during AIDS and how best to restore it are currently questions of great urgency and debate in the medical community.

PATHOGENESIS

A few short pages cannot do justice to the full complexity of the disease progression that characterizes AIDS. Among the models that have been presented to explain AIDS is the idea HIV causes immune suppression by directly invading and killing CD4$^+$ helper cells. Other models stress the ability of HIV to disrupt the immune system by upsetting the production of vital cytokines released by immune cells. Still other possibilities include the idea that HIV brings about the demise of the immune system by inducing autoantibodies or by so stimulating the T-cell component of the immune system that they go into a cell cycle process known as apoptosis. (In apoptosis, cells activate their "self-destruct" mechanisms and die.) And finally, a few investigators, most notably Peter Duesberg, whose views we reviewed in the immunotoxicity chapter, have proposed that the characteristic immune depression of AIDS is not the result of virus at all but is caused by the tremendous overuse of stimulants and other drugs by many AIDS patients. This view is not taken seriously by most clinicians because HIV produces AIDS in hemophiliacs and in patients who have never taken drugs.

Whatever the underlying mechanism, the hallmark of AIDS is by now well known: The $CD4^+$ helper cell population plummets, losing as many as 10 billion cells a day, leading to a state of profound and persistent immunodeficiency. One clue to the rapidity of this decline is the immune status of the host at the time when the HIV organism first takes hold. If the body is already in a state of immunological overdrive, say as a result of concurrent sexually transmitted disease or a malarial parasite infection, HIV finds many more receptive cells much more quickly than in a situation in which the immune system is quiescent. This makes AIDS a much more deadly disease in Africa where parasites are rife than elsewhere. There is also new evidence for a gene (*CKR5*) that affords *resistance* to HIV. Patients with a double dose of *CKR5* lack the critical cell surface marker needed by HIV to infect a cell.

Although still highly controversial, some researchers believe that the loss of immune strength brought about by HIV infection may *not* be a direct result of cell killing by the virus. In this view, immune depression may actually result from a form of autoimmunity in which cells that are infected with HIV are recognized and destroyed by an overvigilant immune system.[1] According to proponents of this model, who are not in the majority, a perverse form of "defense" leads CD8[+] T cells to recognize the distorted cell membranes of HIV-infected CD4[+] cells as foreign and to destroy the cell population. Accordingly, the loss of immune strength results primarily from this overzealous attack on damaged and virus-secreting cells, rather than from a direct HIV-mediated cell killing.

IMMUNE SUPPRESSION

To understand fully the pathogenesis of AIDS, it is important to recognize that the causative organism is a member of the family of retroviruses, that is, viruses that rely on RNA as their genetic information system. Retroviruses as a group have been known to be immunosuppressive since at least 1963.[2] At first, such immune suppression was regarded as a laboratory artifact, or at worst, an ancillary curiosity of viral infection. It was only when researchers linked immune suppression to the development of actual disease that they began to uncover the significance of virus-mediated immune depression.

My own research has shown that other RNA viruses can produce immune depression. The key experiment in question was conducted in 1969 in the University of California Berkeley laboratory of Professor Phyllis Blair, where I was a postdoctoral fellow. Blair and I explored the possibility that mammary tumor viruses (MTV) could depress the immune system after infecting a susceptible mouse host.

Like other RNA viruses, MTV resembles members of a family of viruses known as the myxoviruses, which were responsible for killing millions of rabbits in Australia, and the lymphochoriomeningitis (lymf-ō-kor-ē-o-men-in-gī-tis) virus, which causes an inflammation of the meningeal lining of the brain. All contain RNA instead of DNA in their core, and are hence dependent on the host tissue's DNA for making copies of their key proteins and genetic material. This is typically done through the use of the enzyme reverse transcriptase, which first translates the RNA of the virus into a DNA that can serve as a template for instructions about protein synthesis. The MTV story provides an instructive lens into understanding one view of how HIV participates in the development of AIDS.

When Dr. Blair and I proposed that MTV be studied for its ability to produce immune suppression, the idea was greeted with considerable skepticism. Why would a tumor virus be "interested" in producing immunological disturbances? The answer hinges on the observation that many of the tumors that such viruses produce are actually antigenic to their hosts, i.e., capable of eliciting an immune response. In the case of MTV, an active reaction to the virus or to the tumor could effectively limit its ability to infect and ultimately transmit the virus itself. This is so because MTV is transmitted "vertically," i.e., from mother to offspring via the milk. Early breast tumors actually secrete large amounts of viral particles into the milk, providing an avenue of transmission from one generation to the next. If the tumor virus could depress the immune system, it would afford itself an especially effective avenue of survival and transmission, much as clearing out a machine-gun nest in advance helps prepare a beachhead for invasion.

Indeed, after a full-fledged study of this question, the research team with which I worked succeeded in demonstrating that both antibody production and cellular immunity were depressed by this viral agent.[3]

Later research has shown that the *components* of MTV and other RNA viruses are themselves immunosuppressive. By taking substances from disrupted retroviruses, researchers showed that several classes of extracted proteins or their smaller polypeptides exert a profound immunosuppressive effect both in intact animals and in tissue culture. In particular, CKS-17, a viral component that is found in both mouse and cat leukemia viruses, has proven to have dramatic immunosuppressive abilities. This protein is found across species lines, including ape, cow, and human leukemia viruses.

Ominously, CKS-17 is also present in HIV. If HIV is like these other viruses, then even its lifeless protein components can possibly produce the immunological abnormalities associated with retrovirus infection. Thus, the frightening possibility exists that the immunological abnormalities that arise from HIV infection (including those that lead to opportunistic infections) may not require a live or replicating virus. If so, the immune system will have to clear infective and noninfective particles alike if it is to control AIDS. As evidence for this likelihood, the virus-free blood of AIDS patients is itself immunosuppressive, perhaps because of the presence of similar protein components shed from live virus no longer present. If true, simply reducing or eliminating HIV from the blood, as may be achieved with the new class of protease inhibitors, may not completely reverse the immune depression of AIDS.

Some hints as to the nature of this depression can be gleaned from the work with MTV. When mice are first infected with MTV, their ability to respond to foreign cells such as sheep red blood cells declines. This deficiency was most evident in older mice congenitally infected with MTV. And, in a prophetic but unintentional experiment that anticipated AIDS, injection of mice with MTV-contaminated blood led to the appearance of immune depression within 1 or 2 weeks. When other MTV-infected mice were grafted with foreign skin, the survival of the grafts was significantly prolonged over that of MTV-free, but genetically identical, controls.[4]

This work added to the body of evidence that showed that many non-tumor-producing RNA viruses could depress the immune system. These viruses include cytomegalovirus and Riley virus, an obscure RNA virus that is isolated from small animals. Infection with the Riley virus actually stimulates a mouse's antibody response, while decreasing its ability to recognize foreign tissue antigens. As an explanation for this effect, researchers now know that this virus preferentially infects cells of the immune system in the T-cell lineage.

Most interestingly, virtually all of the RNA-containing viruses studied, including the avian leukosis–sarcoma complex, the murine leukemia–sarcoma complex, and MTV, are immune depressing. These findings were known in the 1970s, providing a prescient window into the attributes of HIV—and raising early warning signs that increasing incidents of RNA viral contamination in our environment bode ill for human well-being. The explanation for immune suppression offered at the time of these dramatic discoveries was the one adopted by most AIDS researchers today: The virus infects susceptible lymphocytes in the host's blood and then enters the immune cell-producing system in the bone marrow itself, directly destroying the $CD4^+$ cells contained therein.[5] Most importantly, certain individuals appear to resist this process (so-called slow-progressors), while others succumb rapidly (fast-progressors) or remain virus-free altogether despite frequent, high-risk exposure.

MECHANISMS

The process by which an initial viral infection leads to a full-blown condition of immune suppression is now known in substantial detail. What is lacking in this model is a deeper understanding of the ways in which genetics, lifestyle, concurrent infections, and other risk factors influence the vulnerability of each at-risk AIDS patient. We do know that one's HLA type is a strong predictor of the progression of disease (see Table Three) and that lifestyle contributes not just to risk, but probably to vulnerability to infection as well. Table Three shows the varieties of HLA types that determine susceptibility to HIV infectivity. Each person will have two alleles that determine a HLA, A, B, C, or D molecule. It is hypothesized that slow and non-progressors carry protective HLA molecules that process and present certain viral antigens to the immune system efficiently, leading to a strong immune response early in infection, while fast progressors have HLA molecules that fail to bind, process, and/or present molecules necessary for an effective immune response. In this light, it is worth taking a second look at Peter Duesberg's proposal that recreational drug use causes most if

Table Three.   *Linkage between HLA Type and Progression of HIV Disease*[a]

	Progressors		
	Fast[b]	Slow[c]	Non[d]
HLA types	A1, A11, A23 A28+TAP2.3; A29+TAP2.1;	A25+TAP2.3; A26, A32	A2, A28
	B8+DR3;B35+Cw4	B5, B14, B27, B51 B57, Bw4	
	DR2, and DR5	DR5, DR6, DR7 DRB1*0201; DR13	DR13

[a]Source: M. Westby, F. Manca, and A. G. Dalgleish, "The role of host immune responses in determining the outcome of HIV infection," *Immunology Today*, 17,120–125, 1997. Note: This table is not meant to imply that carrying a given HLA marker is assurance of safety against HIV infection.
[b]Fast, persons who develop full-blown AIDS within 1–2 years of infection with HIV.
[c]Slow, persons who show delayed development (usually 6+ years) of AIDS (includes persons who develop HIV antibodies without evidence of disease).
[d]Non, persons with multiple and frequent exposure to HIV who nonetheless fail to develop antibodies against the virus.

not all AIDS-associated immune depression. Although wrong in its sweeping generalities, Duesberg's idea that secondary factors impacting the immune system can make full-blown AIDS more likely may profitably be reexamined.

DUESBERG REVISITED

Let us take a fresh look at the possible contribution of drug use and concurrent infection with sexually transmitted diseases to the AIDS epidemic. Many of those people in the highest risk subgroups in whom HIV first incubated clearly used and abused drugs. During the late 1960s and 1970s when AIDS first incubated in the gay and drug-using communities of inner cities, the use of "poppers" (amyl nitrate), marijuana and related cannabinoids, cocaine, and morphine derivatives was prevalent. Such overuse was so widespread CDC scientists gave serious credence to a drug-induced model in the 1983–1984 period. Virtually all such substances, as reviewed in the immunotoxicity chapter, can interfere with immune competence.

Cannabinoids including the major active ingredient in marijuana, tetrahydrocannabinol (THC), have been shown to block the activation of T cells. THC also binds directly to and may incapacitate lymphocytes in the blood, spleen, and tonsils.[6] Cocaine is a potent CNS stimulant that also interferes with several immune functions at psychoactive doses. It induces the secretion of transforming growth factor beta and in so doing appears to enhance the replication of HIV-1 in the mononuclear cell lines of human peripheral blood.[7]

Anecdotal reports support a major role of chronic exposure to morphine in increasing susceptibility to both viral and bacterial infections generally.[8] In keeping with our knowledge of receptors shared between nerve and immune cells (recall our discussion in Chapter Eight), many of these opiate-produced immune alterations could be reversed with naloxone, a chemical that blocks opiate receptors.[9]

Alcohol is also a widely recognized immunosuppressant. In many alcoholics, chronic alcohol ingestion is associated with lung infections and pneumonia. In addition, bacterial infection and bacteremia (blood-borne infection) is also increased in alcoholics and those who engage in binge drinking. Ultimately, it was the fact that hemophiliacs who acquired HIV despite being virtually completely drug free and newborn infants who had acquired HIV congenitally that spelled the end of the Duesberg hypothesis. Moreover, the gay population is not known for ingesting more drugs and alcohol than any particular group of heterosexuals. The final rejoinder, that blood products used to treat hemophilia were also immunosuppressive, has been largely discounted as a viable mechanism of immunosuppression. But concurrent immunosuppression by drugs could certainly accelerate the progression of HIV to AIDS.

INDIRECT IMMUNE DEPRESSION

Given the epidemic of HIV infection, the data on HIV itself as an immunosuppressant should be reexamined. Rolf Zinkernagel (who received the Nobel prize for his immunology research) believes that HIV does not produce enough cell killing to account for the loss of $CD4^+$ cells. A clue to just how HIV affects immunity can be gleaned from an examination of some of the other RNA viruses I have reviewed above. With few exceptions, none of the RNA viruses classically linked to immunosuppression is cytopathic. In plain terms, they do not kill cells.

Could we account for the postulated immune depression by HIV without evoking the cell-killing idea? A possible explanation has been proposed by Zinkernagel, who postulates that RNA viruses in general and HIV in particular are "successful" in depressing the immune system because they incite an immune reaction from the body. According to this view, it is the body's own immune system that goes after HIV-infected helper T cells.

The logic of this thinking is not as offbeat as it sounds. By infecting certain susceptible cells like the $CD4^+$ helper population, we already know that HIV flags their presence to the immune system. Rather than killing off the $CD4^+$ cells directly, all HIV needs to do is label them as "traitors," marking them for immune-mediated destruction. By transforming surface antigens on the $CD4^+$ helper cells and antigen-presenting cells, HIV tricks the immune system into attacking its own kind. The surviving $CD8^+$ cells then carry out a process of selective cell killing that decimates the immune system's reservoir of surviving helper cells and any others that harbor the virus. The resulting immune damage is thus the result of a kind of cellular auto-da-fé.

According to this speculative model, the immune depression that eventually leaves the AIDS patient open to opportunistic infection is thus an autoimmune response from within. HIV itself does little if any of the damage. If true, this process points a finger at the immune system itself as the culprit. As with other diseases reviewed in this book, it is the immune system's own assault that is ultimately detrimental to the host. Contrary to popular conceptions, AIDS patients are not so much bereft of an immune system as lacking one limb of that system. The remainder, especially the $CD8^+$ cells, are remarkably active. Consistent with this view is the paradoxical occurrence of $CD8^+$-mediated autoimmune diseases in otherwise immunologically crippled AIDS patients. Some AIDS patients have cytotoxic T-cell damage to their salivary glands, whereas others have auto-immune forms of arthritis.

An analogy with the previously mentioned lympho-choriomeningitis (LCM) virus is revealing. Here is an organism that infects the brain but causes virtually no damage *unless and until* the infected host (in this case a mouse) mounts an immune assault on it. The resulting pathology from an LCM infection is analogous to AIDS: The degree of damage reflects the balance between the effectiveness of the host's immune response in checking the spread of the virus and viral destructiveness in killing off helper cells that harbor the virus.[10] In theory, if the system were to reach a dynamic equilibrium in which virus would be present—but not spreading—*and* the helper cells would be relatively spared from immune-mediated destruction, long-term survival for AIDS patients, such as those listed in Table Three with favorable HLA response markers, might be possible. This new model may have some big "ifs," but it may be an avenue worth pursuing. To do so, however, requires a wholesale suspension of the traditional belief system that postulates that an all-or-none immunological defensive stratagem will be the only one that works.

A MORE EASTERN VIEW

The new model calls for reaching a détente with the HIV organism. In this view, if HIV titers in blood are low and relatively few cells are infected, a moderate immune response might control infection, giving rise to so-called "slow" or long-term progressors. But if titers are high and many cells are infected—drawing the body's extreme, autoimmune responses—the resulting immunopathology may be extensive, giving rise to "fast" progressors.

Rolf Zinkernagel has also proposed a devilishly logical extension of this model: If HIV does not itself produce cell damage and the immune system does, a *defenseless* host after HIV infection might be the best of all. By this account, an HIV$^+$ person lacking autoimmune capability altogether could *in theory* remain symptom free even as the virus circulated in the blood. Of course, this is purely a hypothesis and requires substantially more study before further direct investigation is done.

If this radical hypothesis were true, the best treatment for AIDS would be a course of immune *suppression* rather than stimulation. The premise behind this idea is in itself startling: Rather than achieving recovery by boosting the immune response to HIV as so many AIDS patients now attempt to do, selectively depressing it could be the answer. This approach, I should emphasize, presupposes that initial infection (where a strong immune reaction would be helpful) has already occurred.

COMMENTARY

The theory of autoimmune attack predicts that breaking the immune response against HIV-infected cells would not result in worse disease but in a kind of suspension of hostilities. The end point might be a further slowing of progression of the disease in HLA appropriate hosts and lead to a "carrier state" in which the HIV organism would coexist with the immune cells of the body. As we saw in the introduction, several viruses, notably hepatitis B and herpesvirus, appear to establish a comparable state of relatively benign coexistence on a regular basis. Indeed, small numbers of chronic HIV carriers have been found who have remained symptom-free for 15–17 years.

Several French researchers indirectly undertook a test of this idea when they instituted a course of treatment in which an immunosuppressant would be used to abort the cell-killing effects from the hypothesized autoimmune attack. In 1987, a team headed by J. M. Andrieu used cyclosporin A, a potent immunosuppressant, to *treat* AIDS patients.[11] Although their early results were promising, the approach has proven too draconian. Some patients have died, and earlier recoveries did not last.

More recent studies have shown that cyclosporin may actually inhibit some HIV functions. Early data showed that a course of treatment with such an immunosuppressive agent aborts the programmed cell death in AIDS patients that is induced by cytotoxic T lymphocytes. In additional patients in which it has been tried, full suppression has proven less salubrious, perhaps because of the damage already done by HIV. Although this radical idea remains highly controversial, the recent finding that immune-suppressed organ transplant recipients have a significantly *lower* incidence of AIDS than would be predicted from their risk status means that immune suppression as a means to slow disease progression still deserves a fair hearing.[12]

Related, albeit anecdotal, support comes from the otherwise inexplicably protracted survival of AIDS patient Jeff Getty. Getty received whole-body radiation to suppress his immune system prior to getting a baboon marrow transplant. Although no baboon cells have been detectable after the procedure was completed, a year later Getty was apparently thriving.[13]

The opposing mainstream view, that a sustained, high-level immune response is beneficial to AIDS patients, is supported by data indicating that patients who maintain a strong cytotoxic T-lymphocyte response are able to stave off disease progression and maintain high $CD4^+$ cell counts.[14] The correlation between efficacy of drugs like cyclosporin in reducing the progression of AIDS appears at odds with the improvement in patients with apparently strong immunity. This paradox can be partially explained. Proponents of the strong immunity theory could say that by depriving HIV of an essential molecule for viral assembly, cyclosporin analogues may directly interfere with the *infectivity* of HIV-1 by reducing the production of functional and infectious particles rather than by producing systemic immune depression.[15,16]

Many clinicians agree on the desirability of an intermediate therapeutic goal: accepting AIDS as a chronic disease in which long-term survival is not so much a result of complete eradication, but of reaching a kind of immunological détente with infection. Such an end point may be achievable with the advent of protease inhibitors that block viral assembly, especially as it relinquishes the presently unattainable goal of eliminating infectious virus entirely. Coupled with appropriate immune-elevating therapies, protease inhibitors could bring the immune system into balance with one or perhaps two viral variants in a state of dynamic equilibrium, achieving an intermediate goal of sustained health in HIV-positive patients. The most rational means of achieving such a goal would of necessity require restoring and strengthening cellular immunity[17] and then ensuring that the resulting immune responses are wide ranging enough to both encompass and control newly emerging HIV variants. Paradoxically, such a control, in my view, would *not* automatically mean a stronger immune system.

New data suggest this idea has some merit. Close examination of the course of disease suggests in some cases that where immunity is "pushed" to control the virus, the results can be counterproductive. Instead of reining in the viral population, a boosted immune response appears to work detrimentally to select for immune-proof viral types. A "tough" immune system seems to coax out more and more HIV variants by knocking out one after another until resistant survivors make further immune retrieval an impossibility.

Such a process comports with the outcome of HIV proliferation followed in six patients. In each of the four cases in which viral activity had spread to several reactive clones, immune strength was especially high, but the patients died. By contrast, in the two long-term survivors, immune reactivity was *lower* and only one or two HIV variants could be found. One interpretation is that survival here could be attributed to immune systems *not* pushing the HIV load too hard, permitting the continued persistence of only one or a few viral types that came to exist in harmony with the body's immune controls.

Further support comes from a collaborative project in Switzerland and the United States headed by Giuseppe Pantaleo and Anthony Fauci. This team found that AIDS patients who put out the smallest quantities of T cells against HIV fare far *better* than those who mount a massive response. The core of the difference for the survivors lies in producing a wide spectrum of T cells rather than a single cell type. This guerilla-style approach appears to anticipate a wider spectrum of HIV types and hold them in check better than does a head-on, full-force attack mounted against only one HIV type.[18]

This experience, albeit limited, could be seen as perhaps reinforcing a totally different, Tao-like philosophy of therapy, one that turns on mutual accommodation rather than annihilation and balance instead of the extremes of traditional notions of "cure." According to this philosophy, AIDS could be put into quasipermanent "remission" even as HIV remained sequestered in the body but held in check by active immune surveillance. Still, such patients would, of course, have to continue to practice "safe sex" so as not to infect others with the disease.

In further support of the potential heuristic value of this more Eastern approach, I offer a number of underappreciated findings about the immune system.

FOURTEEN

$\mathscr{U}$*NANTICIPATED FEATURES*

Paradoxical activities often provide grist for a new way of thinking. Among the provocative discoveries we have already reviewed are the abilities of otherwise "desirable" immune reactions to hurt patients; the reverse effect of heightened immunity in encouraging AIDS or tumor growth; and the apparently supportive functions of immunity during pregnancy. These findings suggest that the common medical adage that strongest is best may need to be reexamined. The surprising fact that immune reactions can damage as well as aid the body has proven to be one of the most difficult lessons for Western medical practitioners to learn.

WRONG THINKING ABOUT IMMUNITY: TUBERCULOSIS AS A MODEL

TB is currently undergoing a worldwide resurgence. From its relatively quiescent state in the 1950s and 1960s, TB now affects some 80 to 100 million worldwide, killing some 3 million people annually. Globally, it is the number one cause of death from infectious disease. In the United States, TB incidence declined by approximately 6 percent per year between 1953 through 1984. Thereafter, TB has progressively increased in incidence reflecting the availability of many more susceptible people, so that currently it affects about 1 in every 10,000 people. Most of these cases have arisen in California, Florida, Illinois, New York, and Texas, the states with the highest prevalence of adults with AIDS.

This resurgence is attributable to at least three concurrent factors: a vast upswelling of cases of immunosuppressed AIDS and institutionalized patients who are at dramatically heightened risk for TB, a wave of new immigrants with disproportionately high numbers of TB-positive persons, and a failure to exert effective control once affected individuals are identified. Part of this failure is in misuse or underuse of antibiotics. Too many clinics currently fail to monitor patients to ensure that a full course of antibiotics is taken. As a result, antibiotic-resistant strains of TB are encouraged to replace susceptible strains, and TB's threat is intensified. The current circumstance was described by a prominent WHO health official as "the most frightening situation I have ever encountered."[1]

But another explanation for this failure is underestimating the potential role of the immune system in controlling TB. Ironically, the potentially lifesaving preventive approach of developing a vaccine to control TB has been effectively shelved, a point to be discussed at greater length in the chapter on vaccines. Here it is useful to discuss the paradoxical role of the immune system in aggravating tubercular illness.

A DOUBLE-EDGED SWORD

Those who have studied the tubercle Mycobacterium most closely know that the main risk to the TB patient stems not from any intrinsic toxicity of the bacterium itself but from the aborted immune reaction to it. When the tubercle bacillus first invades the body, it does so through the lungs. There, special tissue macrophages take it up and begin a process of digestion and elimination. Depending on the level of virulence of the particular strain of TB ingested, the bacterium will either be digested or survive.

If it escapes the intracellular enzymes that normally degrade bacteria, the TB bacillus will begin to divide and replicate *inside* the macrophage itself. Even when this bacterial expansion occurs, full-blown disease may still be avoidable. As long as the bacterium is sequestered within the macrophage, it is relatively harmless. Indeed, the TB bacillus has a special waxy coat that provides it with a relatively impenetrable covering, which, coupled with its previously mentioned ability to alter cellular pH, ensures its ability to thrive ensconced within its host cell. But should the cell be broken or TB escape, the ensuing immune response escalates dramatically.

The immune reaction usually takes one of two forms. In some individuals, the initial reaction is predominantly limited to the release of free TB from bacillus-laden cells. In some of these people, this escape engenders a mild immune response leading to the breakdown of cell walls, a clearing of free bacteria, and minimal cell damage from the mopping up operation by macrophages of residual cells. For others, a full-bore immune response becomes indiscriminate, leading to tissue death and serious collateral tissue damage.[2]

This phenomenon of immune-mediated crisis is called the Koch phenomenon or reaction, after the discoverer of the TB bacillus, Robert Koch (1843–1910). In the Koch reaction described at length below, the resulting massive cell death and necrosis can be fatal.

NATURAL HISTORY OF TB

For most people who become infected with the TB bacillus, the infection remains latent. Normally, only 5–15 percent of infected persons actually develop symptomatic TB over their lifetimes.[3] Most of this risk is concentrated in the first 2 years after acquiring the infection. Thereafter, the risk declines. In children and immuno-compromised hosts in which the first layer of macrophage protection is deficient, the incidence of full-blown TB is greater. Among such patients, the fatality rate can approach 50 percent if the disease is left untreated. The greatest risk of dying from active TB is among AIDS patients for whom a primary infection almost always proceeds inexorably to full-blown clinical disease.[4]

As long as the bacterium stays placid and divides only infrequently, the macrophage and the bacterium enjoy a kind of pathogenic détente. During this period, the macrophage often becomes a giant cell (discussed in Chapter Five). Giant cells signal the beginning of potentially damaging immune reactions as they form a chronic focus of infection.

During the period of latent infection, the immune system holds bacteria in check, and the disease process may stay in remission. As in AIDS, patients can become carriers and may produce antibodies so that they test positive in the common tine test. But the accumulations of inflammatory and giant cells then release cytokines that attract circulating T cells.

These T cells in turn release their own chemical signals, marshaling still more macrophages to the infected part of the lung and hemming in their otherwise itinerant counterparts. The surrounded macrophages inexorably increase in number until one or more burst, releasing contained TB bacteria and their products into the circulation. If repeated often enough, such ruptures can be catastrophic, signaling thousands of surrounding macrophages to sweep into the vicinity to scavenge any free bacteria that may have escaped. And so a vicious cycle is set in train leading to more TB bacteria being released, still greater influxes of macrophages, and so on. T cells may also recruit still more macrophages to this local "hot spot," increasing both the numbers of macrophages and their individual ability to ingest and destroy tubercle bacilli.

At this point, related cytokines carry messages to the brain, creating general malaise and fatigue. In short order, the patient may break a fever, signaling an infectious episode. These episodes can become sufficiently common and cyclic, as Thomas Mann observed in his famous novel, *The Magic Mountain*, that the TB patient can actually "tell time" without a thermometer.[5] When this cycle comes into full swing, the patient becomes symptomatic and truly "sick" with TB.

THE KOCH REACTION

Such symptoms signal that a full-bore immune reaction is under way. But it is right about here in the immune process that things can go seriously awry. What has begun as a successful battle can become a tedious stalemate and, ultimately, a perilously desperate rout. For if the body is not fully successful in eliminating the tubercle bacillus in its first wave of responses, it trips a signal that sets the T cells into an attack on the macrophages themselves.

This T-cell assault is actually a form of autoimmunity akin to what occurs in AIDS and other diseases: Special T cells—the CD8$^+$ cells—go after normal immune constituents and kill them. (Indeed, it may be because so many CD8$^+$ are present in AIDS patients that HIV-associated TB evolves into such a serious disease.) The resulting mayhem spills millions of living, fresh TB bacilli into the surrounding tissue. As the bacilli strike out and infect *healthy* lung tissue, the T cells proceed hot on their heels. Within a matter of hours from the initial abortive assault, T cells are now killing otherwise healthy lung tissue to get at the bacilli replicating in the lung parenchyma. Now whole sectors of the lobes of the lungs begin to liquefy, literally disintegrating before the clinician's X-ray probing eye.

This death process proceeds as long as the immune system perceives an antigenic challenge—in this case the presence of lung tissue infected with tubercle bacilli. The end result is the previously described Koch reaction, a kind of cellular mayhem that leads to massive caseous necrosis (after the cheeselike appearance of the dead tissue) and ultimately to death.

HEPATITIS B INFECTION

The TB example paints an entirely different picture of the immune system than that conveyed in most medical texts. For standard medical books like *Cecil's Textbook of Medicine*,[6] the immune system is described as a largely reactive defense system, one that may be implicated in disease, but only classic autoimmune ones. But as we just saw with TB, sometimes the immune system is more like the Hindu god Shiva, a destroyer as well as a benefactor.

This model is especially apt for viral hepatitis infections. Hepatitis B is perhaps the most prevalent viral disease in the world. It affects at least 300 million people and is responsible for hundreds of thousands of deaths from hepatitis and liver cancer. When hepatitis B virus invades the body, it produces a smoldering, relatively benign infection that normally has an indolent and mild course. Unlike its more cytopathic kin, hepatitis virus does not kill liver cells. As described in Chapter One, hepatitis B can invade the cells of the liver where it resides without causing clinically evident disease for decades.

For some reason, a number of these virally infected persons suffer massive and devastating liver damage following activation of their infective status. Many clinicians now recognize that the key ingredient to this massive cellular destruction is the immune reaction against infected liver cells itself, an attack mounted by both the T- and B-cell arms of the immune system.[7]

Like all other DNA viruses, the hepatitis B virus usurps the DNA machinery of the cell to make copies of its own DNA material. The flag that tells the body about this process is a key molecule that appears on the virally infected cell surface. This viral gene product alerts the T cells of the body about the presence of an intracellular parasite. Normally, this new cell surface protein targets the host cell for T-cell-mediated destruction, just like a laser-guided "smart" bomb tracks its target.

As long as the virus inside the cell remains quiescent, infection is relatively harmless. But should the immune system march into action, mounting an assault on infected liver cells, the ensuing disease process resembles the Koch reaction and can be devastating. An autoimmune-like attack can produce fulminant hepatitis and is commonly heralded by profound weakness, lethargy, and fatigue. If the immune response is "successful," the disease process is severe but mercifully short. In a matter of weeks, an acute episode of hepatitis B can "clear," the damaged liver can regenerate, and the patient may emerge only slightly the worse for wear.

But if the immune assault is unsuccessful, the self-directed attack can become chronic and smoulder unchecked for years. In time, the liver tissue dies and is replaced with nonfunctional scar tissue, producing cirrhosis. For a few unfortunate hepatitis B victims, these cirrhotic areas degenerate into frank carcinoma. In some parts of Asia and Africa, hepatitis B is so common that liver cancer is the major cause of noninfectious deaths.

As in TB, this process of cellular death and destruction is wrought by the T cells of the immune system. In chronic hepatitis, the liver waxes and wanes from the depredations of this infectious cycle. Initially, it produces compensatory cells in an attempt at regeneration. The result is often simply more fresh cells for the B virus to invade and the immune system to attack and the cycle continues.

The two examples of TB and viral hepatitis highlight situations in which an out-of-balance immune system can wreak havoc. Knowledge of this contrarian pathological mechanism should have alerted researchers to similar processes that might be occurring in other diseases, including AIDS. An equally misunderstood property of the immune system is its secondary reactions, once it has fended off a primary disease.

MEASLES AND ASTHMA

Children who get measles are much more prone to other infections during the latent and active periods of their viral illness. Because a measles infection does not depress cell numbers in the immune system, this effect has mystified researchers for years. New data suggest the measles-related spate of secondary illnesses reflects a generalized impairment of cells in the immune system resulting from reduced levels of interleukin 12, the intercellular hormone critical in starting an immune response. When IL-12 levels are low, the body appears vulnerable to secondary infections and to other undesirable immune activity.

One additional phenomenon possibly linked to this IL-12 response is the relation between measles and asthma. Over the last 30 years, allergies, and their related disorder asthma, have increased dramatically in developed countries around the world.[8] Many explanations have been offered for this dramatic increase in aberrant immunological reactivity. Among them are the increase in "tight" homes; greater prevalence of ecological disturbance and accompanying weeds and pollen-bearing plants; living conditions fostering the growth of dust mites and cockroaches; and the lack of protective breast feeding in a significant portion of the newest generation of children.

But the most provocative explanation for this resurgence of allergic reactivity is that something fundamental has changed for the immune system itself. Researchers at the Medical Research Council Environmental Epidemiology Unit in Southampton, United Kingdom, have offered the idea that it is the direct reduction in full-blown *natural infections* during childhood that is responsible. As evidence for this radical hypothesis, the most dramatic increases in asthma and allergies generally have coincided with a decline in natural childhood infections, particularly from measles.

Much of this reduction can be attributed to intensified vaccination programs. In the past naturally acquired infections in the early childhood years might have prevented later allergic sensitization. As infection levels have fallen—in Great Britain the drop has been over 100-fold in the first part of the twentieth century—successive generations of children may have lost a hypothetical "protective" effect of natural infections with viral and some bacterial agents early in childhood.[9] The result is a compensatory but misdirected hyperactivity of the immune system, causing asthma.

This explanation has great heuristic appeal as it equates two changes occurring concurrently in the same system: As the immune system receives fewer and fewer major challenges, as would come from a full-bore assault by natural infections, it may be left with a more highly "strung" level of attentiveness. In theory, this hair-trigger setting could encourage overreaction to otherwise innocuous antigenic challenges, such as those from pokeweed or goldenrod pollen, insect parts or feces, or the danders of animals.

Researchers now know enough about the immune system to have predicted some major differences between natural and artificial immune stimulation. When natural infection occurs, some of the T helper cells provoked are *less* likely to produce allergic-type reactions than is the type of cell that responds to a killed vaccine. In this way, a natural measles virus infection can shift the balance of immune cells away from allergic-type reactions while vaccinations encourage asthmaticlike ones.

Evidence that something like this may in fact be occurring comes from data that show that children who have older siblings—and hence enhanced opportunities for acquiring childhood infections—are much less likely to develop allergies than are those who are in small or single-child families. A critical test of this hypothesis would be to examine the likelihood of allergies developing in a country that has only a rudimentary vaccination program against measles, mumps, and rubella. In such a setting, a substantial number of children still get measles naturally. Those who do, according to the protective model, would be expected to be resistant to developing an allergy.

Such a study was done in the African country of Guinea-Bissau. Among the roughly 50 percent of the children who acquired measles during their childhood years, there was indeed a significant reduction in the response to a typical test of allergic reactivity when the same children were 14–21 years old. Compared with children who did not get measles, those who did had about two-thirds less reactivity to a standard test allergen (dust or grainery mite allergen). Similar protective effects were not seen when children were simply vaccinated against measles, suggesting that the *natural infection* itself was necessary to ensure protection.

Alternative explanations, such as the possibility that vaccination against measles somehow sensitizes the recipient to develop allergies, are, in my estimation, less plausible. The newest data make even clearer the linkage between immunization and asthma. Japanese children who respond vigorously to a TB vaccine, probably because of prior infection, are much less prone to get asthma than are their weakly reactive peers. And children who escape getting natural infections entirely appear the most asthma-vulnerable of all.

COMMENT

These observations suggest a whole new view of an immune system in dynamic equilibrium with the environment and with the body itself. Natural selection—and natural selection alone—is the dominant force shaping the reactions of immunity. And the rapid (in an evolutionary sense), widespread substitution of killed viral or bacterial vaccines for natural infection may have disturbed the natural balance between normally progressive infections and the immune system. As evidenced by the suggestive measles vaccine/asthma link, the introduction of artificial means to provoke lasting immunity may have insidious consequences. A "successful" dead-cell vaccination against one disease can reshape the pattern of the immune system's response to live antigenic challenges from the natural pathogen-ridden world. Lacking the age-old "education" by natural pathogens, the immune system may be left hyperreactive to new antigenic challenges. It may be that there are other causes of allergies and asthma, but the insight that vaccination may hold the key to understanding the upsurge in this sometimes life-threatening illness is a major contribution indeed.

These data, if confirmed by other studies, will provide powerful evidence for the evolutionary importance of spontaneous natural challenges to the immune system or at least reasonable vaccine surrogates (such as attenuated viruses) that do the same thing. Over the millennia of human evolution, no prior occasions occurred in which the immune system has been given the contemporary barrage of killed-cell or so-called capsular vaccines. As valuable as many of them may be (e.g., in protecting against pneumococcal pneumonia), vaccine developers may have overlooked the long-term implications of their wide-scale use. These artificial immunizations provide nonliving, surrogate challenges to natural infection, often for whole populations. As such they offer a qualitatively different challenge to the immune system than does a naturally acquired infection from a living organism. The measles example should give us pause and make us reexamine the role we assign to vaccines in protecting our health.

FIFTEEN

$\mathscr{B}$UILDING ON NATURAL IMMUNITY

THE VACCINE STORY

Without a doubt, vaccines are needed to stem the onrush of infectious disease in the modern world. But what kind of vaccines? In the mid-1790s when Mary Ashley Montagu brought the first reports of the use of cowpox as a defense against smallpox among the Turks to England, she found a receptive mind in the person of physician Edward Jenner. Smallpox had been ravishing all of Europe. Over a 40-year period, it had killed or disfigured close to 25 percent of the population in England alone. At the end of the eighteenth century, the public was clamoring for surcease from this calamity. Jenner adopted the techniques that Montagu had learned about in Turkey, techniques that had been brought to the Mideast from China. According to the great sinologist Joseph Needham, the Chinese had discovered years earlier that dried pustules from smallpox victims could be instilled into the nostrils by tube where they actually cause a natural, but attenuated, form of the disease. The result is typically a lasting immunity with only a few deaths.

In 1798, Jenner made a vast improvement on this story. He was aware that cows developed pustules on their udders during the progression of a kind of bovine form of smallpox known as cowpox—and that cow maids were prone to get a form of the disease, with light fever and pustules that were limited to their hands. Afterwards, the cow maids were surprisingly immune from the ravages of smallpox. In Jenner's own words, "Morbid matter of various kinds, when absorbed into the system, may produce effects in some degrees similar; but what renders the cowpox virus so extremely singular is that the person who has been thus affected is forever after secure from the infection of smallpox."[1]

To test his prescient observation, Jenner turned to the most accessible—and we now would say, vulnerable—members of British society, the children from the poorhouses of London. He obtained several pauper children who were being housed in special quarters. Without further explanation to their parents (assuming they could have been found had Jenner tried), he inoculated them with pus from the cowpox pustules. (Today we call this process "vaccination" after the Latin for cow, *vacca*.) To bring his test to fruition, he then went one step further—a step that many of us today would consider a still greater violation of ethics: He intentionally inoculated vaccinated and unvaccinated pauper children with potentially virulent, dried pustular material taken from actual smallpox victims.

Now, Jenner had reason to know that the smallpox material would be infectious and, under normal circumstances, it could be expected to produce a potentially fatal illness. The first subject of this extreme experimentation was an 8-year-old boy.

In May 1796, he treated this child with material he took from the hand of an infected dairymaid. Sure enough, the boy became slightly ill—developing fever, headaches, and loss of appetite. He was well again a day or two later. After an interval of 1 or 2 months, Jenner inoculated the boy *again* with smallpox material, taken from the pustule of someone suffering from the full-blown disease. Miraculously, the child remained well! Jenner continued these experiments on and off over the next 3 years, firming up the data and reinforcing his conviction that vaccination was in fact a powerful preventive tool for smallpox.

With hindsight, we might share our ethical repugnance at this frank exploitation of the poor, minors, and people in no position to give consent. But Jenner mollified any potential critics by pointing out that the poor received neither the protection of God nor the protection of English society. But his later acts belie even this questionably genteel notion. To prove that his challenge inoculations were actually exposing the children to a bona fide risk of smallpox, Jenner needed a control: To produce one, he intentionally infected an *un*vaccinated patient with smallpox pustular matter. The patient became ill—and presumably suffered at least all of the disfiguring ravages of the full-blown disease. We do not know if he died. Surely this was an ethical breach even by eighteenth century standards! But Jenner's use of naturally attenuated, pustular material, a process known as variolation, became the benchmark against which all other vaccines were measured.

Perhaps understandably given the stakes involved, Jenner's original discovery was greeted with skepticism by the medical profession. By 1807, first Bavaria and then other German prefectures permitted vaccination to be done. One hundred and sixty three years later, in 1970, the successful campaign to eradicate smallpox was undertaken in earnest, leading some 20 years later to the full extermination of the virus from humankind. In 1997, the World Health Organization destroyed the last vestiges of this disease by incinerating the remaining cultures of the smallpox virus.

RABIES

This dramatic discovery was followed by Louis Pasteur's experimentation to develop a vaccine for rabies in the late 1880s. Like Jenner, Pasteur, without ethical concern, vaccinated the poor—and eventually his own children—with rabies material passed through chicken spinal cords. As part of this work, Pasteur cultured bacteria and showed that over time he could "attenuate" or weaken them, making it possible to secure immunization material from even previously pathogenic cultures of bacteria. These developments were greeted with increasing enthusiasm in an industrialized world plagued with contagious diseases that flourished in the confines and dense quarters of the working classes. Indeed, in the mid-1900s, the United States and all of Europe achieved remarkable reductions in the incidence of diseases like whooping cough, diphtheria, measles, and mumps, which only a few decades earlier caused much illness and death among the countries' children.

DIPHTHERIA AS A CASE STUDY

In the early 1900s, one in ten children in the United States were routinely getting diphtheria, a serious upper respiratory infection with a 10 percent mortality rate. Together with TB, whooping cough, measles, and tetanus, these industrial ravages killed over 200,000 people a year in the United States in this period. So prevalent were these diseases that most people who lived in urban settings and survived the early ravages of disease carried a remarkable degree of immunity against subsequent infection. In a typical urban setting, 70–80 percent of dwellers over the age of 15 could be expected to be immune to diphtheria, solely from their almost ubiquitous exposure to the bacterium *Corynebacterium diphtheriae.*[2] Unfortunately, as we have seen with hepatitis and herpesviruses, "successful" recovery from the disease does not ensure eradication of the causative agent. Most individuals who have vaccine-induced immunity, and many with natural immunity, emerge as carriers of the diphtheria bacterium.[3]

With the advent of a widely used vaccine against diphtheria in the 1950s, tremendous reductions in attack rate were achieved both here and abroad, particularly in the war-ravaged Soviet Union. But with the breakup of the Soviet Union in the early 1990s, vaccinations underwent a precipitous decline. As a new generation of children grew up without vaccination in the New Independent States of the former Soviet Union, they experienced a massive upsurge in disease prevalence. The data are shown in Figure Five. According to WHO, between 1990 and 1995, 90 percent of all of the cases of diphtheria *in the world* were reported from this region!

Ironically, the renewed vulnerability of the Soviet people to diphtheria was in part related to an unrecognized but insidious effect of prior mass vaccination programs. The widespread use of a vaccine had led to a diminution of the prevalence of the causative organism. But because vaccine-produced immunity is short-lived, 20–60 percent of adults who might otherwise have been permanently protected as a result of surviving a bona fide natural case of diphtheria lost their vaccine-related im-

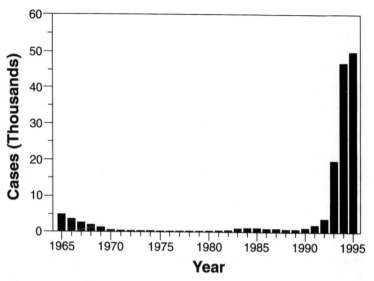

Five.   Reports of diphtheria from the New Independent States of the Soviet Union, 1965 to the present. Note the radical increase in reported cases commencing about 1993, following the cessation of mandatory childhood immunizations in the period 1991–1992. This period coincided with the breakup of the former Soviet Union. Redrawn from Morbidity and Mortality Weekly Report, *copyright © Massachusetts Medical Society, 1996. Reprint rights granted.*

munity and became vulnerable again to infection. Then, when vaccinations stopped and the bacterium reasserted itself among the Soviet children, diphtheria could also strike the previous generation of partially protected adults. This state of affairs has proven disastrous with the breakdown of vaccination programs in the former Soviet Union between 1990 and 1994 (see Figure Five).

It is well to remember that prior to the advent of mass vaccinations in the late 1950s, the Soviet Union had a catastrophic rate of diphtheria. In 1955, 104,138 cases were reported in just the state of Russia alone. By 1965, diphtheria had been all but eliminated: In the entire Soviet Union only 4691 cases were reported, an incidence rate of

2.0 per 100,000. By 1989, there were only 839 cases.[4] But beginning in 1990, when vaccination programs were reaching only about two-thirds of the children in the Soviet states, diphtheria began an inexorable increase, first in Russia and then other Soviet republics. As shown in Figure Five, exponential increases began in 1990–1991, culminating in 47,808 new cases in 1994. In the first half of 1995 this attack rate continued, with a two- to threefold increase over the previous year. About 2.8 percent of the cases in 1994 proved fatal.[5]

The present epidemic began in Moscow in 1990, allegedly among workers in a military construction battalion. It has since swept across 13 time zones, from St. Petersburg to Vladivostok, eventually affecting about 50 in every 100,000 people. (An attack rate of less than 1 in 100,000 is presently the rule in the United States.)

Beginning in 1994, in an effort to stem the tide of illness, vaccination rates were increased 88.1 percent. Thirty million doses of adult-formulation tetanus and diphtheria toxoids were administered in 1994 alone. Despite this massive effort, less than half of the 114 million adults in the Russian Federation received vaccine through 1994, leaving an unacceptably high attack rate, especially in the Ukraine. In countries like Georgia, Azerbaijan, and Armenia, the epidemic was exacerbated because of large numbers of displaced persons and severe shortages of energy and rubles. The highest rates of diphtheria are in Tajikistan and approach 1 per 1000.

The factors that contribute to the epidemic transmission of diphtheria are the same in the Ukraine and Russia as elsewhere: high population density and the movement of people into urban centers from outlying areas, a common pattern for the emergence of disease since the days of the Justinian plague in 571–576 AD. Once diphtheria emerged in the cities, it spread to the countryside, taking a surprisingly high toll among the adult population aged

40–49. In Lithuania and Turkmenistan, the fatality rate reached 23 percent, making it the most serious disease to strike the former Soviet Union since World War II.

The key element in fomenting this massive epidemic, according to a research team investigating the outbreak, is the presence of a large number of highly susceptible children and adults.[6] Reduced childhood vaccinations also contributed to the epidemic. The key social and demographic features of the epidemic—its occurrence in sectors with major socioeconomic instability and a deteriorating health infrastructure—are also likely contributing factors to the outbreak.

LESSONS OF EPIDEMIOLOGY AND IMMUNITY

One paradoxical factor that permitted the exacerbation of the disease is particularly ominous. It is likely that starting and *then stopping* vaccination set in train the epidemic by permitting the emergence of a vulnerable adult population. By breaking the previous cycle of natural childhood disease that would be followed by long-lasting adult immunity, childhood immunization set the stage for the emergence of an adult population only partially protected from infection. With the waning of the short-lived vaccine-induced immunity, a whole population of vulnerable adults was left exposed to possible disease.

This pattern is remarkably similar to the one that exacerbated measles in the United States, leading to a resurgence of measles outbreaks on college campuses in the United States in the 1970s and 1980s. By largely eradicating natural, childhood measles through vaccination of a large but not complete portion of the childhood population, a cohort of young adults emerged who "skipped their shots"—and thereby missed both natural childhood infection and any induced immunity. As shown by the

outbreak of near-fatal measles on some college campuses
in the 1980s and 1990s, this new group is at dramatically
heightened risk of serious adult illness.

CHILDHOOD VACCINATION

According to the Centers for Disease Control and
Prevention, the solution to this disturbing resurgence of
disease will depend on a dramatic increase in the coverage of children with routine doses of the trivalent acellular version of the vaccine known as DTP (diphtheria,
tetanus, and pertussis) and a redoubling of efforts to
ensure that measles, mumps, and rubella vaccines are
given to every schoolchild. At least 95 percent coverage
with four doses of DPT is needed along with a single
dose of a broad-spectrum age-appropriate formulation of
diphtheria toxoid. This last measure alone would go a
long way toward eradicating this scourge from the population.

As recently as the autumn and winter of 1995–1996,
many of the countries in the Soviet Federation still lacked
sufficient doses of vaccine to stem the tide of the diphtheria epidemic just described. Because many countries in
the developed world also have populations susceptible to
diphtheria, the movement of epidemic diphtheria from
the Soviet Federation to North America and Europe is a
real possibility. It would be a true tragedy if this disease,
like tuberculosis, were once again allowed to gain a foothold. Particularly with the advent of the safer acellular
(i.e., cell-free) pertussis preparations, DPT shots appear
to be a particularly valuable weapon against childhood
disease. But the secondary effects of this shift to near-
total reliance on killed vaccines, particularly for asthma,
should not be ignored.

Similar inroads can be made against childhood middle ear infections and meningitis through use of new

vaccines. In particular, improved coverage with *Haemophilus influenzae* type 6 conjugate vaccines could greatly reduce the frequency of meningitis particularly and systemic infection in childhood generally.[7]

MISTAKES AND MISCONCEPTIONS

Along with other myths about the immune system, it is commonly misunderstood that vaccines work to prevent infection by producing a kind of "sterilizing" immunity in which all invading organisms are met with instant death. In fact, immunologist Barry Bloom of the Howard Hughes Medical Institute in New York City has observed that relatively few vaccines actually prevent infection of host cells.[8] Bloom emphasizes that vaccines protect the host in at least two ways: by encouraging a kind of accelerated "mop-up" operation by the immune system that reduces the effective number of newly invading viral or bacterial cells, and by limiting or preventing a second infection by reinforcing the body's early response. Vaccines also shift the balance of immune responses in the body's favor, reducing the damaging sequelae from infection and reducing the likelihood of transmission of the offending agent. To avoid creating a recurrence of the events that led to vaccine-associated allergies in Africa, the key is to provide early *long-lasting* immunity that stimulates the appropriate arm of the immune system (usually Th1 cells) and thereby mimics the natural course of infection.

AIDS AS AN EXAMPLE

Bloom points out that even a modestly effective vaccine, such as one that achieved only a 20–40 percent protection rate, would be a tremendous boon in the case of AIDS. It would be acceptable only if it did not, of course, produce a variant of AIDS itself that might occur from attenuated vaccines or increase the risk of natural disease. He notes that political forces are working to drive investments in AIDS control toward chemotherapeutic products, leaving too few resources for vaccine development.[8] These pharmaceutical approaches to HIV control are, in my opinion, likely to promise a swifter, albeit more short-lived, victory over HIV. Such pharmaceutical approaches are expensive and intrinsically limited by the emergence of viral resistance. Within a few short hours of giving AZT, literally millions of new viruses are produced even as others are killed. Darwinian selection all but ensures that some of the surviving viral particles will have resistance to the chemical. The current spate of protease inhibitors combined with more traditional therapeutic agents will likely help more patients. But resistant and recombinant strains to even these new agents are likely to prove the norm, spelling doom for even the most radical therapies. In my view, for most of the at-risk population around the world, only a vaccine will promise the lasting immunity necessary to provide meaningful protection against AIDS.

A RATIONALE FOR INCREASED VACCINATION

Vaccines have been developed for a surprisingly large number of diseases that afflict the developed world but only a smaller list in the developing one. In addition to the availability of immunization against measles, rubella, and mumps, childhood vaccinations and oral immunization are now routine for diphtheria, pertussis (whooping cough), and polio. As we saw, the newest polio regime, which includes a mixture of oral attenuated virus (Sabin) preceded by two treatments with the killed version developed by Salk, is intended to limit the likelihood of immunologically depressed children from contracting a full-blown case of polio from the attenuated strain.

Vaccines are also available for *Haemophilus influenzae* type B, the cause of many childhood ear infections and smaller numbers of meningitis. So-called "polyvalent" vaccines are also on the market. The pneumococcal vaccines, which include at least 20 different genetic forms or serotypes of potential pneumonia-causing organisms, are particularly important for protecting patients who lack a functional spleen (e.g., those with sickle-cell anemia) or the elderly, who are at especially high risk for pneumonia.

Despite the dramatic success of vaccines in reducing or in some cases (as with polio) virtually eliminating disease, major drug manufacturers have been reluctant to underwrite their development. This is related in part to the concern over liability but also to the relatively long lag time between research, development, and scaleup for mass production. Many vaccines, like those for cholera or malaria, are intrinsically limited in the amount of return that can be expected financially—and because they presently require refrigeration to ensure freshness, they might not get where they are most needed, particularly in the Third World.

A VACCINE FOR TB?

Given the extraordinary prevalence of TB worldwide (affecting some 90 million people in 1995), one would think that the availability of a vaccine to limit its spread would be embraced with open arms. An age-old standby—bacillus Calmette-Guérin (BCG)—has been available for over 40 years. This bacterial strain was developed by two French researchers at the turn of the century at the Pasteur Institute in Paris. Following Louis Pasteur's lead, which demonstrated the weakened pathogenicity of microorganisms that had been subjected to repeated passage, Calmette and Guérin passed virulent bovine TB (*Mycobacterium bovis*) from rabbit to rabbit for 20 generations until they had a strain that would not cause disease. The resulting live, attenuated bacterium became known as BCG.

Over the ensuing decades, many countries—especially Canada—adopted this strain as part of their national immunization program. For children, an early vaccination between the ages of 2 and 5 years can produce lasting immunity, protecting over 80 percent of those immunized from acquiring TB over their lifetimes.[9] Although data on later programs are ambiguous, they suggest only marginal protection for adolescents or adults treated with BCG *after* childhood. Clearly, late BCG immunizations are not as protective as the childhood ones, and BCG administered to adults is not a solution to the TB problem.[10] (Ironically, BCG vaccination *is* remarkably effective in protecting against leprosy, which is caused by a mycobacterium related to the TB one.)

For these and related reasons, a prominent advisory committee to the CDC recommended that BCG *not* be routinely given in the United States.[11] Rare serious complications such as fatal disseminated BCG disease affect between 0.06 and 1.56 cases per million doses of administered vaccine, a very low death rate this group nonetheless found unacceptable. As the deaths were almost entirely confined to severely immunocompromised hosts, it is likely that close surveillance (for instance to ensure that no HIV+ persons were given live vaccine) would ensure even more minimal adverse effects. But even the World Health Organization has recommended childhood vaccination of HIV+ children only in countries where TB is endemic.

Given these data and the fact that TB rates are rising among the poor and ethnically diverse populations of major U.S. cities like New York and Chicago, it was surprising that the CDC did not recommend an immediate improvement in vaccine design, including the addition of a suitable immune stimulant or adjuvant. Certainly in urban areas like these, childhood vaccination of at-risk populations may make great sense, though a certain risk does exist. Instead, the CDC recommended that only ultrahigh-risk children, such as those who cannot be removed from a household with a treatment-noncompliant tuberculous adult, be given the vaccine. As an alternative, the CDC supports the continued reliance on antibiotics as prophylactic treatment. This may be a big mistake.

In urging that rifampin or isoniazid be used to prevent progression of latent disease after a positive tuberculin test, the CDC has inadvertently encouraged still further epidemiological problems. As with the current enthusiasm for chemotherapy for AIDS, such a prophylactic strategy is questionable because it encourages the emergence of multiple-drug-resistant TB. By using often suboptimal doses of antibiotics preemptively, physicians run the risk of selecting for strains able to resist the killing effects of the drugs. The final CDC rationale for limiting BCG vaccinations in the United States is that most people would develop antibodies after their vaccination and thereby render a tuberculin test inaccurate. In my opinion, such a position is hardly a reason to deny a potentially lifesaving boost to the immune system's response to TB.

When considered against the direct and indirect benefits of BCG vaccination, the CDC's decision is questionable. The immune activation achieved by a BCG vaccine may afford a generalized protection against other diseases, perhaps even against some tumors. In contrast, any risk of adverse effects is slight. Although all of the data are not in, some 1960s Canadian data suggested reductions in leukemia incidence in BCG-vaccinated children. But such nonspecific bolstering of immune defenses generally is given short shrift in the United States. Some Canadian clinicians with whom I have spoken believe that such elevation of immune response has a generally salubrious effect on the health of their population and accounts in part for a morbidity and mortality pattern that is better than that of the U.S. population. While this proposition is virtually untestable, given the plethora of confounding variables, a general endorsement of BCG by world governments like Canada should at least prompt more serious inquiry in the United States.

Over three billion doses of BCG vaccine have been given to millions of people worldwide, with an extraordinarily low incidence of side effects, usually limited to pain and swelling at the inoculation site, and more rarely, swollen lymph nodes. Given the resurgence of TB both nationally and globally, greater reliance on this vaccine— or better, an improved version would appear warranted.

Many researchers believe that we now know enough about the nature of the immune reaction engendered by BCG and its component parts to develop a much more effective vaccine.[12] We now know that even a single TB bacterial protein antigen can provide a powerful, protective immunity against TB infection, at least in animals. We also know which cells carry out the protective effect: They are the cytotoxic antigen-specific T-cell population of the Th1 arm. And we know that administration of even a raw DNA that codes for a BCG-related antigen can provide powerful immunity,[13] an approach that should be tried in AIDS.

COMMENTARY

Given the extraordinary prevalence of this most common cause of death from infectious disease, it is remarkable that the health world has not paid more attention to developing an immunological control program.

A common core to such programs would be an increased reliance on new conjugate vaccines that combine several different bacterial antigens. So-called capsular polysaccharide (CP) vaccines that utilize the nonliving coating of bacteria have already proven remarkably effective in limiting infectious disease caused by pneumococci and meningococcal bacteria, especially in the armed forces. These developments were considered so valuable to public health that the innovators of CP vaccines, Drs. John B. Robbins, Rachel Schneerson, Porter Anderson, and David H. Smith, were given the Albert Lasker Clinical Medicine Award in 1996 for their discoveries.

These recommendations add fuel to a simmering fire that pits a powerful faction of public health officials and pharmaceutical manufacturers believing in chemoprophylaxis and treatment against a pitifully small number of outspoken critics, such as myself, who believe that with proper precautions to avoid vaccine-related complications and attention to secondary effects like asthma, vaccines are a powerful and effective means of disease control. Of course a major caveat illustrated by the Russian experience is that once used, one cannot abruptly forgo continuing reliance without courting the risk of disease resurgence. But unlike antibiotics whose overuse guarantees further reliance and dependency through the emergence of resistant strains, vaccines provide a natural and ideally lasting immunity that affords populationwide protection. In fact, there is agreement in most medical circles that vaccines are the most cost-effective medical intervention in our arsenal against conventional illness.

THE POLITICS OF VACCINE DEVELOPMENT

Despite their proven efficacy and value in limiting the prevalence of childhood disease and protecting adults and the elderly from serious debilitating disease, factors like liability and permanence of effect have dampened the enthusiasm of many governments and pharmaceutical companies for embarking on new vaccine development enterprises. In 1986, the drug industry promoted a law that greatly reduces their liability in the event of adverse vaccine reactions but the industry remains vastly under-invested in vaccine-related research.

AIDS is a case in point. In 1995 developing countries spent only 1/20th of 1 percent of their budgets allotted to AIDS last year on vaccine research. Slightly better numbers are available for the United States. In the same period, a meager 10 percent of the budget allotted to NIH to combat AIDS went into vaccine development. Yet, in the NIH view, basic research on vaccines generally is "vastly insufficient."[14] To be sure, in the early heydays of AIDS, new vaccines were rushed to the testing stage but with little or no basic understanding of the mechanism of probable mode of efficacy. In part, for this reason none of the original 15 HIV vaccine prototypes was found to be sufficiently effective to move on to clinical trials. Only in December 1996 did NIH make a full commitment to testing, appointing Nobel laureate David Baltimore to head up the first concerted effort at developing an AIDS vaccine.

It is my hope that this recent recognition "to give immunity a chance" signals a shift toward elevating the immune system to its rightful place as the mainstay of our resistance to disease. Presently these efforts are being stymied by fears, both rational and not, that vaccines extract too high a price in the form of adverse side effects to warrant widespread use.[10] Successful rejuvenation of immunological approaches to prevention will require both a more sophisticated understanding of what the immune system can and cannot do and suitable educational strategies to bring this new perspective to the public.

SIXTEEN

$\mathcal{T}$HE TAO AND THE IMMUNE SYSTEM

This new perspective will require a radical reconstruction of our bodies. In a world where humans constantly strive to control their lives, the immune system is no exception. We develop powerful drugs to knock it down, use certain chemotherapies that damage it, and allow the proliferation of toxic chemicals that erode its strength. We have tried to end-run it through overuse of antibiotics. And we indiscriminately take every nostrum offered that suggests it will somehow be improved. In AIDS, our direct efforts to master it through crudely prepared vaccines have had unfortunate side effects. When we have tried to control it, we have often made disease worse. In our urge to figure out what to do to "help" immunity, we neglect to inquire what, if anything, it needs.

Among the roots of these misplaced efforts is the belief in the perfectibility of nature. This precept has led us to expect both too much and too little of our immune capabilities. We want the immune system to repel every possible incursion of natural pathogens and to respond to human-made substances as if they arose in the natural world. At the same time, we ignore our intrinsic immune strengths and resist bona fide efforts to reinforce them. In organ transplantation, we are still bent on abolishing re-activity altogether when selective tolerance would be a better strategy. When relatively new diseases like asthma and certain forms of autoimmunity strike, we have tried to suppress them rather than redirect their underlying cause.

Although these are all admittedly highly complex problems, some of these often clumsy and shotgun re-sponses stem from ignorance. In our dealings with the immune system, we have missed the Taoist precept that the more we interfere with the balance in the natural world, the more disease and disorder arise. Perhaps it would be well to remember, if left alone, the immune system is wonderfully adept at restoring internal balance. We could also recognize that intrinsic immune capa-bilities and the extraordinary complexity of the external world sometimes call for a period of watchful waiting during which natural healing can occur. A case in point are childhood ear infections, long-recognized abroad in places like Holland as generally self-correcting without antibiotics, though this is not to say parents should shun all drugs in a worsening situation. The roots of this wis-dom are not hard to find.

In its day-to-day encounters with the natural world, the immune system anticipates an enormous number of varieties of antigenic experience and recognizes those that pose genuine challenges to bodily integrity. This sys-tem distinguishes potential disease-causing organisms from those that are beneficial and partitions the natural world into substances it reacts to and those it will ignore. Its "wisdom" in doing so is not so much intentional as a wonderfully adaptive, nondirected system.

It is in this sense that the immune system most closely resembles the philosophy of Taoism. One of the most important and ineffable Taoist precepts is *wu-wei* (woo-way), a method of achieving goals through goallessness. The great masters like Lao-tzu and Chuang-tzu or the Taoist poet Li Po exemplified this standard in their writings and actions. To achieve their goals, these philosophers practiced a kind of detachment. The Way of Tao does not force or interfere with things but lets them work in their own way. The immune system achieves much of its own goals through just such a process. Instead of waiting to make antibodies against new pathogens and directing attacks accordingly, the immune system puts out millions upon millions of potential reactant cells, much as a spider spins a web of great complexity in anticipation of its prey. This wondrous system works in much the same way, preparing to deal with adversity and individual threats by not focusing on any one of them in advance.

In keeping with the philosophy of Lao-tzu, the immune system maintains its "edge" by not being too sharp. Much of its remarkable adaptability is lodged in its imperfectness. To ensure the greatest range of response possible, the immune system does not start out with finely honed cells, primed to make specific antibodies. Rather, as we have seen, it is designed to evolve rapidly after contact with a foreign threat, shaping its reactivity as it "learns" what the invader looks like. Neither the antibodies it produces nor the cytotoxic cells it first generates are "perfect" in their molecular design or destructive prowess. By allowing these attributes to be acquired after contact with an antigen, the immune system permits perfection to be achieved in stages, in keeping with Taoist precepts.

The immune system also has no will or intention of its own. It neither loves the body nor hates its enemies. It quietly culls from its ranks any cells that might recognize the self and thereby reduces the risk of inadvertent attacks that might injure the body. But being imperfect, it can fail. When failure occurs, the error may be readjusted or, if the imbalance persists, full-blown autoimmune disease may flare. It encourages the proliferation of its cells if they contact foreign materials but does not know if these contacts are friendly or harmful. Hence, poison oak, allergies, and asthma may each arise as accidental carryovers from past adaptive responses once directed at bona fide threats to well-being.

The wisdom of the Tao also recognizes that being in and part of the world is essential to life. When Lao-tzu declared, "One disease, long life; no disease, short life," he may have inadvertently captured a truism of the immune system as well. Unless and until the immune system is permitted to have contact with the inimical forces of the real world, it cannot offer the protection that is needed for longevity. Denying access of the immune system to naturally occurring disease-causing organisms, as evidenced by the spate of allergies and asthma in such protected populations, may deny immunity the opportunity for normal development.

COUNTERINTUITIVENESS

As with Taoism itself, much about the immune system runs counter to our preconceived ideas and intuitions about health and well-being. Rather than eradicating all disease-causing organisms, immunity often permits some surviving pathogens to stay safely ensconced within us. The same system is prepared to fight a fetus growing in the confines of the womb but won't unless provoked by abnormal pathology. The immune system's much vaunted role in controlling cancer is also less than perfect, as some immune reactions will stimulate rather than inhibit tumor growth.[1]

At the root of our misbeliefs about immunity is the assumption that it is a perfect defensive system that always has the body's best interest at heart. If what I have postulated in this book proves true, the immune cells may actually have their *own* survival "in mind" when they organize resistance within the body. As such, inadvertent damage through autoimmune reactions might best be handled through re-education of wayward cells, and not blunt attack.

In keeping with this view, the immune system does not know the difference between self and non-self except as it blunders into cell markers from the body in the thymus during its own vulnerable building period. Those that make such contact die, leaving the system temporarily without the cellular assailants to go after body tissues. But like its Taoist counterpart, the immune system is simply disinterested. It does not care about good or evil, health or disease. It simply does its genetically ordained job of eliminating things it does not recognize and ignoring the rest of the world. This view is, of course, not universally shared. In one researcher's view, for instance, the immune system evolved to "combat" infection and to recognize so-called "danger molecules."[2]

Another misconception is that the immune system is hellbent on destruction all of the time. Parasitic, bacterial, and viral invaders are to be annihilated indiscriminately. Of course, were this to happen routinely, damage from immune-caused inflammation and disease symptoms from immunological chemical mediators would be the rule, not the exception. We now have a better idea of why, on occasion, many of the body's worst "enemies" are accommodated by the immune system. Among these are some hepatitis (especially the newly discovered hepatitis G) and herpesviruses that reach a kind of steady state in the host, neither causing disease nor inciting flagrant immune attacks. When such reactions do occur, serious illness is as likely as cure. This state of détente applies to many parasites and microbes like the TB bacillus where sometimes an immune assault can be as damaging as noninvolvement. For these and related diseases, an overpowering immune response often does as much damage as good. As we saw with the lymphochoriomeningitis virus, in many circumstances there may be no disease at all without an immune attack.

The lesson here may be profoundly important. As with the Taoist adage about responding to an enemy's advances, "Force should never be opposed by force," it may be that sometimes the best use of the immune system is to call on it sparingly. As evolutionary biologist S. Ohno of the University of California Davis has declared, "To attack infected cells in which viruses are in the quiescent state of symbiosis with the host is the ultimate folly."[3]

Nor is it self-evident that we can expect a cure by subjecting cancer cells routinely to immune assault. As we saw in the chapter on cancer and immunity, under some circumstances tumor cells thrive under an immune attack. And the newest data from the work of Hammond show that some tumors actually do better (for them) when under immune attack, becoming progressively more malignant as they survive the silver bullets of immune cells. By contrast, in *nonaggressive* immune environments, some tumors will progress much more slowly toward full-blown malignancy.[4]

A NEW VISION

All of this suggests the value of a new perspective on immunity, one that incorporates the Taoist view. In this new view, an immune system that accommodates to rather than vanquishes its targeted "enemies" may sometimes be more valuable to the body. Obviously, this is true in pregnancy, where the fetus can best be supported when the body is not provoked into unbridled immune attack. Some immune responses that stop short of complete destruction may do less damage than ones that annihilate an invading organism. On those occasions where pathogens are "taken prisoner" by macrophages in a kind of reverse Trojan horse gambit, the body may be spared toxins and a flood of released microorganisms. As we saw with TB, serious disease results only when a full-scale "counter-terrorist" attack unleashes the prisoners. The message of all of this seems to be some pathogens may be best controlled when they are pressed back to acceptable levels and not eradicated down to the last cell.

Should we acquire the wisdom of how to modulate this delicate system, such as through a detailed understanding of the feedback loops controlled by cytokines, we will undoubtedly be blessed with unheard-of biological power. We will know more about the factors that lead to the trajectory of immune decline that accelerates with age. We may learn how to restore flagging or lost immune function, especially in chronic diseases like AIDS. Vaccines will cease being hit-or-miss affairs. Immunizations will be made routinely to ensure fertility—or to prevent it. Simple biological factors will be isolated that sustain or augment immune activities. And feedback loops will be encouraged rather than jammed, as can happen in chronic stress. Perhaps, like other components of our bodies, the immune system needs to know the rest of the body is alive and well so as not to overreact.

Although many herbal remedies and homeopathic medicines like echinacea can tone or strengthen the immune system, most others provide unproven and untested means of restoring flagging immune reactions. Indeed, it is one of our most common mistakes to rely on external medications to help immunity. A simple means of maintaining immune strength is open to all who would avail themselves: moderate exercise. The simple expedient of doing Tai Chi ch'uan each day is an age-old Taoist regimen now recognized as a healthy means of toning the immune system. In men, simple exercise programs clearly heighten immune responsiveness.[5] In keeping with the Taoist adage of prevention, this beneficial effect is best seen in those who exercise before they get ill, as suggested by data from AIDS patients.[6,7]

A SYSTEM IN BALANCE

Findings such as these suggest that additional natural factors linking the immune system to the general vitality of the body and mind will be identified and reinforced. Once the rudiments of this knowledge are gleaned, it may be possible to arrest other age-related declines within the immune system's powers. The key to success here will be in learning how to control autoimmune reactions, like those directed against the thyroid gland, that become more common with age and how to sustain the endocrine factors that promote rather than dampen immune responsiveness and sustain the vitality of a waning thymus gland.

Indeed, one of the paradoxes of immunity is that hyperaggressive immune responses, particularly those directed against the body itself, signal a failing system. It is a Taoist maxim that a frightened warrior will reveal his impending defeat by overextending himself. So it is that an immune system that is overstimulated by a chronic "threat" may begin to turn on itself. The autoimmune reactions that progress with advancing middle age may prove to be early warning signs of such failure.

With the advent of more sensitive immunological controls, it should prove possible to restore the normal checks and balances of the immune system to stave off these events, just as minute doses of insulin help to correct age-dependent diabetes.[8] Other factors like human growth hormone will also likely be found to play a dramatic role in immunological homeostasis, fending off the natural diminution of immunological power with age.

Even as we need to work toward preserving immune strength, we must be careful not to push it too far. Danger exists in expecting too much of our immune systems in its "war" against microbial or cellular terrorists. As with hepatitis B and TB, an overaggressive immune system can be too much of a good thing. If survival of latent colonies of pathogens and nests of cancer cells occurs more commonly than we thought, perhaps the answer is to devise a means to "negotiate" a détente and learn to deal with such potential threats on an ongoing basis. It may be that, as with the smoldering and virtually ineradicable infection that ensues with the TB organism or hepatitis C virus, the price we may need to pay for peace is a rapprochement where we can learn to live with our enemies. Until we accept that the immune system's response to some invasions is accommodation rather than eradication, we will be doomed to fight a never-ending battle against near-invisible enemies. If the immune system's way to "win" is to relent, then perhaps we could learn to do the same. As the *Tao-te Ching* says, "That which is most yielding can overcome that which is most strong."

ZEN IN THE ART OF IMMUNITY

The immune system is thus something quite different than the image of a bristling, hypersensitive apparatus finely tuned to recognize and reject all that is not self. Although it has a modicum of such attributes, it may be at its best when it accommodates more than it opposes, accepts more than it rejects, and balances more than it abolishes. The price of such accommodation is that we may be only partially "defended" against nature, but more accepting of our own biological selves.

This new image of immunity makes it at the same time more immediately responsive to change, yet more yielding and accepting of difference than we had previously believed. And if the adages of the Taoist sages are correct, by not overextending, overexerting, or overcommitting the immune system, it may serve us longer into old age than is now the rule.

BALANCE

The view of the immune system as a balancing mechanism designed to maintain homeostasis rather than one that seeks and destroys is radical. This is so because of the way we students of medical science were taught: We learned to view the body as a collection of parts; as an entity in opposition to nature and at war with itself. In a sense, this old vision is unfortunate because for so long it stymied a view of immunity that would have recognized its ability to accommodate and integrate rather than always to destroy and annihilate. Such an outlook is more than simply a gentler view of the world. It is one more in keeping with the vision of living systems as integrated, balanced networks in constant harmony, rather than as organisms in a lifelong battle against an inimical nature.

This new view, if widely adopted by the medical establishment, is likely to permit more effective innovation and wiser use of immunity by harnessing the growing panoply of immunological modifiers and intercellular hormones to balance immune responses. It is my hope that, with time, medicine will come to recognize this model of immunity. When this happens, medical practitioners may be better equipped to encourage the regeneration of those devastated immune systems that now plague AIDS patients and victims of silicone and other environmental assaults. Once so accepted, the immune system will once again be regarded not simply as the bastion of our defense against an antagonistic world, but as a highly responsive system that ebbs and flows in response to the ever-shifting patterns of life on a beneficient planet.

$\mathscr{E}$NDNOTES

INTRODUCTION

1. See M. Lappé, Chapter 12 in *Evolutionary Medicine*, Sierra Club Books, San Francisco, CA, 1995, for documentation and discussion.
2. Ibid.
3. Susan Sontag, *Illness as Metaphor and AIDS and its Metaphors*, Doubleday Anchor Press, New York, 1995.
4. P. Jaret, "Our immune system: The wars within," *National Geographic*, June 1986, pp. 702–736.
5. D. E. Cressman, L. E. Greenbaum, R. A. DeAngelis, *et al.*, "Liver failure and defective hepatocyte regeneration in interleukin 6 deficient mice," *Science* 274: 1379–1383, 1996.

6. Barry Bloom, "A perspective on AIDS vaccines," *Science* 272: 1888–1890, 1996.

7. This post-polio syndrome has been recently documented. See M. C. Dalakas, "The post-polio syndrome as an evolved clinical entity: Definition and clinical description," *Annals of the New York Academy of Sciences* 753: 68–80, 1995.

8. See T. I. Michalek, C. Pasquinelli, S. Guilhof, and F. V. Chisari, "HIV B virus persistence after recovery from acute viral hepatitis," *Journal of Clinical Investigation* 93: 230–239, 1994.

9. B. Rehermann, C. Ferrari, C. Pasquinelli, and F. V. Chisari, "Hepatitis B virus persists for decades after patients' recovery from acute viral hepatitis despite active maintenance of a cytotoxic T-lymphocyte response," *Nature Medicine* 2: 1104–1108, 1996.

10. J. B. Wyngaarden and L. H. Smith, *Cecil Textbook of Medicine*, 17th edition, W. B. Saunders, Philadelphia, 1985.

11. This statistic is cited in *Cecil Textbook of Medicine*, Chapter XIX, Infectious Diseases, p. 1528.

12. A. D. Ericsson, "Carotid artery atherogenesis," *Raum & Zeit* 3: 15–22, 1992.

13. A. D. Ericsson, "Stroke: The immune response," *Raum & Zeit* 3: 5–10, 1992.

14. See A. Maseri, "Inflammation, atherosclerosis, and ischemic events—exploring the hidden side of the moon," *New England Journal of Medicine* 336: 1014–1015, 1997.

15. Cited by Naomi Pfeiffer, "Spectra team finds common genetic basis for syndrome," *Genetic Engineering News* 16: 28, 1996.

16. M. Hotopf, N. Noah, and S. Wessely, "Chronic fatigue and minor psychiatric morbidity after viral meningitis: A controlled study," *Journal of Neurology, Neurosurgery and Psychiatry* 60: 504–509, 1996; and P. White, S. Grover, H. Kangro, *et al.*, "The validity and reliability of the fatigue syndrome that follows glandular fever," *Psychological Medicine* 25: 917–924, 1995.

17. William R. Clark, *At War Within, the Double Edge Sword of Immunity*, Oxford University Press, New York, 1995, end piece.

CHAPTER ONE

1. R. M. Zinkernagel, "Immunosuppression by a noncytolytic virus via T cell mediated immunopathology: Implication for AIDS," *Advances in Experimental Medicine and Biology* 37: 165–171, 1995.
2. Cited in S. K. Stanley *et al.*, "Effective immunization with a common recall antigen on viral expression in patients infected with HIV1. *New England Journal of Medicine* 334: 1222–1230, 1996.
3. See A. Cumano, F. Dieterlen-Lievre, and I. Godin, "Lymphoid potential, probed before circulation in the mouse, is restricted to caudal intraembryonic splanchnopleura," *Cell* 86: 907–916, 1996.
4. J. L. Heeney, C. Brock, J. Goodsmith, *et al.*, "Immune correlates of protection from HIV infection and AIDS," *Immunology Today* 18: 4–8, 1997.
5. See V. Stephan, V. Wahn, F. LeDiest, *et al.*, "Spontaneous reversion of T-cell gene defect in atypical X-SCID," *New England Journal of Medicine* 355: 1563–1567, 1996.

CHAPTER TWO

1. See R. D. Campbell and J. Trowsdale, "A map of the human major histocompatibility complex," *Immunology Today* January 1997, insert.
2. R. M. Zinkernagel, "MHC-restricted T-cell recognition," *JAMA* 274: 1069–1071, 1995.
3. See R. J. Graff, M. A. Lappé, and G.D. Snell, "The influence of the gonads and adrenal glands on the immune response to skin grafts," *Transplantation* 7: 105–111, 1969.
4. New data offers some support for Pauling's original idea. See R. Rawls, "Chemical instruction may have a role in antibody selectivity," *Chemical and Engineering News* 16 June 1997, p. 10.
5. J. W. Kappler, N. Roehm, and P. Marrack, "T cell tolerance by clonal elimination in the thymus," *Cell* 49: 273–280, 1987; B.

Stockinger, "Neonatal tolerance mysteries solved," *Immunology Today* 17: 249, 1996.

6. See D. Adams, "How the immune system works and why it causes autoimmune disease," *Immunology Today* 17: 300–302, 1996.

7. The genetic control of this complex sequence is described in a recent article: T. Boehm, M. Nehis and B. Kyewski, "Transcription factors that control development of the thymic microenvironment," *Immunology Today* 16: 555–556, 1996.

8. See J. Kling, "Immunization of mucosal barriers leads to novel classes of vaccine products," *Genetic Engineering News* 16: 1, 21, June 15, 1996.

9. D. R. Tough, P. Borrow, and J. Sprent, "Induction of bystander T cell proliferation by viruses and type 1 interferon in vivo," *Science* 272: 1947–1950, 1996.

CHAPTER THREE

1. D. Adams, "How the immune system works and why it causes autoimmune disease," *Immunology Today* 17: 300–302, 1996.

2. See J. M. Grange, J. L. Stanford, and G. A. Rook, "Tuberculosis and cancer: Parallels in host responses and therapeutic approaches," *Lancet* 345: 1350–1352, 1995.

3. See G. M. Shearer, "Redirecting T-cell function," *Nature* 377: 16–17, 1995.

4. This second tier protection involves a special molecule known as B7 which binds to a CD 28 molecule: See F. W. Symington, W. Brady, and P.S. Linsley, "Expression and function of B7 on human epidermal Langerhans cells," *Journal of Immunology* 150: 1286–1293, 1993.

5. See for instance Chapter 69 of the *Tao-te Ching*, which describes how an army achieves its ends by balancing its response to the enemy's advances and acting without undue aggressiveness. R. G. Henneks, *Tao Te Ching*, Modern Library Edition, New York, 1989, p. 171.

6. See E. Pennisi, "Number 12 steps up to bat," *Science News* 146: 121, 1994.
7. Ibid., pp. 120–122.

CHAPTER FOUR

1. See G. Beck and G. S. Habicht, "Immunity and the invertebrates," *Scientific American* 275: 60–66, 1996.
2. See R. M. Zinkernagel, "Immunology taught by viruses," *Science* 271: 173–178, 1996.
3. See R. M. Zinkernagel, "Response" to a letter in *Science* 272: 635, 1996.
4. M.A. Lappé, "Possible significance of immune recognition of preneoplastic and neoplastic cell surfaces," *National Cancer Institute Monographs* 35: 49–55, 1972.
5. W. A. Hammond, J. R. Benfeld, H. Tesluk, *et al.*, "Tumor progression by lung cancers growing in hosts of different immunocompetence," *Cancer Journal*, 8: 130–138, 1995.
6. See letter from K. A. McKean, L. Nunney, and M. Zuk, "Immunology taught by Darwin," *Science* 272: 634–635, 1996.
7. See M. Lappé, *Evolutionary Medicine*, Sierra Club Books, San Francisco, CA, 1995.

CHAPTER FIVE

1. See W. H. Hildemann, " Some new concepts in immunological phylogeny," *Nature* 250(462): 116–129, 1974.
2. See John J. Marchalonis, *Immunity in Evolution*, Harvard University Press, Cambridge, MA, 1977, pp. 251 et supra.
3. These reactions are explained in J. G. P. Sissons, "Superantigens and infectious disease," *Lancet* 341: 1627–1628, 1993.
4. K. E. Ellerman and A. A. Like, "Staphylococcal enterotoxin-activated spleen cells passively transfer diabetes in BB/Wor rats," *Diabetes* 41: 527–532, 1992.
5. R. D. Inman, B. Chiu, M. E. Johnston, S. Vas, and J. Falk,

"HLA class 1 related impairment on IL-2 production and lymphocyte responses to microbial antigens in reactive arthritis," *Journal of Immunology* 142: 4256–4260, 1989.

CHAPTER SIX

1. M. Lappé, *Evolutionary Medicine*, Sierra Club Books, San Francisco, CA, 1995.
2. S. M. Behar and S. A. Porcelli, "The immunology of inflammatory arthritis," *Science and Medicine* 3: 12–21, 1996.
3. M. Lappé, "Silicone reactive disorder: A new autoimmune disease caused by immunostimulation and super antigens," *Medical Hypothesis*, October 1993.
4. Ibid.
5. See C. M. Black and C. P. Denton, "Overview of current therapeutic concepts," in: "Systemic sclerosis: Current pathogenic concepts and future prospects for targeted therapy," *Lancet* 347: 1453–1458, 1996.
6. See G. R. Botstein, G. K. Sherer, and E. C. LeRoy, "Fibroblast selection in scleroderma: An alternative model of fibrosis," *Arthritis and Rheumatism* 26: 189–195, 1982.
7. J. A. Snowden, J. C. Briggs, and P. M. Brodes, "Autologous blood stem cell transplantation for autoimmune disease," *Lancet* 348: 112–113, 1996.
8. C. M. Black, "Conclusion," in: "Systemic sclerosis," cited above.

CHAPTER SEVEN

1. W. T. Boyce, M. Chesney, A. Aikon, *et al.*, "Psychobiologic reactivity to stress and childhood respiratory illnesses: Results of two prospective studies," *Psychosomatic Medicine* 57: 411–422, 1995.
2. W. T. Boyce, S. Adams, I. M. Tschann, *et al.*, "Adrenocortical and behavioral predictors of immune responses to starting school," *Pediatric Research* 38: 1009–1017, 1995.
3. See Paul H. Black, "Central nervous system–immune sys-

tem interactions: Psychoneuroendocrinology of stress and its immune consequences," *Antimicrobial Agents and Chemotherapy* 38: 1–67, 1994.

4. See Hans Selye, *Stress*, Acta, Inc., Montreal, 1950.

5. See H. Selye, "A syndrome produced by diverse nocuous [sic] agents," *Nature* 138: 32–34, 1936.

6. Details of these complex interactions are neatly summarized in P.H. Black, "Psychoneuroimmunology: Brain and immunity," *Science & Medicine* November/December 1995, pp. 16–20.

7. Black, "Psychoneuroimmunology."

8. See in particular J.F. Sheridan, N. Feng, R.M. Bonneau, *et al.*, "Restraint-induced stress differentially affects anti-viral cellular and humoral immune responses in mice," *Journal of Neuroimmunology* 31: 245–255, 1991.

9. See R. Glaster and J. K. Kiecolt-Glaser (eds.), *Handbook of Human Stress and Immunity*, Academic Press, San Diego, CA, 1994.

10. W. B. Cannon, *Bodily Changes in Pain, Hunger, Fear, Rage*, Appleton & Co., New York, 1929.

11. Sheridan.

12. Reviewed in S. R. Pruett, D. K. Ensley, and P. L. Crittenden, "The role of chemical-induced stress responses in immunosuppression," *Journal of Toxicology and Environmental Health* 39: 163–192, 1993.

13. See J. O. Keith and C. A. Mitchell, "Effects of DDT and food stress on reproduction and body condition of ringed turtle doves," *Archives of Environmental Contamination and Toxicology* 25: 192–203, 1993.

14. C. Brown, W. B. Gross, and M. Ehrich, "Effects of social stress on the toxicity of malathion in young chickens," *Avian Diseases* 30: 679–682, 1986.

15. Tom Boyce, personal communication of January 17, 1997.

16. See V. M. Sanders and F. E. Powell-Oliver, "Beta adrenoceptor stimulation increases the number of antigen-specific precursor B lymphocytes that differentiate into IgM secreting cells without affecting burst size," *Journal of Immunology* 148: 1822–1828, 1992.

17. See R. Ader, D. Felten, and N. Cohen, "Interaction between

the brain and the immune system," *Annual Review of Pharmacology and Toxicology* 30: 561–602, 1990.

18. C. Surridge, "Science tracks down the training dangers," *Nature* 382: 14–15, 1996.

19. These data were summarized in a report on the 2nd Symposium of the International Society of Exercise and Immunology held in Brussels, Belgium, on November 17–18, 1995. See R. Brines, L. Hoffman-Goetz, and B. K. Pedersen, "Can you exercise to make your immune system fitter?" *Immunology Today* 17: 151–155, 1996.

CHAPTER EIGHT

1. These ideas are described in S. Greer, "Cancer and the mind," *British Journal of Psychiatry* 143: 535–543, 1983; and M.N. Swartz, "Stress and the common cold," *New England Journal of Medicine* 325: 654–655, 1991.

2. See J. K. Kiecolt-Glaser, P. T. Marucha, W. B. Malarkey, *et al.*, "Slowing of wound healing by psychological stress," *Lancet* 346: 1194–1196, 1995.

3. This case was reported in the May 4, 1996, issue of Lancet: L. Cohen, S. Mouly, P. Tassand, *et al.*, "A woman with relapsing psychosis who got better with prednisone," *Lancet* 347: 1228, 1996.

4. For a review, see D.N. Khansari, A.J. Murgo and R.E. Faith, "Effect of stress on the immune system," *Immunology Today* 11: 170–175, 1990.

5. C. C. Chen, A. S. David, H. Nunnerley, *et al.*, "Adverse life events and breast cancer: Case–control study," *British Medical Journal* 311: 1527, 1995.

6. See S. Geyer, "Life events prior to manifestation of breast cancer: A limited prospective study covering eight years before diagnosis," *Journal of Psychosomatic Research* 35: 355–363, 1991.

7. Ibid.

8. L. Xiao and P. Eneroth, "Tricyclic antidepressants inhibit human natural killer cells," *Toxicology and Applied Pharmacology* 137: 157–162, 1996.

9. See P. H. Black, "Central nervous system—immune system interactions: Psychoneuroendocrinology of stress and its immune consequences," *Antimicrobial Agents and Chemotherapy* 38: 23, 1994.

CHAPTER NINE

1. See K. Kannan, K. Senthilkumar, and B. A. Loganathan, "Elevated accumulation of tributyltin and its breakdown products in bottlenose dolphins found stranded along the U.S. Atlantic and Gulf coasts," *Environmental Science and Technology* 31: 296–301, 1997.
2. See especially R. A. Malmgren, B. E. Bennison and T. W. McKinley, "Reduced antibody titers in mice treated with carcinogenic and cancer chemotherapeutic agents," *Proceedings of the Society of Experimental Biology and Medicine* 79: 484–488, 1952.
3. See Joseph G. Vos and Henk Van Loveren, "Markers for immunotoxic effects in rodents and man," *Toxicology Letters* 82/83: 385–394, 1995.
4. See Michael I. Luster, C. Portier, D. G. Pait, *et al.*, "Risk assessment in immunotoxicology. II. Relationship between immune and host resistance tests," *Fundamental and Applied Toxicology* 21: 71–82, 1993.
5. See Michael I. Luster, A. E. Munson, P. T. Thomas, *et al.*, "Development of a testing battery to assess chemical-induced immunotoxicity: National Toxicology Program's guidelines for immunotoxicity evaluation in mice," *Fundamental and Applied Toxicology* 10: 2–19, 1988.
6. Response to questionnaire dated June 6, 1996, from Michael I. Luster, Chief, Toxicology and Molecular Biology Branch, National Institute for Occupational Safety and Health.
7. See Luster and Munson, *et al.*
8. See S. M. Levy, R. B. Herberman, J. Lee, *et al.*, "Persistently low natural killer activity, age and environmental stress as predictors of infectious morbidity," *Natural Immunity and Cell Growth Regulation* 10: 289–307, 1991.
9. H. Tryphonas, "Immunotoxicity of polychlorinated bi-

phenyls: Present status and future considerations," *Experimental and Clinical Immunogenetics* 11: 149–162, 1994.

10. Ibid.

11. See J. Raloff, "Pesticides may challenge human immunity," *Science News* 149: 149, 1996.

12. M. Potter, S. Morrison, F. Wiener, *et al.*, "Induction of plasmacytomas with silicone gel in genetically susceptible strains of mice," *Journal of the National Cancer Institute* 86: 1058–1065, 1994.

13. See C. S. Rabkin, S. Silverman, G. Tricot, *et al.*, "The National Cancer Institute Silicone Implant/Multiple Myeloma Registry," *Current Topics in Microbiology and Immunology* 210: 385–387, 1996.

14. See J. G. Vos and M. I. Luster, "Immune alterations," in: *Halogenated Biphenyls, Terphenyls, Dibenzodioxins and Related Products*, R. D. Kimbrough and M. A. Jensen (eds.), Elsevier Science Publishers, Amsterdam, pp. 285–322, 1995.

15. M. Lovik, H. R. Hohansen, P. I. Gaarder, *et al.*, "Halogenated organic compounds and the human immune system: Preliminary report on a study in hobby fishermen," in: *Toxicology—From Cells to Man*, J. P. Seiler, O. Krofotva, and V. Eybl (eds.), Springer, Berlin, 1996.

16. See S. Tanabe, H. Iwata, and R. Tatsukawa, "Global contamination by persistent organochlorines and the exotoxicological impact on marine mammals," *Science of the Total Environment* 154: 154–177, 1994.

17. R. J. Letcher, R. J. Norstrom, S. Lin, *et al.*, "Immunoquantitation and microsomal monoxygenase activities in hepatic cytochromites and chlorinated hydrocarbon contaminant levels in polar bear," *Toxicology and Applied Pharmacology* 137: 127–140, 1996.

18. Tanabe.

19. See F. Yamashia and M. Hayashi, "Fetal PCB syndrome: Clinical features, intrauterine growth retardation and possible alteration in calcium metabolism," *Environmental Health Perspectives* 9: 41–45, 1985.

20. See N. Shigematsu, S. Ishimura, R. Saito, *et al.*, "Respiratory involvement in polychlorinated biphenyls poisoning," *Environmental Research* 16: 92–100, 1978.

21. See P. H. Chen and S. T. Hsu, "PCB poisoning from toxic rice bran oil in Taiwan," in: *PCBs and the Environment*, J. S. Waid (ed.), Volume 3, CRC Press, Boca Raton, FL, 1986, pp. 207–213.

22. See K. H. Chang, K. H. Hsieh, T. P. Lee, *et al.*, "Immunologic evaluation of patients with polychlorinated biphenyl poisoning: Determination of lymphocyte subpopulations," *Toxicology and Applied Pharmacology* 61: 58–63, 1981.

23. R. Stiller-Winkler, H. Idel, G. Leng, *et al.*, "Influence of air pollution on humoral immune response," *Journal of Clinical Epidemiology* 49: 527–534, 1996.

24. See S. A. Kafafi, H. Y. Afeefy, A. H. Ali, *et al.*, "Binding of polychlorinated biphenyls to the aryl hydrocarbon receptor," *Environmental Health Perspectives* 101: 422–425, 1993.

25. S. H. Smith, V. M. Sanders, B. A. Barrett, *et al.*, "Immunotoxicological evaluation of mice exposed to polychlorinated biphenyls," *Toxicology and Applied Pharmacology* 45: 330, 1978.

26. Reviewed in Tryphonas.

27. The film starring John Ritter was aired in 1988.

28. Attributed to Sanjay S. Baliga, coauthor of *Pesticides and the Immune System: The Public Health Risks*, World Resources Institute, Washington, DC, 1996. Cited in *Chemical and Engineering News* March 18, 1996, p. 23.

29. Peter Duesberg, "Retroviruses as carcinogens and pathogens: Expectations and reality," *Cancer Research* 47: 1199–1220, 1987.

CHAPTER TEN

1. L. Thomas, "Discussion," in: *Cellular and Humoral Aspects of the Hypersensitive States*, H. S. Lawrence (ed.), Harper, New York, 1959, p. 592.

2. R. T. Prehn and J. M. Main, "Immunity to methylcholanthene induced sarcomas," *Journal of the National Cancer Institute* 18: 769–778, 1957.

3. See S. Sugiyama and R. Taketoshi, "Immunosuppression after single and multiple pulse doses of 7,12 dimethylbenz(a)anthracene in the rat," *Gann* 64: 397–400, 1973.

4. See J. K. Ball, N. R. Sinclair, and J. A. McCarter, "Prolonged immunosuppression and tumor induction by a chemical carcinogen injected at birth," *Science* 152: 650–651, 1966.

5. See M. A. Lappé and D. S. Steinmuller, "Depression of weak allograft immunity in the mouse by neonatal or adult exposure to urethan," *Cancer Research* 30: 674–678, 1970.

6. See M. A. Lappé, "Evidence for the antigenicity of papillomas induced by 3-methylcholanthrene," *Journal of the National Cancer Institute* 40: 823–846, 1968.

7. T. Stewart, S. J. Tsai, H. Grayson, *et al.*, "Incidence of de novo breast cancer in women chronically immunosuppressed after organ transplantation," *Lancet* 346: 796–799, 1995.

8. This phenomenon is known as the Hammond Effect. See W.G. Hammond, J.R. Benfield, H. Tesluk, *et al.*, "Tumor progression by lung cancers growing in hosts of different immunocompetence," *Cancer Journal* 8: 130–138, 1995.

9. H. C. Outzen, R. P. Custer, and R. T. Prehn, "Spontaneous and induced tumor incidence in germ-free nude mice," *Journal of the Reticuloendothelial Society* 17: 1–9, 1975.

10. See G. Parmiani, G. Carbone, and R. T. Prehn, "In vitro spontaneous neoplastic transformation of mouse fibroblasts in diffusion chambers," *Journal of the National Cancer Institute* 46: 261–269, 1971.

11. See for instance O. Stutman, "Immunodepression and malignancy," *Advances in Cancer Research* 22: 261–269, 1975.

12. Thomas Kuhn, *The Structure of Scientific Revolutions*, University of Chicago Press, Chicago, 1970.

13. R. T. Prehn and M. A. Lappé, "An immunostimulation theory of tumor development," *Transplantation Review* 7: 26–34, 1971.

14. See R. T. Prehn, "On the probability of effective anticancer vaccines," *Cancer Journal* 8: 284–285, 1995.

15. R. T. Prehn, "Stimulatory effects of immune reactions upon the growth of untransplanted tumors," *Cancer Research* 54: 908–914, 1994.

16. Hammond.

17. See the provocative piece by R. T. Prehn and L. M. Prehn, "The autoimmune nature of cancer," *Cancer Research* 47: 927–935, 1987.

18. See M. A. Lappé, R. G. Graff, and G. D. Snell, "The importance of target size in the destruction of skin grafts with weak incompatibility," *Transplantation* 7: 372–377, 1969.
19. C. K. Chai, "Hyperplastic growth in skin grafts of rabbits," *Journal of Heredity* 73: 304–308, 1982.
20. See C. D. Steele, R. J. Wapner, J. B. Smith, *et al.*, "Prenatal diagnosis using fetal cells isolated from maternal peripheral blood: A review," *Clinical Obstetrics and Gynecology* 39: 801–813, 1996.

CHAPTER ELEVEN

1. See M. Kasahara, M. F. Flajnik, T. Ishibasni, *et al.*, "Evolution of the major histocompatibility complex: A current overview," *Transplantation Immunology* 3: 1–22, 1995.
2. W. D. Billington, "Species diversity in the immunogenetic relationship between mother and fetus: Is trophoblast insusceptibility to immunological destruction the only essential common feature for the maintenance of allogeneic pregnancy?" *Experimental and Clinical Immunogenetics* 10: 73–84, 1993.
3. See P. M. Johnson, "Immunobiology of the human placental trophoblast," *Experimental and Clinical Immunogenetics* 10: 118–122, 1993.
4. This finding was made by R. L. Simmons and P. S. Russell, "The antigenicity of mouse trophoblast," *Annals of the New York Academy of Science* 99: 717–732, 1962.
5. See A. Tafuri, J. Alferink, P. Moller, *et al.*, "T cell awareness of paternal alloantigens during pregnancy," *Science* 270: 630–633, 1995.
6. See G. T. Waites and A. Whyte, "Effect of pregnancy on collagen induced arthritis in mice," *Clinical and Experimental Immunology* 67: 467–476, 1987.
7. L. Salter-Cid and M. F. Flajnik, "Evolution and developmental regulation of the major histocompatibility complex," *Critical Reviews in Immunology* 15: 31–75, 1995.
8. See W. P. Dmowski, "Immunological aspects of endometriosis," *International Journal of Gynecology and Obstetrics* 50 (suppl. 1): S3–S10, 1995.

9. See A. Torchinsky, A. Fein, and V. Toder, "Immunoteratology: I. MHC involvement in the embryo response to teratogens in mice," *American Journal of Reproductive Immunology* 34: 288–298, 1995.

CHAPTER TWELVE

1. See N. Cereb, C. June, and H. J. Deeg, "Effect of gamma and ultraviolet irradiation on mitogen induced intracellular calcium mobilization in human peripheral blood leukocytes," *Clinical Research* 35: 901A, 1987.
2. See D. H. Pamphilon, A. A. Alnaqdy, and T. B. Wallington, "Immunomodulation by ultraviolet light: Clinical studies and biological effects," *Immunology Today* 12: 119–123, 1991.
3. See M. J. Magee, M. L. Kripke, and S. E. Ullrich, "Inhibition of the immune response to alloantigen in the rat by exposure to ultraviolet radiation," *Photochemistry and Photobiology* 50: 193–199, 1989.
4. See A. Garssen, W. Goettsch, F. R. deGruijl, *et al.*, "UVB suppresses immunity and resistance against systemic infections in the rat," *Photochemistry and Photobiology* 57: 75S, 1993.
5. See W. Goettsch, J. Garssen, A. Deijns, *et al.*, "UV-B exposure impairs resistance to infection by Trichinella spiralis," *Environmental Health Perspectives* 102: 298–303, 1994.
6. See H. L. Gensler and H. Chen, "Enhanced growth and experimental metastasis of chemically induced tumors in UV irradiated, syngeneic mice," *Photochemistry and Photobiology* 53: 695–700, 1991.
7. See S. Yasumoto, Y. Hayashi, and L. Aurelian, "Immunity to Herpes simplex virus type 2: Suppression of virus-induced immune responses in ultraviolet B irradiated mice," *Journal of Immunology* 213: 615–620, 1987.
8. See M. S. H. Giannini, "Suppression of pathogenesis in cutaneous leishmania by UV irradiation," *Infection and Immunology* 51: 838–841, 1986.
9. Y. Denkins, I. J. Fidler, and M. L. Kripke, "Exposure of mice to UV-B radiation suppresses delayed hypersensitivity to

Candida albicans," Photochemistry and Photobiology 49: 615–620, 1989.

10. See F. P. Noonan, E. C. DeFabo, and M. L. Kripke, "Suppression of contact hypersensitivity by UV radiation and its relationship to UV-induced suppression of tumor immunity," *Photochemistry and Photobiology* 34: 683–690, 1981.

11. See E. C. DeFabo and F. P. Noonan, "Urocanic acid: On its role in the regulation of UVB-induced systemic immune suppression," in: *Effects of Changes in Stratospheric Ozone and Global Climate*, James G. Titus (ed.), Volume 2, Stratospheric Ozone, U.S. EPA, 1986.

12. Ibid.

13. See F. P. Noonan, E. C. DeFabo, and H. Morrison, "Cis-urocanic acid, a UVB irradiation product, initiates an antigen presenting cell defect in vivo," *Photochemistry and Photobiology* 43 (suppl.): 18S, 1986.

14. DeFabo.

CHAPTER THIRTEEN

1. See R. Huss, "Inhibition of cyclophilin function in HIV-1 infection by cyclosporin A," *Immunology Today* 17: 259–260, 1996.

2. See S. Haraguchi, R. A. Good, and N. K. Day, "Immunosuppressive retroviral peptides: Cyclic camp and cytokine patterns," *Immunology Today* 16: 595–598, 1995.

3. See P. B. Blair, M. L. Kripke, and M. A. Lappé, *et al.*, "Immunologic deficiency associated with mammary tumor virus infection in mice," *Journal of Immunology* 106: 364–370, 1971.

4. Ibid.

5. Ibid.

6. See S. Munro, K. L. Thomas, and M. Abu-Shaar, "Molecular characterization of peripheral receptor for cannabinoids," *Nature* 365: 61–65, 1993.

7. See P. K. Peterson, G. Gekker, C. C. Chao, *et al.*, "Cocaine potentiates HIV-1 replication in human peripheral blood mononuclear cell cultures: Involvement of transforming growth factor-beta," *Journal of Immunology* 146: 81–84, 1991.

8. See P. K. Arora, E. Fride, J. Petitto, *et al.*, "Morphine-induced immune alterations in vivo," *Cellular Immunology* 126: 343–353, 1990.

9. See R. J. McDonough, J. J. Maden, A. Falck, *et al.*, "Alteration of T and null lymphocyte frequencies in the peripheral blood of human opiate addicts: In vivo evidence for opiate receptor sites on T lymphocyte," *Journal of Immunology* 125: 2539–2543, 1980.

10. See R. M. Zinkernagel, "Are HIV-specific CTL responses salutary or pathogenic?" *Current Opinion in Immunology* 7: 462–470, 1995.

11. See J. M. Andrieu and W. Lu, "Viro-immunopathogenesis of HIV disease: Implications for therapy," *Immunology Today* 16: 5–7, 1995.

12. Huss, *loc. cit.*

13. Dan Levy, "Baboon marrow recipient thrives," *San Francisco Chronicle* December 14, 1996, pp. A14, A19.

14. Reported by S. Riddell to R. Huss; see ref. 1.

15. Huss, *loc. cit.*

16. See M. Thali, A. Kukovsky, E. Kondo, *et al.*, "Functional association of cyclophilin A with HIV-1 virions," *Nature* 372: 363–365, 1994.

17. See G. M. Shearer and M. Clerici, "Rethinking AIDS and cancer" (letter), *Science* 274: 163–164, 1996.

18. See S. Sternberg, "Course of AIDS foretold by T cells," *Science News* 151: 36, 1997.

CHAPTER FOURTEEN

1. M. Ashurst, "WHO warns that multidrug resistant TB will spread," *British Medical Journal* 313: 9, 1996.

2. J. M. Grange, J. L. Stanford, and G. A. Rook, "Tuberculosis and cancer: Parallels in host responses and therapeutic approaches," *Lancet* 345: 1350–1352, 1995.

3. See W. W. Stead, T. To, R. W. Harrison, *et al.*, "Benefit–risk considerations in preventive treatment for tuberculosis in elderly persons," *Annals of Internal Medicine* 107: 843–845, 1987.

4. See P. A. Selwyn, D. Hartel, V. A. Lewis, *et al.*, "A prospective study of the risk of tuberculosis among intravenous drug users with human immunodeficiency virus infection," *New England Journal of Medicine* 320: 545–550, 1989.

5. Thomas Mann, *The Magic Mountain*, Knopf, New York, 1953.

6. J. B. Wyngaarden and L. H. Smith, *Cecil Textbook of Medicine*, 17th edition, W. B. Saunders, Philadelphia, 1985.

7. This point is stated categorically by immunologist William R. Clark in his work, *At War Within, the Double Edged Sword of Immunity*, Oxford University Press, New York, 1995, p. 115, from which many ideas in this chapter are drawn.

8. See P. G. J. Burney, S. Chinn, and R. J. Rona, "Has the prevalence of asthma increased in children? Evidence from the national study of health and growth, 1973–1986," *British Medical Journal* 300: 1306–1310, 1990.

9. See S. O. Shaheen, P. Aaby, A. J. Hall, *et al.*, "Measles and atopy in Guinea-Bissau," *Lancet* 347: 1792–1796, 1996.

10. Randall Neustaedter, *The Vaccine Guide: Making an Informed Choice*, North Atlantic Books, Berkeley, CA, 1996, pp. 193ff.

CHAPTER FIFTEEN

1. See H. Bloch, "Edward Jenner (1749–1823): The history and effects of smallpox, inoculation and vaccination," *American Journal of Diseases of Children* 147: 772–774, 1993.

2. See W. H. Frost, "Infection, immunity and disease in the epidemiology of diphtheria, with special reference to some studies in Baltimore," *Journal of Preventive Medicine* 2: 325–343, 1925.

3. See L. W. Miller, J. J. Older, J. Drake, *et al.*, "Diphtheria immunization: Effect upon carriers and control of outbreaks," *American Journal of Diseases of Children* 123: 197–199, 1972.

4. See Centers for Disease Control and Prevention. Diphtheria outbreak—Russian Federation, 1990–1993. *MMWR* 42: 840–841, 1993; and the "Update" that appeared in *MMWR* 45: 693–697, 1996.

5. These data are presented in a review by I. R. B. Hardy, S. Dittmann, and R. W. Sutter, "Current situation and control strategies for resurgency of diphtheria in newly independent states of the former Soviet Union," *Lancet* 347: 1739–1744, 1996.

6. Ibid.

7. J. B. Robbins, R. Schneerson, P. Anderson, *et al.*, "Prevention of systemic infections, especially meningitis, caused by *Haemophilus influenzae* Type 6," *JAMA* 276: 1181–1185, 1996.

8. B. R. Bloom, "A perspective on AIDS vaccines," *Science* 272: 1888–1890, 1996.

9. These data are summarized in the publication, "The role of BCG vaccine in the prevention and control of tuberculosis in the United States," a joint statement by the Advisory Council for the Elimination of Tuberculosis and the Advisory Committee on Immunization Practices, U.S. Department of Health and Human Services, CDC, *MMWR* 45: 1–14, 1996.

10. See I. M. Orme, "Prospects for new vaccines against tuberculosis," *Trends in Microbiology* 3: 401–404, 1995.

11. Ibid.

12. See P. W. Roche, J. A. Triccas, and N. Winter, "BCG vaccination against tuberculosis: Past disappointments and future hopes," *Trends in Microbiology* 3: 397–401, 1995.

13. R. E. Tascon, M. J. Colston, S. Ragno, *et al.*, "Vaccination against tuberculosis by DNA injection," *Nature Medicine* 2: 888–898, 1996.

14. Cited in H. R. Shephard, "Still needed: An AIDS vaccine," *Wall Street Journal* December 3, 1996, p. A22.

CHAPTER SIXTEEN

1. See R. T. Prehn and L. M. Prehn, "Immunostimulation of cancer versus immunosurveillance," *Medicina* (Buenes Aires) 56 (Suppl. 1): 65–73, 1996.

2. See P. Matzinger, "Tolerance, danger and the extended family," *Annual Review of Immunology* 12: 991–1045, 1994.

3. See S. Ohno, "MHC evolution and development of a recog-

nition system," *Annals of the New York Academy of Science* 712: 13–19, 1994.

4. See W. G. Hammond, J. R. Benfield, H. Tesluk, *et al.,* "Tumor progression by lung cancers growing in hosts of different immunocompetence," *Cancer Journal* 8: 130–138, 1995.

5. See R. Brines, L. Hoffman-Goetz, and B. K. Pedersen, "Can you exercise to make your immune system fitter?" *Immunology Today* 17: 255–259, 1996.

6. H. Ullum, cited in Brines.

7. A. Laperrier, cited in Brines.

8. New advances in treating autoimmune disease have concentrated on restoring the immune system's homeostasis. See J. Isaacs, "Immune system harnessed for therapy," *Lancet* 349: 1674, 1997.

INDEX

Acquired immunodeficiency
    syndrome (AIDS) (*cont.*)
  mutations in, 33
  mysteries of, 41
  pathogenesis of, 220–222
  pregnancy and, 208
  progression, 226*t*
  T cells and, 27, 59, 234
  tuberculosis and, 28, 220,
      236, 238
  tuberculosis vaccine and,
      259
  UV light and, 215
  vaccine for, 10, 256–257,
      263
ACTH, 135
Adams, Duncan, 70
Adaptive immune system,
    65–66, 71
Addison's disease, 120*t*, 140,
    153
Adrenal gland, 48, 133, 134,
    140, 147
Adrenaline, 135, 156
Adrenaline surge, 137–138
Adrenocorticosteroids, 49
Africa, 220, 221, 256
African Americans, 21
Agency for Toxic Substance
    Disease Registry, 166
Agent Orange, 174, 175, 180
Agent provocateur analogy,
    124
Aging, 30
AIDS: *See* Acquired
    immunodeficiency
    syndrome
Alachlor, 167
Alcohol use, 228

Aldicarb, 167
Algae, 101, 102
Alleles, 204–205, 226
Allergic encephalitis, 135
Allergies, 5, 63–64, 268
  autoimmunity and, 115
  C3F gene and, 20
  immunological memory
      and, 73
  immunotoxicity and, 172,
      173
  vaccines and, 244–245
Allografts, 193
Alopecia areata, 120*t*
Amino acids, 70
Amitriptyline, 155
Amoebas, 97–98
Amoebiasis, 97
Amyl nitrate, 227
Anaphylactic reactions, 63–
    64
Anaplastic tissue, 89
Ancient mimicry model, 109–
    111
Anderson, Porter, 262
Andrieu, J. M., 231
Andromeda strain (fictional
    germ), 36
Anemia, 114
  autoimmune hemolytic,
      121*t*
  pernicious, 121*t*
  sickle–cell, 258
Anemones, 101
Ankylosing spondylitis, 50,
    117, 154
Antarctica, 171, 176
Antibiotics, 236, 262
Antibodies, 5, 51–53, 267